DEVELOPMENT AND FINANCIAL REFORM IN EMERGING ECONOMIES

SCEME Studies in Economic Methodology

Series Editor: *Matthias Klaes*

Titles in this Series

DEVELOPMENT AND FINANCIAL REFORM IN EMERGING ECONOMIES

EDITED BY

Kobil Ruziev and Nicholas Perdikis

Routledge
Taylor & Francis Group

LONDON AND NEW YORK

First published 2015 by Pickering & Chatto (Publishers) Limited

2 Park Square, Milton Park, Abingdon, Oxfordshire OX14 4RN
52 Vanderbilt Avenue, New York, NY 10017

Routledge is an imprint of the Taylor & Francis Group, an informa business

First issued in paperback 2020

BRITISH LIBRARY CATALOGUING IN PUBLICATION DATA

Development and financial reform in emerging economies. – (SCEME studies
in economic methodology)
1. Economic development – Developing countries. 2. Developing countries –
Economic policy. 3. Finance – Developing countries.
I. Series II. Perdikis, Nicholas, editor. III. Ruziev, Kobil, editor.
338.9'0091724-dc23

ISBN-13: 978-1-84893-458-0 (hbk)
ISBN-13: 978-0-367-66907-2 (pbk)

Typeset by Pickering & Chatto (Publishers) Limited

CONTENTS

LIST OF FIGURES AND TABLES

LIST OF CONTRIBUTORS

Alexandr Akimov is Senior Lecturer at the Department of Accounting, Finance and Economics, Griffith Business School, Griffith University. He holds a PhD in financial economics from the University of New England and a CFA professional designation. His main area of research expertise is in emerging market finance, specializing in post-communist financial developments in the central Asia region. He has published in journals such as *Emerging Market Finance and Trade*, *Comparative Economic Studies*, *Economic Change and Restructuring*, and *Problems of Economic Transition*. His other research is in the areas of energy and carbon markets, and economics of local government. Alexandr has held academic appointments in Australia and Uzbekistan, as well as a financial industry appointment at the National Bank of Uzbekistan.

Victoria Chick is Emeritus Professor of Economics at University College London. Her work is to be found in three books, *The Theory of Monetary Policy* (1973 and 1977); *Macroeconomics after Keynes: A Reconsideration of The General Theory* (1983); and *On Money, Method and Keynes: Selected Essays of Victoria Chick* (P. Arestis and S. C. Dow, eds, 1992) and numerous articles on monetary theory and policy, methodology and the economics of Keynes. She has served on the Council and Executive Committee of the Royal Economic Society and on the editorial boards of several journals, and was co-founder of the Post-Keynesian Economics Study Group. She has had visiting appointments at several universities, including the Bundesbank visiting professorship in Berlin. A two-volume festschrift was prepared in her honour, edited by P. Arestis, M. J. Desai and S. C. Dow: *Money, Macroeconomics and Keynes* and *Methodology, Microeconomics and Keynes* (2001).

M. Jahangir Alam Chowdhury is Professor in the Department of Finance and the Executive Director of the Center for Microfinance and Development, University of Dhaka. He received his B.Com (Hons) and M.Com in Finance and Banking from the University of Dhaka and received his PhD in banking and finance from the University of Stirling. Prof. Chowdhury's research focuses on microfinance, poverty and entrepreneurship. His research has been funded by the Association of Commonwealth Universities, SANDEE, University of Stirling, Royal Economic Society, Asian Scholarship Foundation, Government of Japan, Bureau of Business Research, Partnership for Economic Policy, and Grand Challenges Canada. Professor Chowdhury has published in various scholarly journals, including *Progress in Development Studies, Journal of Small Business and Entrepreneurship, Journal of Business Studies*, and *Journal of Finance and Banking*. Prof. Chowdhury has acted as a consultant to national and international agencies including the World Bank, CIDA, DFID, FAO, UNDP and Palli Karma Shahayak Foundation.

Malay K. Dey is currently a visiting assistant professor of finance at the University of Illinois at Urbana Champaign and the CEO of FINQ LLC, a diversified financial technology startup. He previously held faculty positions in multiple US universities including Cornell University, NYIT, and Morgan State University. Dey received his PhD (finance) degree from the University of Massachusetts Amherst in 2001. His research focuses on theoretical and empirical issues related to institutional trading and liquidity in equity markets. Dey has published in *Emerging Markets Review, Review of Quantitative Finance and Accounting, Journal of Trading*, and *Journal of Business Finance and Accounting* and also presented his research at prestigious conferences and workshops including the NBER, INQUIRE Europe, Bocconi University, and IGIDR.

Dr Khurshid Djalilov is Lecturer at the Bournemouth University Business School. He obtained his PhD in management from King's College London (University of London) and his MA in economics is from University of Colorado (USA). His research interests are in the areas of strategic management, international business, emerging markets and transition countries. He is also the coordinator of Palgrave Dictionary of Emerging Markets and Transition Economics.

Alexander Dow is Adjunct Professor at the University of Victoria in Canada. He was formerly Professor of Economics, Glasgow Caledonian University, and has taught at the University of Manitoba, the University of Toronto and the University of Stirling. Graduating from the University of St Andrews in Scotland in 1968 with an Honours degree in History and Political Economy, he completed an MA in economics at Simon Fraser University in British Columbia then worked as a Research Officer for the Commonwealth Secretariat in London. He earned a PhD in economics at the University of Manitoba. Research interests and publications have included the economic history of Canada, Keynesian economics, British economic performance and Scottish political economy. He is editor (with Sheila Dow) of *A History of Scottish Economic Thought* (2006).

Sheila Dow is Emeritus Professor of Economics at the University of Stirling in Scotland and Adjunct Professor of Economics at the University of Victoria in Canada. Her main research interests lie in the history and methodology of economic thought and the theory of money and banking. Recent books are *Economic Methodology: An Inquiry* (2002), and *Foundations for New Economic Thinking: A Collection of Essays* (2012). She is co-editor of the WEA's online journal, *Economic Thought*, and co-convenor of SCEME. Past roles include chair of the International Network for Economic Method, co-chair of the Post Keynesian Economics Study Group and special advisor on monetary policy to the UK Treasury Select Committee.

Daniela Gabor is an associate professor in economics at the University of the West of England, Bristol. Her research explores discourses and practices of central banking through a critical political economy approach; the IMF's conditionality and advice on governance of cross-border financial interconnectedness particularly in relationship to global banks' market-based activities; shadow banking activities through the repo market, and the implications for central banking, sovereign bond markets and regulatory activity, including Financial Transaction Taxes. Her research has been cited in the financial media, and received funding from European and British sources. Daniela has organized several conferences and workshops on critical finance questions. She disseminated her research through active blogging and tweeting activities, alongside traditional academic journal outlet.

Roy H. Grieve graduated in political economy and history from the University of Glasgow in the early 1960s. Subsequently became a long-standing member of the Department of Economics at Strathclyde. Now retired. Grieve has been involved in teaching and research also in China (China Foreign Affairs University, Beijing), Pakistan (Government College University, Lahore), Nepal, Bangladesh and Albania. His main interests are in the areas of history of economic thought, macroeconomics and development; in several papers he has argued for the superiority of ideas of the Keynesian and old classical traditions over the mainstream modern focus on the neoclassical or marginalist approach. He remembers Dipak as an esteemed colleague and is also grateful to him for his support and encouragement of his daughter while an undergraduate at Stirling twenty or so years ago.

Jens Hölscher is Professor of Economics and Head of Department of Accounting, Finance & Economics at Bournemouth University. Previously he taught at the Universities of Berlin, Swansea, Birmingham, Chemnitz and Brighton. He held visiting professorships at the Universities of Halle (Institute of Economic Research IWH), Perugia, East Europe Institute Regensburg, Danube University, Bonn (ZEI), Bolzano-Bozen, Frankfurt (Viadrina), New Brunswick in Cairo, Almaty (KIMEP and KBTU) and the Centre of Economic Research at the Deutsche Bundesbank. He is interested in institutional and transition economics, both areas in which he published widely. He is the co-editor of Palgrave's (Macmillan's Global Publishing) book series 'Studies in Economic Transition'.

Prasanta K. Pattanaik is Emeritus Professor in the Department of Economics, University of California, Riverside. His current research interests include welfare economics and the theory of social choice, decision theory, the measurement of deprivation and living standards, and development of economics. He is a fellow of the Econometric Society, and, in 2006–7, he served as President of the Society for Social Choice and Welfare. In addition to his many papers in journals, he has written or edited ten books, including his most recent book, *Essays on Individual Decision-Making and Social Welfare* (2009).

Nicholas Perdikis is Professor of International Business and the former Director of the School of Management and Business at Aberystwyth University. He received his degrees from Cardiff University. He is a research associate at the Estey Centre for International Law and Economics in Saskatchewan and has worked as a consultant for UNCTAD and the UK Foreign Office and the British High Commission in India. His principal research interests lie in the impact of trade policies on firms exports and the international flow of goods as well as their impact on transition and developing economies.

Kobil Ruziev is Senior Lecturer in Economics at the University of the West of England, Bristol. He obtained his first degree from the Tashkent Institute of Finance in Tashkent, Uzbekistan where he studied Banking. He studied at Vanderbilt University in Nashville, TN in the USA for his MA in Economics. He obtained his PhD in economics from Stirling University, Stirling, Scotland. His research interests are in the areas of financial development and reform in emerging economies, SME use of formal and informal finance, institutional economics, and economic transformation in the former Soviet Union. Prior to joining the University of the West of England, he worked at various higher education institutions in Uzbekistan, Scotland, and Wales, and also had a banking industry appointment at the National Bank of Uzbekistan.

Jan Toporowski is Professor of Economics and Finance at the School of Oriental and African Studies, University of London. He studied economics at Birkbeck College, University of London, and the University of Birmingham, UK. Jan Toporowski is Visiting Professor of Economics at the International University College in Turin, and the University of Bergamo. He has written widely on financial macroeconomics. His most recent book is *Michal Kalecki: An Intellectual Biography. Volume 1, Rendezvous in Cambridge 1899–1939* (2013).

Radha Upadhyaya is an economist with extensive research and teaching experience. She is currently a research fellow at the Institute for Development Studies (IDS), University of Nairobi. At IDS, Radha is a member of the SAFIC (Successful African Firms and Institutional Change) research project. This project aims to understand how successful African firms in the food-processing sector develop. Radha completed her PhD at the School of Oriental and African Studies (SOAS), University of London. Her PhD focused on the Banking Sector in Kenya and the thesis showed how social factors are essential to understanding competition in the banking sector. She is a development economist with unique combination of research, teaching, public policy and private sector experience. The scholar has been involved in policy reform, the restructuring of a failed Kenyan bank, and has also served on the board of the Institute of Economic Affairs. Currently she is a member of the Programme Investment Committee (Board) of the Financial Sector Deepening Trust (FSDK) which is an independent Trust established to support the development of inclusive financial markets in Kenya. Dr Upadhyaya has PhD and MSc from SOAS, University of London, and BA from University of Cambridge. She is also a CFA Charterholder.

David Vazquez-Guzman is a tenured professor serving in the Economics Division of the Social Sciences Department of the Autonomous University of Juarez City in Mexico since 2009. He is a former CONACyT fellow, and he got his PhD in economics from the University of Stirling, in Scotland, UK. Professor Vazquez works in areas related to economic development, methodology and microeconomic theory, focusing on issues of welfare and vulnerable groups.

Chaoyan Wang received her PhD in economics from the University of Stirling in 2008. She worked as a post-doctoral associate at the Department of Economics, University of York and a senior lecturer in finance at the University of Bedfordshire and a research associate at FINQ LLC. She is currently working as Teaching Associate at the School of Contemporary Chinese Studies of the University of Nottingham. Her research is mainly focusing on market microstructure and market regulation on emerging stock market.

FOREWORD

It is an honour for me to be asked to write the foreword to *Development and Financial Reform in Emerging Economies*, which the editors, Dr Kobil Ruziev and Professor Nicholas Perdikis, have dedicated to the memory of Dipak Ghosh. Dipak was a close friend whom I knew for more than three decades. Like his many other friends and colleagues, I admired him immensely for his scholarship, his passionate belief that economics could be a powerful instrument for improving the life of the poor all over the world, his deep concern for the welfare of his students, and, above all, his compassionate and gentle personality. He was always eager to explore new ideas and ready to share his ideas with anybody who might be interested. Only a few weeks before his death, he wrote to me to ask me whether I would like to join him as a coauthor of a paper that he was planning to write on the implications, for welfare economics, of having individual preferences which might change with a change in the distribution of property rights.

This volume spans some of the major research interests of Dipak. The chapters in Part I explore a number of important issues in development economics. A highly interesting feature of many of these chapters (see, for instance, Chapters 1, 2, 3 and 6) is that they delve into the history of economic thought and highlight insights from the contributions of thinkers such as Smith, Hume, Keynes and Kalecki. The chapters in the second part of the volume study financial markets in many different parts of the world, including Kazakhstan, Uzbekistan, China, India, Bangladesh and Africa. A valuable addition to the literature on economic development and financial reforms in developing and transition economies, *Development and Financial Reform in Emerging Economies* is a fitting tribute to the memory of Dipak.

PRASANTA K. PATTANAIK

INTRODUCTION

Kobil Ruziev and Nicholas Perdikis

Economic crises, be they large like the 1929 Great Depression or the Global Financial Crisis (GFC) of 2008, or small, are costly in terms of lost economic opportunities. They are also painful as they lead to unemployment and increase personal and social tensions, damaging the lives of millions of ordinary people. Ironically, major crises provide an impetus to challenge orthodox thinking which can lead to new ideas with radically different policy conclusions. The Great Depression, for example, inspired John Maynard Keynes to write *The General Theory* (1936). In this pioneering work, Keynes rigorously explained, in terms of fundamental uncertainty, monetary production and investor psychology, why market-based monetary economies were inherently unstable and proposed measures to tame excessive fluctuations in aggregate demand.

Success, however, often breeds complacency. This is a common trait in academic disciplines and is no less true of economics. The economic success in advanced economies during the post-World War II period and the subsequent 'triumph' of Keynesianism in the 1950s and 1960s led to the detachment of economic theorizing from reality. Economists started treating restrictive formal models, and the results of simulations based on them, as if they represented reality. Unfortunately, the economic problems of the late 1970s and the early 1980s, which could not be explained by the traditional Keynesianism, did very little to change this trend. With the collapse of Keynesianism, the detachment from reality actually widened with the rise and subsequent dominance of the neoclassical orthodoxy during the so-called Great Moderation, which preceded the GFC. Orthodox theories not only failed to predict the scale and the magnitude of the GFC, but, with their insistence (or preaching) of the inherent stability of market-based economies, can also be blamed for indirectly contributing to it.

Although the GFC has been interpreted as the second biggest crisis since the Great Depression in terms of its depth, probably it is the biggest ever in terms of its breadth as it affected almost all countries in the world in one way or another.

The hope and expectation is that, similar to the Great Depression, the GFC will motivate economists to challenge the established orthodoxy in economics and help bridge the gap between economics and the real world. Although the status quo is proving a lot more difficult to change than expected, the dissatisfaction with the neoclassical orthodoxy is gradually gaining momentum.

In this sense, this volume of collective essays aims to contribute to this process; specifically so in the context of development economics in general and the financial sector reforms in emerging economies in particular. Modern development strategy, led by international financial institutions in charge of policy advice to emerging economies, is built heavily around uncompromising orthodox economic ideas that are succinctly summarized by the words 'Washington Consensus', the term coined by Williamson. By putting its dogmatic faith in sheer market efficiency, this approach gives only marginal importance to the role and vitality of institutions in the economic process, and ignores largely the complex and time-consuming nature of institutional capacity building. It does not fully engage with the ideas of alternative schools of thought on the operation and functioning of modern economies despite the repeated failures of its policy recommendations in emerging economies since the 1960s.

By revisiting the contributions of past influential economists, and evaluating unintended consequences of reforms in some of the transition and developing economies, this volume aims to reassert the importance of historic experiences in generating a more realistic and dynamic world view about the way modern economies function and hence the way development strategy should be formalized. Recognition of the constantly changing nature of the economic relations and the associated evolution of institutions, including money, banking and finance, in the economic process is of paramount importance in this regard. Improving our general understanding of the potential sources of economic growth and the essential inputs required to develop the productive capacity of economies should also help us to design and shape better economic policies. One of the key and critical conclusions to emerge from this volume is that improvements in our understanding of the interdependence between the changing nature of economic relations and the development of ideas which form the basis of policy prescription can lead not only to the adoption of better and more relevant policies, but also to more accurate anticipation and analysis of their likely impact. The book is aimed at a broad audience, including academics, postgraduate students, policymakers and professional practitioners.

This essay collection would not have come into existence if it were not for the respect and admiration the contributors had for the work of Dipak Ghosh who died when the idea of this book was being conceived. He was a passionate fellow academic who worked tirelessly in areas of our academic interests. He was an inspirational colleague, a compassionate and reliable friend, and a very kind gentleman; a rare combination of qualities to possess in modern academia. During his productive career spanning more than twenty years at the University of Stirling, Dipak inspired many people. He published his work in various economics journals including *Manchester School, Scottish Journal of Political Economy, Journal of Post Keynesian Economics, Journal of Economic Methodology, Progress in Development Studies, Problems of Economic Transition, Studies in Economics and Finance, Savings and Development, Development Southern Africa, Economic and Political Weekly, Journal of Business Finance and Accounting, Journal of Small Business Management, Economic Notes, Australian Economic Papers, Indian Economic Journal, Central Asian Survey, Economies et Societes, Acta Oeconomica* and *the Bulletin of Economic Research*. He was an active member of various scholarly associations and research centres including the Post Keynesian Study Group (PKSG), Stirling Centre for Economic Methodology (SCEME), the Bangladesh Economic Association, Development Studies Association, International Institution for South Asian Studies, Royal Economic Society, Scottish Economic Association, Scottish Local Government Academic Network, and South Asian Social Research Forum. The volume presents a selection of methodological and critical essays discussing pertinent issues in development economics and financial sector reforms in emerging economies, areas of research Dipak Ghosh felt passionately about and contributed extensively to in his lifetime. It is to his memory that this book is dedicated.

The critical essays collected here are organized under two broad themes: economic development; and financial sector reforms in transition and developing economies. Part I discusses the relationship between economic development and the development of ideas and experiences. It attempts to show how appreciation of this process can contribute to a better understanding of the working of modern economies, advanced and developing, and as a result the prescription of relevant policies. Included in this part are contributions by Sheila Dow and Alexander Dow, Roy Grieve, Dipak Ghosh, David Vazquez-Guzman and Jan Toporowski. Regarding Dipak Ghosh's two contributing chapters, the drafts of these chapters existed at various stages of development and these were completed by Victoria Chick and Kobil Ruziev. Part II covers financial sector reforms in selected emerging economies, and also includes a discussion of the importance of the role of money and finance, and that of financial regulation, in market-based emerging economies. Contributions include those of Kobil Ruziev and Sheila Dow, Daniela Gabor, Jens Holscher and Khurshid Djalilov, Alexandr Akimov, Chaoyan Wang and Malay Dey, Jahangir Chowdhury and Radha Upadhyaya.

Finally, we would like to thank all our authors for their excellent contributions and also for being patient with our demands during the editorial process, some of which, we admit, were raised out of pure ignorance. We enjoyed reading the individual chapters immensely and remain hopeful that this will be shared by our readers.

1 ECONOMIC DEVELOPMENT IN THE SCOTTISH ENLIGHTENMENT: IDEAS AS CAUSE AND EFFECT

Alexander Dow and Sheila Dow

Man, it was postulated, not only made himself *and his institutions: he and his institutions in an important sense* were themselves made *by the circumstances in which from time to time and from place to place he happened to find himself.*

Ronald L. Meek, 1976[1]

Dipak Ghosh was a friend and colleague to both of us, and an intellectual companion over many years. He was a true scholar, motivated by the scope for economic ideas to promote economic and social development. Given this long-held concern with development issues, as well as his fondness for Scotland, we offer the following analysis of a peculiarly Scottish contribution to ideas on development in the hope that he would approve.

In characterizing the European Enlightenment, Ronald Meek, as quoted above, identifies as 'perhaps the most important' idea, that of adding 'a new dimension to the problem of man and society': the significance of context. In this chapter we apply this insight to an analysis of the particular characteristics of Enlightenment thought as it developed in Scotland, and specifically to the theory of economic development. In particular we argue that both the existence of cultural mix in Scotland, and the nature of Gaelic thought as part of that mix, influenced Scottish Enlightenment thought.

While Scottish Enlightenment thought developed as part of a wider intellectual movement in Europe in the eighteenth century, it had distinctive features. It was arguably on account of these distinctive features that innovative ideas emerged within a range of disciplines. A notable contribution which arose from this distinctive intellectual environment was the seminal contribution to thinking about economic growth and development in the form of Adam Smith's *Inquiry into the Nature and Causes of the Wealth of Nations.* Other Enlightenment figures, notably Sir James Steuart, David Hume, James Anderson and Adam Ferguson, contributed to the debate on issues of growth and economic development.

The contribution of Scottish Enlightenment figures to the later development of economics was substantial, and is thus the subject of a vast literature, with a range of interpretations. Here we focus on the particular ideas with respect to economic growth and development which refer to ideas themselves. One of Smith's key contributions was to develop and apply the principle of the division of labour, which he elucidated as one of the key engines of growth. The concept was in fact first introduced in the context of division of labour in the generation of ideas, and only later extended to the mode of production. On this foundation was built the theory of trade-led growth in an expanded market, and hence a vent-for-surplus theory of economic development. Indeed this marked the idea of economic development itself as an object of study. But possible feedbacks of the division of labour in the form of diminishing moral sensitivities, and the consequence of this for economic development were also discussed in the period. There was considerable concern that economic growth and moral virtue would be incompatible. Another key idea was that economic development itself is a precondition for ideas conducive to economic development: consumption aspirations on the one hand and innovations to improve productivity in order to meet these aspirations on the other. To what extent, then, was the Scottish Enlightenment itself, as a set of ideas, the product of prior economic development?

The aim here, therefore, is to explore the interdependencies between the particular economic experience of Scotland and the ideas for economic development which arose in the eighteenth century, focusing particularly on the role of ideas themselves in economic development. There has been disagreement in the literature on the Scottish Enlightenment as to the relative influences of civic humanism and natural law (between particularity and generality). Here we will find a circularity between the general forces which influenced the Scottish Enlightenment thinkers and the particularities of their circumstances. Indeed we will suggest that an absence of dualism, such as between particularity and generality, was a central feature of Scottish thought. In the process we address an issue being given increasing attention in the literature: how far were these ideas for economic development a veiled analysis of 'improvements' in the Highlands and Islands? We extend the discussion by addressing the further question, as to how far the distinguishing characteristics of the Scottish Enlightenment were themselves a product of the particular cultural backdrop.

We start by considering some of the distinctive characteristics of Scottish Enlightenment thought, where theories of economic development arose out of moral philosophy. In the following section we focus on the particular ideas as to economic development which relate to the importance of ideas as a mechanism for productivity growth. We then provide some background to these ideas in the form of the socio-economic conditions leading up to the Scottish Enlightenment, paying particular attention to the Highland–Lowland distinction. This focus is in line with a renewed attention in intellectual history on the Highlands in relation to the rest of eighteenth-century Scotland.[2] In the process, we address the debate as to how far economic development was instrumental in facilitating the Enlightenment itself. Finally, we consider the extent to which the form the ideas of the Scottish Enlightenment took, on economic development as well as on knowledge more generally, were influenced by the cultural composition of Scotland at that time. We are therefore considering ideas, not as something independent of material reality, nor as fully determined by material reality. Rather we consider the important mutual influences between ideas and reality, mediated by moral philosophy (and thus culture).

The themes that run through the discussion are first the interplay between ideas and context, so that we consider how the Scottish experience (including its cultural diversity) served to spawn the particular set of ideas of the Scottish Enlightenment, which included ideas about the interplay between development and ideas; and second, the interplay between particularity and generality – between general trends in ideas and economic reality on the one hand and the particularity of the Scottish reality and of the ideas of the Scottish Enlightenment – which included ideas about generality and specificity.

The Distinctive Characteristics of the Scottish Enlightenment

The eighteenth-century Enlightenment was a general European intellectual movement which took the form of a challenge to the authority of the Church in matters of science (or knowledge more generally), and established alternative foundations for knowledge, most particularly in reason and evidence. Just as in other emerging fields of enquiry, this approach to knowledge was applied to the functioning of the economy. The origins of this intellectual movement are complex, and the currents of thought within Europe spread from one country to another.

However, this movement took a range of forms, such that the Scottish Enlightenment differed in several important respects from the Enlightenment elsewhere, most notably in France.[3] This occurred in spite of the strong influence from Continental thought through a variety of channels, not least from direct, extended, contacts in France on the part of Hume, Steuart and Smith. Indeed it could be argued that it was Hume's (ultimately unsuccessful) attempts to grapple with French Enlightenment rationalism that encouraged him to develop an alternative approach to knowledge. Under the influence of Descartes, the French Enlightenment prioritized reason as the foundation for knowledge. Hume eventually concluded that reason could not provide the proof of existence which was necessary for science applied to the real world; this was the pinnacle of his scepticism.[4]

Hume therefore turned to his project of developing a science of human nature to provide the alternative basis for knowledge in conventional belief, based on generations of experience. In contrast to Descartes's pure reason, conventional belief was not the outcome of demonstrable truth. Brian Loasby refers to this as 'Hume's Impossibility Theorem: "It is impossible ... that any arguments from experience can prove this resemblance of the past to the future; since all these arguments are formulated on the supposition of that resemblance".[5] Experience itself was subject to the problem of induction. In Hume's hands, this problem was not simply a matter of unobserved instances, but the more profound problem that reality is too complex, and underlying causal mechanisms too deeply hidden, for any knowledge of them to be held with certainty.[6]

Using the Newtonian 'experimental' method, knowledge could be built using systematic study of experience (detailed historical study) combined with reason.[7] Where reason was combined with imagination to identify patterns and fill in evidential gaps, the outcome was conjectural history. But prior to experience and reason were conventional belief, the imagination required to conceive of cause in the first place, and then to engage in abstract reasoning, and, as Smith explained in the *History of Astronomy*, the sentiment to motivate the search for knowledge.[8] Then, as Smith explained in his *Lectures on Rhetoric and Belles Lettres*, this knowledge had to be communicated in such a way as to persuade different audiences, appealing to their prior knowledge and to the imagination.[9] This was far removed from French rationalism, which consisted of applying classical logic to axioms held to be true, as well as from the empiricism without abstract theory more characteristic of the English Enlightenment.

This approach to knowledge was both influenced and reinforced by the system of higher education.[10] Students entered higher education in their mid-teens, and were provided a structured approach to knowledge built on early teaching of moral philosophy. This philosophy emphasized the absence of a single rationalist truth, but rather took a historical approach to explain the different possible ways of building knowledge. This carried forward into other subjects, which were also taught historically, exposing students to the idea that knowledge can be built in different ways best suited to problems at hand. It is this approach, arguably, which underpinned the inventiveness of the period.

In his *Lectures on Jurisprudence* (1762–3), Smith developed the idea of the division of labour in terms of knowledge: 'Genius is more the effect of the division of labour than the latter is of it. The difference between a porter and a philosopher in the first four or five years of their life is, properly speaking, none at all'.[11] While anyone was capable of becoming a philosopher, this activity was facilitated by education. Further, it appealed more to the sentiments of some than to others, who then went on to specialize in pursuing particular lines of enquiry with a higher input of reason. The difference between philosophers and others then became an issue for rhetoric: how to persuade different types of audience, with different experience, different familiar knowledge, and different inclinations to apply reason, to accept particular ideas.

The key characteristics which Scottish Enlightenment thinkers brought to economic questions followed from this overall approach to knowledge. First, knowledge was provisional since it could not be demonstrated to be true. In particular, principles could be teased out of detailed study of societies in different times and places, but these might require adaptation in the light of new circumstances and when applied to new cases. Second, the focus on society ensured that economic questions were approached from the standpoint of moral philosophy; and indeed for Francis Hutcheson and Smith their economic ideas developed as applications for moral philosophy teaching. The focus on society also meant that economic questions were also integrated with social, psychological and political questions. It was only later that these lines of enquiry emerged as separate disciplines.

Finally, the methodological approach differed not only from the French deductivism characteristic of the Cartesian approach, but also from English empiricism based on a different understanding of Newton.[12] Knowledge was derived from experience, but with the aid of imagination and reason it could be systematized and communicated for more general, albeit provisional, application. Hume and Smith were thus able to develop a theory of human nature which drew out what they identified as common features of humanity, while demonstrating how these features were manifest in different ways in different societies. Smith argued in the *History of Astronomy* (appeared 1795) that aesthetically-pleasing systems drawn from first principles, and connecting with what is already understood, would be most persuasive to audiences. Yet persuasion was distinct from the process of theory formulation itself. However, the provisional nature of theory emerging from the Scottish Enlightenment arguably became communicated in a more deterministic manner than was intended, because that was aesthetically appealing. We shall consider this possibility in terms of the theory of economic development.

Theories of Economic Development

The first idea on which we focus is the idea of economic development itself, which arguably was the first contribution from the Scottish Enlightenment thinkers. (Indeed, it could be argued that the notion of an economy as such only emerged during the Enlightenment, as something distinct relative to the polity.)[13] Before Smith, indeed with origins dating back to ancient times, there had been discussion of change in the means of subsistence and associated modes of organization by means of stages of development.[14] But the eighteenth century saw a much greater focus on understanding economic history in terms of advance from one stage of development (one mode of economic organization) to another: the hunting and gathering, pastoral and agricultural stages, leading to the final stage of commercialization. Indeed this discussion emerged within a new discourse, on economic development.[15] In the French stadial approach, notably Turgot, the emphasis was on agriculture.[16] But Smith changed the focus from agriculture to one of growth in prosperity once the fourth stage, commercialization, had been reached. He introduced the idea, drawing on natural law philosophy, that such growth might be the normal condition for commercial societies.

There were differences of opinion as to whether such growth was indeed sustainable, and Smith himself considered a range of moderating factors. A key feature of this discourse followed from Scottish Enlightenment thought, that it emerged out of moral philosophy. Economic development was not discussed in isolation, but in conjunction with an emphasis on moral sensibilities as a practical question of norms and conventions. Thus Hume and Smith both aimed to encourage debate as to the best way to secure both virtue and prosperity, their mentor Hutcheson having expressed concerns that commercial society was incompatible with virtue.[17] There was debate as to whether prosperity would support, or even promote, moral sensibilities, or whether it would erode them.[18] It was therefore seen as necessary that appropriate social institutions be developed in parallel to economic development. This debate resurfaced much later as the Adam Smith Problem,[19] referring to the apparent incompatibility of Smith's moral philosophy and his economics.[20] The sustainability of the commercial economic process is now primarily discussed in the economic literature in terms of how far market forces can be relied on to generate socially optimal outcomes. Would the unintended consequences of self-interested behaviour produce a good outcome for society, without reference to moral values? But in the eighteenth century the focus was at least as much on production and whether the emergent specialized mode of production in commercial society was independent of social institutions and moral concerns.

The key principle applied to thinking on economic development, referring to production, was the principle of the division of labour. This principle was present in others' thinking before Smith.[21] But it was Smith who developed the principle, drawing on a wide range of evidence from different societies in order to establish how generally it could be applied. The division of labour allowed division of tasks and thus specialization and productivity growth. The surplus thus generated could then be used for investment in order to specialize productive functions further, yielding ever more surpluses. This process was facilitated by commercialization, which extended markets, and Smith focused on the market process. If markets could be extended overseas, then exports would provide even more latitude for division of labour. Economies then could reap the benefits of economies of scale at a macro level and experience growth in prosperity at an aggregate level. From this theory emerged the emphasis on vent-for-surplus and capital accumulation which proceeded to underpin classical economics. There is a difference of opinion as to whether priority should be given to the division of labour in Smith's theory of economic development, or capital accumulation.[22] Here we focus on the division of labour; this follows from a focus on the connections between Smith's economics and his epistemology, and is reinforced by the fact that Smith gave such prominence to the division of labour, placing it right at the start of the *Wealth of Nations*. Nevertheless, accumulation prior to the Scottish Enlightenment (albeit brought about by the division of labour) played a key role in providing the conditions for the Enlightenment.

It is through the exercise of practical reason that particular innovations in the division of labour emerged. New connections were conceived by the imagination, within a learning-by-doing process. The resulting innovations required a process of persuasion in order for them to be applied,[23] leading to increasing returns at economy-wide level.[24] John Rae was later to take this up,[25] developing a theory of invention, chastising Smith for, as he saw it, prioritizing capital accumulation instead as the cause of the division of labour.[26] But the foundations are there in Smith's recourse to the human capacities for imagination and persuasion in explaining the division of labour.

Hume and Smith had identified human capacities as being held in common in different societies, though manifest in different ways. At a basic level these capacities included imagination, sentiment and reason. According to Hume and Smith, the imagination is crucial to developing a moral sense, through sympathy,[27] and it is only through moral sensibility that society can function. While Hutcheson had argued that moral sensibility is innate,[28] Hume and Smith were concerned about the consequences of changing economic organization for moral sense. Indeed appropriate social norms which relied on moral sense were necessary for a successful system of market exchange. (This is the normal resolution of the Adam Smith Problem, that is, social behaviour and self-interest are generally complementary rather than conflicting.) While imagination is essential to the development of moral sense, imagination can also be applied to self-interest, even if it involves self-deception, and the wish for self-improvement. Thus Smith offers the account of the poor man's son who strives for riches, imagining that these will bring him happiness.[29] Whether he achieves happiness or not, he is led, as by an invisible hand, to promote economic improvement.[30] This aspiration for self-improvement is activated by exposure to luxury goods. Thus, as societies develop and international trade expands, the process is fuelled by increasing aspirations encouraging efforts to improve productivity, an argument developed by Steuart, Hume and Smith.[31]

The emergence of commercialization itself is promoted by the human propensity, which Smith identified, to 'truck, barter and exchange one thing for another'.[32] But Hume identified particular social and economic benefits from the changes in mode of production brought about by the division of labour. He saw the social discipline of employment itself as being a civilizing force, and that work itself, rather than a burden, was a source of feelings of self-worth. Employment in turn would encourage what he referred to as 'arts', by which was meant such things as knowledge, inventiveness, skill, technique and technology. Trade in turn would increase communication between societies, spreading the benefits of this civilizing force, and thus the capacity further to increase productivity.[33] In his essay 'On Money', Hume emphasized the stimulating effects of a trade surplus in terms of spurring on further industry; money inflows were the sign of productivity improvements which had led to increased sales abroad rather than themselves the causal force behind increased expenditure.[34]

Hume was in fact less sanguine about the sustainability of economic development than Smith. Success in international trade meant that foreign societies were aspiring to the imports to which they were increasingly exposed, so that they too would employ the division of labour to improve the competitiveness of domestic production, and thus substitute for imports.[35] Steuart was particularly concerned that markets, and thus scope for further growth, could be lost.[36] Indeed Hume and Steuart saw economic development as a catching-up process, rather than Smith's ongoing process. While Hume emphasized the need for government to promote stability and security to underpin commercial activity, he was also concerned about the scope for government unduly to exercise its power to tax and to issue debt. Commercial activity itself he saw as promoting social responsibility.

Others, however, raised concerns as to the wisdom of taking the division of labour too far, not just in terms of potential conflict between prosperity and virtue, but also in terms of prosperity itself. Smith himself qualified the role for specialization, foreseeing that agricultural improvement would go hand-in-hand with manufacturing growth. Others, such as James Anderson, argued for even more balance so that each sector provided a market for the others' products, particularly between different activities within agricultural improvement, and within smaller, regional, geographical areas.[37] This focus on the particularity of local context as throwing up exceptions to the general argument for specialization was also a feature of Steuart's *Principles*, from which Smith purported to distance himself in the *Wealth of Nations*. But, while Smith himself aimed to set out an aesthetically pleasing system, he too took pains to point out exceptions to his (provisional) general principles according to context.

There was a more fundamental objection to the division of labour on social grounds, put most forcefully by Adam Ferguson.[38] He argued that the division of labour threatened to erode moral sensibilities and the social fabric in such a way as to threaten the security necessary for commercial society to function effectively. Indeed he raised the possibility of developed societies reverting to barbarous despotism.

It is here indeed, if ever, that man is sometimes found a detached and a solitary being: he has found an object which sets him in competition with his fellow-creatures, and he deals with them as he does with his cattle and his soil, for the sake of the profits they bring.[39]

This was relevant to the contemporary issue of how to organize military defence. Ferguson argued that economic advance would be threatened by greater risk of military attack in the case of a standing army.[40] He focused on the need for a militia, which would retain a balanced moral sense, while Smith argued for a specialist standing army.[41] Ferguson did not regard corruption as the inevitable consequence of commercialization, but rather emphasized the need for institution-building to counteract its damaging effects on society; like Hume, Ferguson saw the role of government as central to providing a secure backdrop for commerce. Smith certainly appreciated the danger of specialist production work being alienating, and the need for education to counteract this.[42] But Ferguson's argument is a more general one. Smith had argued that the social aspects of behaviour are necessary for the functioning of markets.[43] Ferguson was raising questions as to the sustainability of these social aspects of behaviour under the division of labour, with more relevance for production than exchange. For him there was a long-term trade-off between prosperity and virtue, and indeed the erosion of virtue could eventually undermine prosperity. On balance nevertheless, Ferguson believed that the division of labour would bring about progress.[44]

How far were these ideas influenced by the local context? There is a large literature now on the particular background in Scotland to the Enlightenment, emphasizing such influences as the different philosophical traditions and the removal of the political action to London following the Act of Union in 1707.[45] But here we focus on the particular cultural history behind the apparent Highland–Lowland divide as a possible influence. There is a clue to this cultural influence in that the thinkers who most emphasized concerns over the division of labour, and also the scope for variety of development experience (Ferguson, and Anderson) had Highland connections to varying degrees. In fact, if we enquire more closely into how social and economic organization in the Highlands was organized, it becomes hard to sustain the interpretation of stages as a natural and inevitable linear progression. Indeed Allan Macinnes offers an illuminating account of the shift from feudalism to capitalism in the Highlands and Islands from the perspective of Gaeldom, as a 'convulsive rather than evolutionary or revolutionary' process.[46]

Here perhaps we have a reflexive case study for variety of epistemology, due to particular circumstances, which was a feature of the Scottish approach itself. In what follows, we consider the ideas for economic development again against the backdrop of the particular Scottish context, in terms of ontological and epistemological differences within Scotland. But first, a brief account of the background to that context is provided.

The Scottish Economy up to the Enlightenment

As with all history, there are conflicting accounts, but it would be a fair characterization to describe the Scottish economy as poor relative to England in the period before the Enlightenment.[47] There was limited experience of luxury goods, yet commercialization was emerging alongside agricultural innovation, facilitated by changing institutional arrangements with respect to land ownership and tenancy, and an indigenous banking system which had emerged in response to the needs of a growing economy with relatively poor stocks of specie.[48] The changes in land tenure were particularly significant, dating back to the sale of church property following the Reformation. More recently, improvement in the form of division, consolidation and enclosure followed from a series of Acts during the second half of the seventeenth century. The tenancy relationship became one of pecuniary rent, rather than payment in kind and (mutual) feudal obligation, and landowners came to see their property as a means of accumulating wealth rather than social standing. Until early in the eighteenth century land was still often divided into strips (runrigs), held by multiple or joint tenancies which were periodically reallocated to ensure equality within the community. However, movement of landowners to London encouraged a drive for higher rents, and higher efficiency, and tenancies were increasingly held on an individual pecuniary basis.

Natural resource endowments were significant for general relative poverty, but also for the pattern of economic activity. There was in particular a physical difference between central Scotland, which was more suitable for arable cultivation, and the more mountainous north and south, which were more suitable for stock rearing, such that the central Lowlands could be thought of as progressing towards the third stage of economic development more readily than the north. Further, the presence of urban development in the Lowlands became associated with more commercial activity (the fourth stage) than the more rural areas. It became common for Scotland to be thought of more generally in dualistic terms,[49] with a contrast between the more developed Lowlands and the less developed Highlands, and for this difference to correspond to a cultural difference allegedly between Presbyterian Scots speakers and Roman Catholic or Episcopalian Gaelic speakers, which reached its nadir in the rebellions of 1715 and 1745. To the extent that this was the understanding in the eighteenth century, it is highly relevant to the emergence of Enlightenment thought. However, it is debatable how dualistic the Highland–Lowland divide was, or was perceived to be, even in the Enlightenment.

The understanding of pre-Enlightenment history in terms of a Highland–Lowland divide has been challenged, suggesting that the distinction (such as it existed) was a creation of the seventeenth and eighteenth centuries, imposed on a less divided national society. As Newton puts it: 'It is possible to see the conscious recognition in earlier times of the features of a common Scottish tradition springing from Gaelic, and wider Celtic, roots'.[50] Some, notably John Campbell, Roy Campbell and Devine, have argued variously that a dualistic account of Scottish culture only emerged as a result of suppression of the Highlands and Islands, with attempts to limit the power of the clan system, and in particular the changes in land tenure. But even then the hill country in the south of Scotland had much in common with the physical conditions in the Highlands, and the rebellions did not in fact follow a strict Highland–Lowland divide.

Devine also challenges the view that the Highlands and Islands were backward in terms of economic development.[51] He notes the improving efforts of entrepreneurial Highland landowners (notably the Campbells), with their early engagement in cattle trade, and thus in commerce more generally, in order to satisfy the demand for imported goods, such that commercialization (for example, pecuniary rents rather than rent in kind) reached rural areas of the Highlands before the rural areas of the Lowlands. Indeed, as part of the efforts of 'improvement' there were clearances of population from the Lowland rural areas as well as the Highlands. Nevertheless it could be argued that traditional social structures were more enduring in the Highlands and Islands (for a variety of reasons), and that there was therefore more resistance to new technology in the Highlands if it disrupted existing social structures.[52]

However, these social structures themselves were changing. The erosion of the traditional system of justice and conflict resolution in the Highlands and Islands meant that, during the dearth of 1695–1700, Highland marauding resumed without adequate checks. The resulting impression of Highlanders as warlike was reinforced by the rebellions, which were exercises in resistance to suppression of a way of life.[53] These rebellions (the second of which at the time did have the potential to succeed) confronted Lowland society with the direct experience of the potential for armed conflict. The resulting determination further to suppress Highland and Island culture brought about further structural change in the Highlands and Islands, with direct implications both for culture and the economy.

By then, Union with England and Wales had removed political power from Scotland as a whole, diverting energies to such matters as economic improvement, and the Union opened up new markets which also acted as a spur to increased output and innovation, as the theory of development would predict. But there had been significant improvement before then, according to Devine, in that significant agricultural surpluses had been achieved already during 1680–1740.[54] Various societies were formed to promote ideas for agricultural improvement, starting with the Honourables the Society of Improvers during 1723–45. Hume and Smith were involved in the Edinburgh Society for Encouraging Arts, Sciences, Manufactures, and Agriculture in Scotland, which had grown out of the Select Society founded in 1754 (by the portraitist, Allan Ramsey). Campbell emphasizes the importance of intellectual input as helping Scotland overcome its relatively poor resource endowment.[55] But both he and Devine emphasize innovation prior to the Enlightenment, such that surpluses and commercialization had already advanced significantly by the mid-eighteenth century.[56] They therefore come to the conclusion that, rather than the Enlightenment being the cause of Scotland's rapid economic advance from the eighteenth century, it was on balance the effect. But, to the extent that the Enlightenment proceeded to provide the basis for further advance (for example in generating ideas for Highland 'Improvement') we see an interplay between the two. This conclusion would itself be consistent with the theory of economic development which emerged in the Scottish Enlightenment.

In the next section we come back to the special characteristics of the Scottish Enlightenment generally, and the theories of economic development it spawned, to consider how far these special characteristics reflected the particular circumstances in Scotland.

Economic Improvement and the Highlands and Islands

The apparent consensus in the economic history literature, that economic development predated and facilitated the Enlightenment in Scotland, is consistent with the content of Enlightenment thought: that the process of economic development, with its spur to the imagination, generates new connections in thought. However, in the Enlightenment, Scottish epistemology evolved in a way that was particularly helpful for addressing practical problems. As Campbell argues,

> The Scottish intellectual tradition's contribution to industry lies less in a series of specific inventions which had some industrial application and more in the emergence of a new methodology, a scientific method, which could perceive the advantages of new methods of production even when it was not always possible to provide convincing explanations of why that should be so.[57]

What we want to consider here is how far the particular socio-economic background in Scotland coloured the particular ideas that emerged. As noted above, the Scottish approach to knowledge was to derive general principles (albeit provisionally) from a range of experiences. There was a disparity of economic experience across Europe, between Scotland and England, and in the new colonies which influenced their thinking, as well as over time. Hume and Smith in particular drew on their extensive familiarity with the classical period. Meek draws attention to the particular focus at the time on the experience of North American Indians as providing insights into the organization of subsistence in the first of the four stages which could previously only be imputed from ancient literature.[58] Indeed Meek argues that experience of contemporary differences, combined with the speed of economic change in eighteenth-century Europe, help explain the development of the stadial approach in Europe more generally.[59]

Here we are concerned to understand the particularity of Scottish Enlightenment ideas, and so focus on the particularly Scottish experience. It is increasingly argued that the Scots ideas of economic improvement were implicitly directed at the particular question of improvement of the Scottish Highlands.[60] Caffentzis, for example, points out that Hume's *Political Discourses* were written while he was in Edinburgh at the time of the Annexing Act of 1752, whereby thirteen estates were annexed to the Crown, and the rents and profits from Highland estates were to be used for 'civilizing' the inhabitants.[61] When reference was made to 'rude' and 'civilized' societies, they had in mind the Highlands and Lowlands respectively, within a more general categorization of societies. It could be argued therefore that the Highlands were understood in terms of an earlier stage of development than the Lowlands (within the stadial approach).

The argument that the focus of theorizing about development was on the Highlands can be overstated. Nevertheless, while the sweep of evidence drawn on for formulating a theory of development was wide, immediate experience (as Smith's epistemology attests) must have been the greatest influence on their thinking about economic development. Several of the key thinkers (Smith, Hume and Anderson) were actively engaged in policymaking for Highland improvement. The Scottish Enlightenment took much of its character from the spur to its epistemology from the need to address practical problems.

However, while the expression 'civilizing' the Highlands was current in some circles, consistent with the policy of suppressing Highland culture (outlawing Highland language, dress etc.), this is not the sense we get from Hume (albeit in defensive mode, responding to Samuel Johnson's criticism of the Highlands):

> I shall be sorry to be suspected of saying any thing against the manners of the present Highlanders. I really believe that, besides their signal bravery, there is not any people in Europe, not even excepting the Swiss, who have more plain honesty and fidelity, are more capable of gratitude and attachment, than that race of men.[62]

Given that Hume's family was involved in introducing improvements to their farm at Ninewells in the Borders (south of the Lowlands), he had direct knowledge of the process, and also of a context where commercialization had only recently developed, that is, where economic advance was ahead of some parts of the Highlands, but only by recent developments.

Similarly, Adam Ferguson discussed North American Indian society as being at an earlier stage of development, but not in terms of identifying the stages with degrees of progress.[63] John Miller argued further (contra Rousseau) that the stages of development should not be analysed in terms of moral judgement.[64] This indicates a less materialist, determinist interpretation of the stages than later emerged, in line with the natural law approach, with Marx.[65] Taking instead the civic humanism approach, Philipson advocates instead a moderate interpretation of the stages approach: 'It was clear to them that savages, living in pre-political, tribal societies were capable of experiencing a sense of moral autonomy.'[66] He argues that the Enlightenment figures were trying to make sense of intellectual life in Scotland, which was now remote from politics; the science of man implied that we can learn from 'savage' society. There was for example a concern that commercialization would threaten individual liberty by shifting power to the state. Movement through the stages should therefore not be seen as a simple matter of progress.

This was relevant to the interventionist approach to Highland Improvement, particularly following the 1745 Rebellion. Gray concludes his study of the Highland economy by referring to the damaging effects of the encroachment of emerging capitalism as being uncontroversial: 'That the old way of life held much that was valuable and that many of the policies that helped to break it were mistaken and short-sighted, even greedy, need not be challenged'.[67]

Hume, with his deep understanding of the importance of social custom, advocated a more cautious approach to the imposition of 'improvement' policies in the Highlands, which respected particularities of context. As Philipson puts it:

> No commercial society could be stable, Hume thought, whose government did not recognize and respect the variety of its social and regional structure. No citizen could possibly think of himself as virtuous unless he acknowledged that his own happiness and that of society at large were interconnected, unless he realized the importance of pursuing political stability in respecting the regional integrity of the different communities of the kingdom.[68]

Smith and Hume's advocacy of the benefits of commercialization cannot be interpreted as Whiggism, in the sense of belief in the inevitable progress of society, tempered as such progress was by concerns about social estrangement, and threats to competition, morality and security. By comparing the Highlands and Lowlands they could see at first hand the problems with commercialization within a particular context: the breakdown of clan-based mechanisms for social control in the Highlands, the breakdown of traditional society in towns, and so on. Even although agricultural improvement, entrepreneurship and commercialization arguably were as advanced in some parts of the Highlands as in the Lowlands before the suppression following the 1745 rebellion, traditional Scottish culture had been preserved longer in the Highlands. They could witness the disruptive, and sometimes self-defeating (social and economic) effects of attempts to apply the principle of the division of labour in unqualified form.

Davis draws attention to different Enlightenment approaches to understanding the individual.[69] On the one hand, René Descartes and Locke posed the self and ideas in dualistic distinction from reality: the inner and outer worlds. On the other hand, Davis characterizes Smith's thought as an attempt to bring the two together, with the concept of the invisible hand as a process of the unintended consequences of subjective interest. Indeed we see in Scottish philosophy more generally a resistance to dualistic distinction and an avoidance of absolutist conclusions, both of which arguably reflects the influence of Scotland's cultural background.

This background, as we have suggested, is one of cultural difference, encouraging a sceptical epistemology. The content of Highland culture itself may also have been influential. Foucault identifies Hume and Smith as being on the cusp of the emerging modern episteme, at the end of the age of resemblance.[70] The former is characterized, among other things, by categorization, and means/end separation, compared to the more organic approach to life of the latter, where resemblances and connections are emphasized.[71] The Highland Improvement movement involved attempts to introduce modernism in a non-modernist society, and, where new technologies threatened the traditional way of life, they were resisted.[72] Being on the cusp, Hume and Smith had privileged knowledge of both epistemes. In addition, belonging to a society within which both epistemes were represented, and where there was active discussion of policy with respect to Highland society, must have had some impact on their thought. It is hard therefore to understand them as out-and-out modernists. Yet the modernism which subsequently developed may account for the interpretation of their economics in modernist terms (something which Smith himself would have understood, from his analysis of rhetoric). In particular, the provisionality of principles, the importance of context and the resistance to thinking in dualistic terms, all came to be disregarded.

There are many particular features of the context which can explain the characteristics of the Scottish Enlightenment, and the resulting theory of economic development. But this set of cultural-socio-economic factors relating to the regional make-up of Scotland would help to explain the particular combination of uses of natural law philosophy and civic humanism, such that general principles were sought for, but always understood as being provisional in the face of particular circumstances (in space and time). While the focus was on economic advance with a view to increasing prosperity, the difficulties that this advance would create, and the benefits of prior forms of organization lost, were also given prominence. There was a modesty about the principles, and more generally about the scope for demonstrable knowledge, reflecting an understanding of the complexity of reality and our understanding of it. At the same time there was an emphasis on the socio-psychological foundations for knowledge, which were necessary in the absence of scope for demonstrable truth.

Conclusion

Scottish Enlightenment thought is distinctive (within the broad movement known as the Enlightenment) in a way that can be understood against the particular context. Here we have focused on the argument that the experience of the main Enlightenment figures of the socio-economic differences within Scotland at a time of remarkable change (social, institutional, political and economic) helps us to understand that distinctiveness. In particular it helps us understand the provisional nature of the principles employed and the attention to context. It was Smith's systematizing of theory which proved most influential for subsequent modernist thought, at the expense of attention to the concerns about commercialization which he shared with his contemporaries, among whom were key figures with more experience of the different conditions in different parts of the country. Similarly, in contrast to the attitude of Hume and Smith, the Whig interpretation of the Scottish theories of economic development has failed to recognize fully the respect shown for societal difference in the face of the social repression which followed the rebellions.

It is increasingly conventional in intellectual history more generally, and the history of economic thought in particular, to explore the context within which ideas were developed. In considering the ideas of the Scottish Enlightenment a neglected aspect of that context has been explored: the cultural mix in Scotland, particularly with respect to the Highlands and Lowlands. We have also drawn attention to the significance, as well as the sometimes misleading nature, of the construction of a Highland–Lowland divide in some portrayals of the eighteenth century.

This chapter has concentrated on the aspects of the Scottish theory of development which focused on knowledge rather than resource endowments, emphasising connections between the theory of knowledge and the theory of economic development proposed by Scottish Enlightenment thinkers. Perhaps the greatest contribution was to steer a path between general principle on the one hand and particularity on the other, and we have tried to follow that path in our interpretation of their ideas.

Acknowledgements

This paper has benefited from comments made on earlier versions presented to the Annual HETSA Conference, Brisbane, July 2007, the Annual ESHET Conference, Prague, May 2008, and the Department of Philosophy at the University of Athens, April 2009.

2 NEARER TO SRAFFA THAN MARX: ADAM SMITH ON PRODUCTIVE AND UNPRODUCTIVE LABOUR

Roy H. Grieve

Introduction

The purpose of this chapter is to shed light on Adam Smith's famous – perhaps one should say 'notorious'[1] – distinction between 'productive' and 'unproductive' labour. It is appropriate to begin by setting Smith's analysis in context.

An essential feature which distinguishes classical from neoclassical economics is that classical economists envisaged production as a *circular* process – that is to say, as a process in which the commodity inputs to production are themselves products of the production system. This classical conception contrasts sharply with the neoclassical representation of production as a *one-way* process of transformation of natural resources, through the application of labour and capital, into final goods. When inputs are viewed in classical terms as products of the system the idea of an 'overplus' or '*surplus*' readily emerges when the quantity of outputs is compared with the necessary input quantities of the same commodities. Such a conception – the very hallmark of the classical understanding of a modern economic system – is of course absent from the neoclassical model. In practical terms a surplus, output in excess of what is necessary to reproduce that output, is vital in providing for the support of members of the community who do not contribute to the production of their own subsistence, and it provides also the means whereby, through savings and capital accumulation, the productive capacity of the economy can be expanded.

In the literature, reference had been made, long before publication of Smith's *An Inquiry into the Nature and Causes of the Wealth of Nations* (1776), to the concept of a surplus,[2] but Smith, while sharing with predecessors and successors within the classical tradition the recognition of the central importance of the phenomenon of surplus production, did not himself employ the terminology of 'production with a surplus'; his discussion[3] runs instead in terms of a differentiation between 'productive' and 'unproductive' labour. Smith's handling of the productive/unproductive distinction has, however, proved problematical to many scholars, and has generally received a poor press. Marx, who was sympathetic to Smith's approach, nevertheless expressed reservations, while members of the later marginalist school totally failed to appreciate what Smith was trying to say and regarded the productive/unproductive labour distinction as completely misconceived. Even today 'inconsistency' is emphasized as characterizing Smith's discussion.[4]

Investigation and elucidation are called for. In this chapter the view is taken that there is more sense in Smith's distinction than the critics have generally allowed. It is argued here that Smith chose to describe as 'productive' that labour which, over and above replacing the goods and services it used up in the course of its operations, produced a net surplus of the resources (real or financial) essential for growth of the economy. On the other hand, he classified as 'unproductive' labour which merely consumed resources without contributing to their reproduction (though allowing that such labour might in other ways contribute to society).

Productive and Unproductive Labour: The Smithian Classification

The terms 'productive' and 'unproductive labour' first appear in the *Wealth of Nations* in Smith's – much quoted – pronouncement that the nation's labour force can be regarded as falling into two distinct categories:

> There is one sort of labour which adds to the value of the subject upon which it is bestowed: there is another which has no such effect. The former, as it produces a value, may be called productive; the latter, unproductive labour. Thus the labour of a manufacturer [i.e. a workman] adds, generally, to the value of the materials he works upon, that of his own maintenance, and of his master's profit. The labour of a menial servant, on the contrary, adds to the value of nothing.[5]

Smith's thesis is clear – it is by employing productive labour that an investor not only recoups the funds invested, but may indeed gain a net profit from the surplus value created. Smith goes on to cite further features or properties which characterize the product of productive labour. Contrasting the very different results of employing productive and as compared with unproductive labour, he observes that the labour of the 'manufacturer',

> fixes and realises itself in some particular object or vendible commodity, which lasts for some time at least after that labour is past. It is, as it were, a certain quantity of labour stocked and stored up to be employed, if necessary, upon some other occasion. That subject, or what is the same thing, the price of that subject, can afterwards, if necessary, put into motion a quantity of labour equal to that which had originally produced it. The labour of the menial servant, on the contrary, does not fix or realise itself in any particular subject or vendible commodity. The services of the menial generally perish in the very instant of their performance, and seldom leave any trace or value behind them, for which an equal quantity of service could afterwards be procured.[6]

Here Smith is attributing distinctive additional properties to productive labour: its product can be carried forward for future use, and not only that, its product is capable of supporting in employment at least as much labour as was engaged in its production. By contrast, when unproductive workers are employed nothing is contributed for their support in the future.

For emphasis, Smith forcefully – and provocatively - reiterated the proposition that the present contribution of unproductive labour – however eminent the labourers may be – will not ensure that contribution in the future:

> The labour of some of the most respectable orders in the society is, like that of menial servants, unproductive of any value, and does not fix or realise itself in any permanent subject, or vendible commodity, which endures after that labour is past, and for which an equal quantity of labour could afterwards be procured. The sovereign, for example, with all the officers both of justice and of war who serve under him, the whole army and navy, are unproductive labourers ... Their service, how honourable, how useful, or how necessary soever, produces nothing for which an equal quantity of service can afterwards be procured ... In the same class must be ranked, both some of the gravest and most important, and some of the most frivolous professions: churchmen, lawyers, physicians, men of letters of all kinds; players, buffoons, musicians, opera-singers, opera-dancers, etc. ... Like the declamation of the actor, the harangue of the orator, or the tune of the musician, the work of all of them perishes in the very instant of its production.[7]

Productive Labour: Distinguishing Characteristics

To summarize: the characteristics said by Smith to distinguish productive from unproductive labour are:

(i) productive labour 'adds to the value of the subject upon which it is bestowed', so that the value of the product not only repays the cost of materials together with the wage bill, but yields a value surplus which constitutes a profit to the capitalist employer.

(ii) productive labour 'fixes and realizes itself' (is 'embodied' we might say) in the form of the commodities it produces, commodities which possess a certain degree of durability and so can be 'stocked and stored up' for future use.

(iii) the product of productive labour can 'put into motion' a quantity of labour (at least) equal to that by which it was originally produced.

Let us work through the list.

Criterion (i)

Productive labour is said to yield a net profit to the capitalist employer. What lies behind this proposition? Essentially a simple fact of common observation: Smith is making the point that while the employment of unproductive workers, such as 'menial servants', costs the employer money, putting labour to work in industry offers a very good prospect of making a profit. Workers who are employed by capital in industrial or commercial operations can generally be expected, Smith believed, to return a profit to their employer. Smith was not blind to the possibility of such ventures failing to live up to the hopes of the entrepreneur, bringing losses not gains, but took the view that, as a rule, outcomes are successful.

So, putting capital to work in employing labour is a pretty sure way of making money; how does profit arise? Although Smith does not explain the source of surplus value by reference to the labour theory of value as did Marx, his explanation is not dissimilar. As Smith sees the situation, capitalist employers possess the economic power which enables them to appropriate the lion's share of the value added in production; only a mere subsistence wage is left for the workers.[8] In principle, labour is thus productive of surplus value in *any* sphere of capitalist operation; what is produced is irrelevant. The significance of the surplus-value condition is, of course, that the employment of such labour is potentially good for economic progress: the capture by the capitalists of surplus value puts in their hands finance to extend their operations.

Before concluding on the surplus-value criterion, we should note an inconsistency in what Smith says about service labour. There is no question that 'menial servants', returning no profits to their employers, properly fall into the unproductive category, but what about the 'players, buffoons, musicians, opera-singers, opera-dancers' whom he also lists as unproductive along with 'the sovereign, the officers of justice and of war', etc? While the sovereign and the rest of the establishment are not employed in profit-seeking ventures, players, buffoons, musicians, opera-singers, opera-dancers normally are. The fact that their product is intangible, and that they have not worked-up materials ('adding to the value of the subject on which their labour is bestowed') would seem irrelevant to their status as 'productive' labour: they *do* generate surplus value. Smith evidently, by his own criterion, got this wrong.[9]

It may be noted that Marx likewise judges labour 'productive' if its employment yields surplus value to the employer. But, for Marx, the creation of surplus value was the sole distinguishing feature of productive labour: he proposes no other conditions for labour to qualify as 'productive'.[10] On that, Smith's position, as we have seen, was different: he specified two further conditions, referring both to the product's durability and to its ability to support labour in employment.

Criterion (ii)
Smith requires (or so it looks), as a characteristic of productive labour, that its produce must be of a material or durable nature: 'productive labour fixes and realizes itself in some particular object or vendible commodity, which lasts for some time at least after that labour is past'. Apparently, therefore, labour which produces services which 'perish in the very instant of their performance' fails – however useful these services may be – to qualify as productive. But that

conclusion does not necessarily follow: although intangible services cannot be directly stored up like tons of potatoes or stockpiles of coal, services rendered in the course of production *can* in effect be carried forward through time when 'embodied' in material products.

It is not surprising that this criterion has proved controversial; questions are asked. What about the 'materiality' of the product? Was Smith saying that labour supplying services cannot count as productive? What about 'durability'? Does the production of *any* durable product justify classification of labour as 'productive'? These questions will be examined further below.

Criterion (iii)

This criterion requires that for labour to be classed as 'productive' its product must be such as to 'put labour into motion'. To appreciate what Smith has in mind here, we need to understand the nature of the economic system as Smith envisaged it. His conception is of a surplus-producing economy which, over an annual cycle of production, produces more output than suffices to replace the materials used-up in the course of that production.[11] The surplus thus created may be used for the support of 'unproductive' members of the community who make no contribution to the production of that output or, alternatively, used to add to the community's stock of productive resources.

Even though Smith doesn't directly describe the features of the system in these terms, it is not difficult to make out what he has in mind. The idea of outputs returning to production as inputs is of course implicit in the condition that labour is productive if its product can 'put labour into motion'. The following passage makes the point explicitly:

> if a quantity of food and clothing, which were consumed by unproductive, had been distributed among productive hands, they would have reproduced, together with a profit, the full value of their consumption. . . . there would have been a reproduction of an equal value of consumer goods.[12]

And again: if an excessive amount of current output is consumed unproductively, and not enough returned to maintain the cycle of production by supporting productive workers, 'the next year's produce', Smith warns, 'will be less than that of the foregoing'[13] From the Smithian perspective production is a surplus-producing process. That is evident from Smith's observation: 'The sovereign, for example, with all the officers both of justice and war who serve under him, the whole army and navy, are unproductive labourers. They are the servants of the public, and are maintained by a part of the annual produce of the industry of other people'.[14] In another instance, Smith laments the fact that, in the past, so much of the nation's surplus output has been wasted in unnecessary wars, rather than applied with greater benefit to building up the capital stock of the country:

> So great a share of the annual produce of the land and labour of the country, has, since the revolution [of 1688], been employed ... in maintaining an extraordinary number of unproductive hands. Had not these wars given this particular direction to so large a capital, the greater part of it would naturally have been employed in maintaining productive hands, whose labour would have replaced, with a profit, the whole value of their consumption ... More houses would have been built, more lands would have been improved ... more manufactures would have been established.[15]

A surplus-producing capability implies a potential for growth, though that capability may not be used to the best advantage.

We must now ask: what is the labour which, in this context, qualifies as 'productive' by reason that it 'puts labour into motion'? Labour is 'put into motion', i.e. supported in employment, by the efforts of the workers who supply means of subsistence (food, clothing, shelter), plus those of the workers who provide the materials and equipment necessary for carrying out productive operations. These workers are in turn supported by others who supply to them the subsistence, materials and equipment they require. And so on. All these workers count as 'productive' by virtue of their contribution to the support of labour in employment.

'Productive' workers, engaged in the many interdependent industries comprising the economy, support each other through their respective contributions to production. The engineering industry, for instance, supplies machines to the textile industry, which manufactures clothes for the engineering workers, and both engineering and textiles depend on the services of the transport industry, which in its turn makes use of goods produced by the textile and engineering sectors. The labour of productive workers collectively throughout the system keeps the economy in operation, maintaining, period by period, the supplies of necessary inputs – of materials, fuel, equipment and wage-goods needed to support the workforce in employment – replacing (and more than replacing) what is constantly being used up. On the other hand, workers who manufacture luxuries for consumption by the wealthy do not count as productive in that their produce does not go, either as producers' goods or wage-goods, to support themselves or other workers in employment.

The set of interdependent industries in which productive labour is employed (with the labour in each industry mutually supporting the labour in the others) may be viewed as forming a self-sustaining 'core' of the production system, a key sector which supplies (replacing as they are used up) all its own resource needs, and via the surplus of its output over its own input usage, makes possible economic growth through investment both in this core sector itself and in other non-essential lines of activity. This core sector essentially corresponds to what Piero Sraffa[16] identifies as the 'basic sector'. While the idea of such a sector is implicit rather than explicit in Smith's analysis, he certainly does recognize the essence of the concept that a certain set of workers - productive labour by criterion (iii) - produce and re-produce the 'necessary' goods required to 'put labour into motion', and in so doing supply a surplus of these goods which makes possible capital accumulation in addition to maintaining 'unproductive' members of the community.

Smith was fully aware of the complex interaction and interdependence of activities characteristic of a modern industrial system. Consider, as highly relevant in this context, his famed account of how the manufacture of simple products such as a labourer's woollen coat involves 'the assistance and co-operation of many thousands' of workmen across the economy; how, that is to say, it involves the assistance and co-operation of many thousands of *productive workers*, the products of whose labour 'put into motion' labour in a vast range of activities, ultimately helping to 'put into motion' the workman who comes to wear the coat. There isn't space here to quote the complete passage, but note the following:

> The shepherd, the sorter of wool, the wool-comber or carder, the dyer, the scribbler, the spinner, the weaver, the fuller, the dresser, with many others, must all join their different arts in order to complete even this homely production. How many merchants and carriers, besides, must have been employed in transporting from some of those workmen to others who often live in a very distant part of the country! ... What a variety of labour too is necessary to produce the tools of the meanest of those workmen ... what a variety of labour is requisite in order to form that very simple machine, the shears with which the shepherd clips the wool. The miner, the builder of the furnace for smelting the ore, the feller of the timber, the burner of the charcoal to be made use of in the smelting house, the brick-maker, the bricklayer, the workmen who attend the furnace, the mill-wright, the forger, the smith, must all of them join their different arts in order to produce them.[17]

Such is the number of workers (Smith says 'beyond all computation') who – to repeat the point at issue – contribute to putting our labourer into motion by providing him with his woollen coat. We emphasize that all labour, working within an interdependent industrial system, producing the inputs, including wage-goods, necessary to maintain the system in operation (or expand it), satisfies Smith's criterion (iii) and therefore qualifies for classification as 'productive labour'.

Let us call criterion (iii) the 'necessary goods' criterion; labour which produces the 'necessary goods' required to 'put labour into motion' qualifies as 'productive'.

This criterion points to a property of productive labour not demanded by the previous two criteria. Specifically, if labour meets this criterion, its contribution renews – and indeed more than renews – the necessary goods (and services) used-up in current production. From this perspective, productive labour puts in place *resources of a character appropriate to maintaining and (via a surplus of necessary goods) increasing the current level of output*. Labour engaged in producing, say, fine porcelain, sedan chairs or wedding hats would not count as productive but labour producing more mundane consumption goods – working clothes, porridge oats – or equipment such as improved spinning machines, would.

This 'necessary goods' criterion points to an interesting theoretical link. What we suggest (as hinted above) is that Smith, in groping in this direction for a characterization of productive labour, was heading towards recognition of a distinction introduced years later by Sraffa – the distinction, that is to say, between the 'basic' and 'non-basic' sectors of an economy.[18] It looks very much as if the 'necessary goods' criterion of productive labour suggested by Smith's analysis, if applied in the context of the Sraffa system, would identify as 'productive' the labour employed in what Sraffa describes as the basic sector of the economy. In Sraffa's model, the basic sector of industry supplies to itself and to the rest of the economy 'basic' goods – essential commodities without which no industry can operate. *Without such basic goods labour cannot be 'put into motion'.* The surplus of basic goods over the basic sector's own requirements supports all non-basic and non-producing sectors of the economy, as well as supplying investment goods for capital accumulation. The interpretation of Smith that we are suggesting is that the goods produced by labour identified by his 'necessary goods' criterion as productive, are in fact analogous to Sraffa's 'basic'goods, and correspondingly, the labour which in Smith's analysis produces these necessary goods is equivalent to the labour employed the basic sector of the Sraffa system.

Let us adapt our terminology, and, emphasizing the Sraffa connection, re-designate 'necessary goods' as 'basic goods' and rechristen the 'necessary goods' criterion as the 'basic goods' criterion.

Taking Stock

There are no serious problems with criteria (i) and (iii). Criterion (i) makes the point – more or less clearly – that a significant characteristic of what Smith describes as productive labour is that its employment yields surplus value to its capitalist employer. Criterion (iii) is straightforward – labour rated by this criterion as productive is engaged in the production of necessary/basic goods, which as inputs are essential for the continued operation of the economic system, and for its expansion. Included within the category of basic goods are materials and equipment, together with wage-goods, as required to support labour 'in motion' in the basic industries of the industrial system. Luxury – non-essential – goods which do not contribute to the support of labour, of course fail to meet the condition imposed by criterion (iii).

Criterion (ii) is more problematical. The way Smith puts the matter rather invites the misinterpretation that workers who produce services as distinct from material commodities are debarred from the productive category. On closer investigation, it is, however, evident that service provision, at least the provision of services which contribute to the production of the basic goods of criterion (iii), is *not* relegated to the category of unproductive labour. In discussing 'the different employment of capitals' Smith[19] observes that capital may be employed (amongst other uses) 'in transporting either the rude or manufactured produce from the places where they abound to those where they are wanted, [and] in dividing particular portions of either into such small parcels as suit the occasional demands of those who want them'. Given his dictum that 'whatever part of his stock a man employs as capital ... [h]e employs it ... in maintaining productive hands only', it is evident that Smith is fully prepared to regard as 'productive' the labour providing services which constitute an essential part of the production process.

There is a further difficulty as regards the durability of products. Durability *per se* cannot be an attribute of a product which qualifies the producer as productive: a statue in marble does not help to put labour into motion. The relevant consideration is whether the product in question serves (or may eventually serve) to do so. On both these counts, therefore, criterion (ii) appears to add nothing to what is covered under criterion (iii).

Do the specified criteria identify a single unambiguous concept of productive labour? The answer is that they seem not to do so: not one, but two different concepts of productive labour appear to be indicated. Taking criterion (i) on its own, productive labour is identified as labour that produces surplus value; taking criteria (ii) and (iii) together, productive labour is defined as labour that produces necessary goods which 'put labour into motion'. Both concepts offer perfectly reasonable characterizations of productive labour, but they refer to different properties and need not denote exactly the same sets of workers. Labour, which from one perspective rates as productive, may not do so from the other. For instance: labour engaged in the manufacture of basic goods can be expected normally to return a profit to the employer, but, on the other hand, say, actors in the theatre, while generating profit for a capitalist, are doing nothing to renew supplies of the necessary goods which they consume. In terms of the surplus-value criterion, both groups qualify, but, by the basic goods criterion, one set of workers rates as productive and the other does not.

Objections and Difficulties relating to Smith's Concept of Productive Labour

Confusing 'Useful Labour' with 'Productive Labour'

Probably the most famous objection made to Smith's analysis is that it is nonsense to characterize, as Smith does, many eminent and important members of the community as 'unproductive' – on the grounds that they fail to meet *any* of the specified criteria. It is no wonder that the supposedly pejorative implication of the term 'unproductive' provoked complaint. For instance, Sir Alexander Gray[20] dismisses the distinction between productive and unproductive labour as 'an evil legacy of the Physiocrats', and warns readers that 'there may be all manner of occupations which are unproductive in the Smithian sense, but yet indirectly are of the highest productivity'.[21] Those who took exception to Smith's description of respected members of the community as 'unproductive' were, of course, missing his point. The usefulness or otherwise, in terms of consumer satisfaction or social benefit, of particular sorts of labour was *not* the issue with which he was concerned: as the objectors should have noticed, Smith explicitly makes the point that his classification of an activity as 'unproductive' does not imply that it is of no use or value to the community, allowing in fact that so-called 'unproductive' activities may well be 'honourable', 'useful' or 'necessary'.[22] What did concern Smith was waste of resources through excessive unproductive employment, with the wealthy spending on 'baubles and trifles' and maintaining armies of servants, and politicians being prone to squander wealth on 'unnecessary wars'.

Issues of Materiality and Durability

Interpreted quite literally as a proposal that labour be recognized as productive only if its direct product possesses physical durability, criterion (ii) has troubled commentators. John Stuart Mill,[23] for one, asked, 'why refuse the title [of productive] to the surgeon who sets a limb, the judge or legislator who confers security, and give it to the lapidary who cuts and polishes a diamond?' If, as pointed out above, we look beyond the particular passage in which Smith enunciates this criterion, it is clear that commentators who have expressed concern about this materiality criterion have taken Smith's words in too literal a sense. Smith did rate labour as 'productive' when, even if its own immediate contribution was of an intangible character, it assisted directly or indirectly in 'putting labour into motion'. In other words, while 'menial servants', 'the officers both of justice and war' etc., are confirmed as 'unproductive', the carter delivering materials to the factory, the retailer providing a convenient supply of consumption goods to members of the workforce are at the same time placed in the category of productive labour.

Marx on Smith

While Marx was full of praise for Smith's identification of the generation of surplus value as a characteristic of productive labour, he was all against Smith's other concept of productive labour, depending as it did on the nature of what labour produced: that, in Marx's opinion, was a mistake. He accused Smith of hanging on to notions of a Physiocratic character. Marx saw the question of productive labour solely from the angle of income distribution: as surplus value could be extracted from labour by capital *in whatever industry* labour was employed, there was no point in differentiating between activities in which labour might be employed.

However, as we have seen, Smith was taking a broader view of the contribution of productive labour – seeing productive labour not only as the source of surplus value, but as being also of vital importance in providing for the growth of the economy. He therefore, appropriately, includes in the 'productive' category labour whose contribution in terms of producing real, physical output he recognized as essential to the achievement of economic progress. Thus in criticizing Smith for giving attention to the 'material characteristics' of the product of labour, Marx was apparently thinking too narrowly in terms of his own theoretical concern, thus missing the point of what Smith was saying.

It is interesting that in recent years Marxist theorists have come to see the virtue of Smith's inclusion within the productive category of labour engaged in the production of basic commodities. Note that a number of scholars, even though approaching the issue from a Marxian perspective, actually prefer a Smithian to the Marxian approach. Specifically, they show a readiness to abandon Marx's position that productive labour is characterized solely by an ability to create surplus value, and accept that the nature of the product may be a relevant consideration.

Ian Gough,[24] drawing on works by Joseph Gillman,[25] Jacob Morris[26] and Justin Blake,[27] takes the view that if we are thinking about economic growth (as of course Smith was), while labour employed in Marx's Departments I and II (producing respectively equipment and wage-goods), may properly be classified as productive, labour of Department III (luxury goods) – which, as creating surplus value, is rated productive in Marx's own terms – should be excluded from the productive category.

Gough (p. 67) continues:

> Blake [1960, p. 173] suggests that for a political economy of growth, a sufficient definition of productive labour is 'labour whose products can re-enter the cycle of production as elements of variable and constant capital ... even when such employment does not directly produce surplus value' ... This is a logical development of the neo-Smithian concept, but one which serves to divorce it clearly from the Marxian concept.

As Gough recognizes, this amounts to a revival of Smith's 'basic goods' concept of productive labour, as appropriate in the context of capital accumulation and growth, in preference Marx's definition solely in terms of the creation of surplus value. Smith, we may be sure, can be cleared of Marx's charge that differentiating between productive and unproductive labour on the basis of the type of output produced amounts to no more than a misguided irrelevance.

Inconsistent Definitions or Concepts of Productive Labour

As already noted, Smith's criteria point to two distinct definitions or concepts of productive labour – (a) as creating surplus value and (b) as producing the basic goods that put labour into motion. Unfortunately, these concepts appear to conflict in that labour which qualifies as productive in terms of one concept may not pass the other Smithian test. How, for instance, are we to regard labour whose employment yields a profit to the capitalist, but whose output (say, a Fabergé Easter egg) is neither a piece of equipment which 'aids and abridges' labour in production nor a subsistence good? Such labour, even though rated as productive according to criterion (i) is certainly not, as required by criterion (iii), producing a 'basic' good which can 'put labour into motion'. Labour employed in such activities would appear by Smith's criteria to be at the same time both 'productive' and 'unproductive'.

We seem to have arrived at a rather unsatisfactory situation. Smith does not, it would appear, provide an unambiguous identification of precisely what labour rates and does not rate as 'productive'; complaints have certainly been made. Looking at the issue from a Marxist perspective, Isaak Ilyich Rubin [28] observes that 'Smith is obviously unaware that he is putting forward two definitions [of productive labour] that do not fully concur with one another'. Maurice Dobb was evidently unimpressed by Smith's attempt to define what he understood by 'productive labour'. Dobb comments:

> in explaining wherein the difference between 'artificers and manufacturers and merchants', on the one hand, and 'menial servants' consisted, Adam Smith is far from clear. Here he introduces two distinct, if largely overlapping, definitions, involving (as Marx pointed out) certain contradictions between them, or at least displaying no clear boundary between the productive and the unproductive.[29]

Eric Roll is similarly critical:

> Throughout chapter iii of the second book [of the *Wealth of Nations*], two separate definitions of productive and unproductive labour are intermingled ... Productive labour is ... defined both as labour which creates value and as labour which creates a surplus for the employer. With this confusion there is mixed up another. Smith also defines productive labour as that which 'fixes and realises itself in some particular subject or vendible commodity'.[30]

So, is Smith confused as to what precisely the term 'productive labour' is meant to mean? An inconsistency in Smith's account of productive labour has already been noted in that labour which produces certain services at a profit is nevertheless represented as unproductive. Despite that element of confusion we take the view that Smith essentially had in mind two different, *but nevertheless complementary*, concepts of productive labour.

The Fabergé egg case exemplifies the anomaly which has particularly troubled the critics: labour engaged in the production of luxury goods is unproductive (by the basic goods concept of productive labour), but at the same time, in returning profit to the entrepreneur, is productive (surplus value concept of productive labour). This does look awkward for Smith, but it has been suggested that he may have avoided an accusation of inconsistency by the simple expedient of leaving problematic workers of that sort out of the picture. Thus Hla Myint argues: 'The classical economists were working on the basis of an economic system where the bulk of material commodities consisted of "necessities" or basic wage-goods, and where "luxuries" were mainly made up of the services of the menial and professional classes'.[31] In other words, if, in addition to suppliers of luxuries supported out of revenue, the number of employees of capitalist operations producing bejewelled Easter eggs and comparable baubles was negligible, it would have been quite natural, and legitimate, for Smith to ignore them. If so, no contentious profit-producing luxury workers would be present to complicate the story.

As a defence the argument is ingenious. However, we doubt that Smith would have assumed such workers out of existence; reviewing in some detail the spending patterns of '[men] of fortune',[32] he clearly recognized that much labour was commercially employed in the manufacture of luxury items of a material character. The suggestion we now make is that it is not necessary to resort to stratagems such as proposed by Myint – for the reason that the alleged inconsistency in Smith's treatment of the concept of productive and unproductive labour is, arguably, more apparent than real.

The point on which Smith's critics focus is that the groups of workers identified by his two concepts of productive labour are not the same – they overlap to a considerable extent, but not completely. We propose that, in coming to a view on this alleged inconsistency, the focus should be on what is *common* to the two concepts rather than on their differing implications regarding the people employed. Thus: both concepts identify labour as productive by virtue of possessing a property, or properties, of the first importance for the attainment of economic growth: (a) an ability to create surplus value, essential for saving to be possible and investment to be financed, and (b) an ability to create a surplus of basic goods, of which an increased quantity is required if the productive capability of the economy is to increase. Workers possessing either property produce what is essential for capital accumulation and growth; the two sorts of surplus-production in fact complement each other in putting in place the resources required for growth.

We therefore propose that the term 'productive labour' be interpreted in a comprehensive sense to include, in one general category, *both* concepts of productive labour as identified by Smith. That, we suggest (even if he did not formulate his proposition with absolute precision) is exactly what Smith's analysis of 'productive labour' comes to – productive labour is labour which produces a valuable surplus, regardless of whether that surplus is of the one sort or the other. From the broader perspective, it doesn't matter if, as would be expected, the different subcategories do not comprise the same productive labourers: their specific contributions are different, but they are all 'productive' in that they replace the resources (real or financial) they use up, and produce a surplus (of whatever kind) without which economic progress cannot be achieved.We therefore take the position that although Smith does indeed use the term 'productive labour' in different senses to describe two different sets of workers, as these are subsets of a more general category of productive labour, no inconsistency is involved.

While this comprehensive conception of productive labour attributed to Smith is seen as logical and acceptable, it has to be said that it would have made for greater clarity had Smith stated explicitly that his concept of productive labour did include two subcategories of productive labour: that while *all* labour profitably employed in commercial operations generated surplus value, *some* of that labour made an *additional* contribution in the form of a surplus of basic goods. That clarification would have taken care of the 'Fabergé egg' issue[33] and would also have allowed recognition (obscured by the broad definition) that the growth prospects of the economy could be enhanced not only by reallocating labour from unproductive to productive activities, but also by transferring productive labour from merely surplus-value-producing employment to employment in the doubly-productive basic sector. Nevertheless the broad definition is consistent with and serves to explain Smith's strong emphasis – as an absolutely fundamental point – on the negative implications of employing, whether in the public or private sector, undue quantities of unproductive labour. ('According, therefore, as a smaller or greater proportion of [the national resources] is in any one year employed in maintaining unproductive hands, the more in the one case and the less in the other will remain for the productive, and the next year's produce will be greater or smaller accordingly').[34]

So far we have looked into a number of 'objections and difficulties' concerning Smith's concept of productive and unproductive labour. Smith's treatment, although not altogether fault-free, generally stands up to the objections raised by the critics. The classification according to Smith's criteria of certain categories of labour as 'unproductive' does not imply condemnation of the labour of unproductive workers as of no value to society. Likewise, interpretation of the term productive as applying only to labour producing tangible commodities derives from a misreading of Smith: although the point is not over-emphasized, Smith did indeed recognize the essential contribution of all sorts of service providers in putting labour into motion. Again, Marx's objection to Smith's taking the product of labour as relevant to determining the status of labour, is ill-founded: given Smith's interest in the necessary conditions of economic growth it was entirely appropriate that he should do so. Finally, we have suggested that, taking an all-encompassing view of productive labour as all labour which produces a surplus, in value or in real terms, capable of engendering growth, no issue of inconsistency arises if certain workers qualify as productive by reason of their contributing to one surplus, without contributing to the other.

Conclusion: A Meaningful Distinction

Smith's differentiation of productive from unproductive labour has not always been well-received. This paper, however, offers a positive view - recognition that his analysis demonstrates a penetrating insight into the conditions which, on the one hand, favour and promote economic growth, and which, on the other, frustrate it. The discussion in which productive and unproductive labour feature is all about how 'the annual produce of the land and labour of any nation' may be increased. That can be achieved, Smith explains,

> only by increasing either the number of its productive labourers, or the productive powers of those labourers who had been before employed. The number of its productive labourers, it is evident, can never be much increased, but in consequence of an increase in capital, or the funds destined for maintaining them. The productive powers of the same number of labourers cannot be increased, but in consequence either of some improvement to those machines and instruments which facilitate and abridge labour; or of a more proper division and distribution of employment. In either case an additional capital is almost always required.[35]

Investment, that is to say, is the key to growth. This is where the concept of productive and unproductive labour fits in. A value surplus and a surplus of necessary goods (fixed and working capital) which support labour in employment are both required – the former to permit the purchase of additional capital goods, the latter to ensure their supply. The significance of productive labour is that, without its (double) contribution, investment, capital accumulation and an increase of the annual produce of the nation simply cannot occur. Smith says it all in the title of Chapter iii of Book II: 'Of the Accumulation of Capital, or of productive and unproductive Labour'.

In classifying labour as productive if its employment yields surplus value to the employer, there is evidently an affinity between Smith and Marx; but what is common to them both regarding the concept of productive/unproductive labour does not extend beyond that. Marx, as we have seen, was strongly opposed to Smith's specifying further grounds for differentiating between productive and unproductive labour by reference to the nature of the product which labour produced. In this, it would appear, Marx was blind to Smith's understanding of the significance of an additional category of productive workers, those engaged in the production of the commodities which 'put labour into motion'.

It is remarkable how Smith anticipated – at least in essence - the distinction Sraffa would later draw between basic and non-basic activities. As the perception that labour can be divided into two categories, one which produces and re-produces essential commodities, the other which uses-up such essentials without replacing its consumption, was fundamental to Smith's conception of the economic system, so is its equivalent in Sraffa's system. We are not of course arguing that Smith anticipated the depth and rigour of Sraffa's analysis – Smith has, for instance, no idea of a notional 'standard system' in which the properties of the actual system are revealed – but the essential features of the Sraffa model (which, to repeat, are of surplus production of basic goods by a key sector comprising numerous interdependent, mutually-supporting activities) can be discerned in Smith's depiction of the working of the contemporary economy.

Finally, in concluding this chapter, note the phrase in the title – 'nearer to Sraffa than Marx'; the point, which should, it is hoped, by now be obvious, is that when we compare the views of Smith against those of his two greatest successors within the classical tradition, we find that his perceptive understanding of the essential conditions for increasing 'the wealth of nations' places him much closer to Sraffa than to Marx. Marx did not appreciate what Smith was getting at in his analysis involving productive and unproductive labour; Sraffa – had he published his thoughts on Smith – might very well have identified a precursor working along similar lines.

It is regrettable that Smith's distinction between productive and unproductive labour has so often been dismissed as a confusing aberration. Essentially Smith's thesis was that employment of *productive labour* which though its activities *not only renews but increases* a country's productive resources (real and financial), rather than *unproductive labour* which consumes such resources without reproducing them, is the route to increasing the value of the annual produce of the nation. The truth of the matter is that his analysis was original and perceptive, and – although admittedly not altogether free of elements of confusion and obscurity – reveals nevertheless a deep understanding of the structure and working of a surplus-producing economic system, of an economy possessing the characteristics of the then-emerging capitalist, industrial economy.

Appendix: Productive and Unproductive Labour – An Illustration

Consider the anatomy of a simple (Sraffa-type) surplus-producing economic system, in terms of which we may interpret different identifications of productive and unproductive labour, and observe the implications for growth of different deployments of labour.

Suppose the economy in question to consist of six industries or sectors, namely *iron* (representing engineering), *coal* (representing fuel and energy), *corn* (standing for agriculture and the production of food, textiles, leather, etc), *transport* (providing essential logistical support), a *luxury* sector producing 'non-essential' goods of all kinds, and finally, a non-industrial sector of *domestic services*. The iron, coal, corn and transport industries are interdependent in that some portion of the goods and services they produce enter as inputs into each other's production; by contrast, the luxury and domestic services sectors produce only goods for final consumption. Production takes place period by period over time, with part of each period's output returning, as replacement for resources used-up, to the production process in the following period.

This is obviously a highly-stylised representation of a real-world economic system. A major simplifying assumption is that all inputs, even items such as machinery, are treated as working rather than, more realistically, as fixed capital. That assumption – after Sraffa (1960) – serves to simplify the model without affecting its validity as a representation of a surplus-producing system. Commodities are broadly defined: for instance, in producing 'iron' the iron industry is understood to manufacture materials and intermediate goods as well as final goods.

The community consists of (wealthy) *capitalist employers*, who derive profits from their industrial operations, *industrial workers* paid a standard wage, and *domestic employees* ('menial servants') who are paid the same wage as the industrial workers. Total population consists of 5,300 'labour units' (or families), comprising 3,800 dependent on industrial employment, 1,000 employed in domestic services and 500 well-to-do employers. It is supposed that the real wage over the production period per unit of labour is made up of a package of 2 iron + 1 coal + 4 corn + 1 transport; only the employers can afford luxury goods and domestic services.

Input-output relationships are shown in Table 2.1. The rows show a sector's inputs as required to produce the current volume of output, and the columns show the lines of production to which each product is applied. Each sector uses, per period of time, certain physical quantities of inputs (measured, as appropriate, in tons, ton-miles or man-hours). In each period of production the economic system produces (i.e. *reproduces*) the total industry usage of inputs (including subsistence goods for the maintenance of industrial employees); in addition a surplus of subsistence goods over industry's requirements is supplied, and used for the support of employers and domestic servants, plus a quantity of luxury goods which, together with domestic services, are purchased only by the employer class.

Table 2.1: The economy as a whole.

	Iron	Coal	Corn	Trans	Lux	Labour	
Iron uses:	2340 +	2800 +	600 +	1200 +	0 +	334	to produce: 18400 iron
Coal uses:	1000 +	2000 +	400 +	700 +	0 +	237	to produce: 15800 coal
Corn uses:	750 +	660 +	3000 +	800 +	0 +	429	to produce: 29200 corn
Trans uses:	800 +	4000 +	2000 +	600 +	0 +	400	to produce: 10000 trans
Lux uses:	2910 +	1040 +	2000 +	1400 +	0 +	2400	to produce: 18000 lux
D-ser uses:	0 +	0 +	0 +	0 +	0 +	1000	to produce: misc. non-marketed services

	Iron	Coal	Corn	Trans	Lux
Commodity usage of industrial sector:					

material inputs (excluding wage goods):

Iron	Coal	Corn	Trans	Lux
7800	10500	8000	4700	0

wage goods (with labour usage in industrial sector = 3800):

Iron	Coal	Corn	Trans	Lux
7600	3800	15200	3800	0

total material inputs (including wage goods):

Iron	Coal	Corn	Trans	Lux
15400	14300	23200	8500	0

Surplus output of industrial sector:

Iron	Coal	Corn	Trans	Lux
18400	15800	29200	10000	18000
less	less	less	less	less
15400	14300	23200	8500	0
3000	1500	6000	1500	18000

The surplus output of the industrial sector – what remains after all costs of production, including the support of the workforce, have been met from current production – is available for use by the owners/employers, as they choose, for their own consumption, for investment, or for the maintenance of servants.

If all labour the employment of which yields surplus value is deemed productive, then - assuming all industrial operations yield a common (positive) rate of profit - the workers in all five sectors of the industrial system, iron, coal, corn, transport and luxuries, fall into the productive category.

Now introduce Sraffa's (1960) distinction between 'basic' and 'non-basic' industries. *Iron, coal, corn* and *transport* form an interdependent set of industries which together comprise the 'basic' sector of this economy – 'basic' in the sense that these industries provide essential inputs, including wage-goods, to every industry operating within the economy. By contrast a 'non-basic' industry (*lux*), while itself dependent on the output of the basic sector, makes no contribution to the production of that sector. Here the products of the basic sector – iron, coal, corn and transport services – constitute the 'basic goods' of the economy.

The basic sector is itself surplus-producing, replacing its own usage of resources, and supplying also the basic goods essential for keeping the non-basic sector in operation, as well as subsistence goods for all members of the community. Maintaining the supposition that each unit of labour is paid per period a real wage package consisting of 2 iron + 1 coal + 4 corn + 1 trans, the *total material inputs* (inclusive of wages paid) of the basic sector, its *output* and the *surplus* it produces, are as shown in Table 2.2.

Table 2.2: The basic sector.

	Iron		Coal		Corn		Trans		[Labour]	
Iron uses:	3008	+	3134	+	1936	+	1534	+	[334]	to produce 18400 iron
Coal uses:	1474	+	2237	+	1348	+	937	+	[237]	to produce 15800 coal
Corn uses:	1608	+	1089	+	4716	+	1229	+	[429]	to produce 29200 corn
Trans uses:	1600	+	4400	+	3600	+	1000	+	[400]	to produce 10000 trans

Total material usage of basic sector (including wage goods for support of the workers):

7690	10860	11600	4700	[1400]

The surplus produced by the basic sector:

	Iron	Coal	Corn	Trans
(gross output):	18400	15800	29200	10000
	less	less	less	less
	7690	10860	11600	4700
(surplus output):	10710	4940	17600	5300

It is evident that the work of the 1,400 labour employed in the basic sector is of the highest importance to the rest of the community (in number equivalent to another 3,900 labour). While the basic sector is self-sustaining, the 2,400 labour in the luxury sector, plus the 1,000 domestic servants – not to mention the 500 employers – are vitally dependent on what is supplied from the basic sector; none of these groups could survive without that sector's contribution.

It is the productivity of the basic sector – its ability to produce a surplus of its particular products over its own need for them – that determines the surplus-producing capability of the economy as a whole. The system's ability to accumulate capital, and its ability to support all sorts of non-productive activities, are governed by the availability from the basic sector of a sufficient supply of essential materials of production and means of subsistence. The particular make-up or form which the surplus product of the economy actually takes depends on how the available surplus of basics is deployed between the possible alternatives.

Thus, in the case of our illustrative economy (see Table 2.3), the surplus of basics is used to 'put into motion' labour in the luxury sector, as well as directly supporting the servants and their masters.

Table 2.3: Use of the basic surplus.

Iron (10710): 4800 as wage goods for labour in *Lux* sector;
3000 as basic consumption for employers and servants;
2910 as material inputs to *Lux* sector.

Coal (4940): 2400 as wage goods for labour in *Lux* sector;
1500 as basic consumption for employers and servants;
1040 as material inputs to *Lux* sector.

Corn (11600): 9600 as wage goods for labour in *Lux*;
6000 as basic consumption for employers and servants;
2000 as material inputs to *Lux* sector.

Trans (5300): 2400 as wage goods for labour in *Lux* sector;
1500 as basic consumption for employers and servants;
1400 as inputs to *Lux* sector.

In the situation represented, the surplus-producing capability of the system as a whole is directed solely to meeting the needs and desires of the employing class. That particular way of utilizing the basic surplus may do a lot for the comfort of that class, but doesn't do anything for the growth of the economy. If growth is wanted, a different deployment of the surplus is essential – it must be used to put into motion labour applied in other, more appropriate, activities. If some of the household servants were re-employed on construction work – building roads or harbours – their diversion to the creation of useful infrastructure could foster economic progress. Again, by switching luxury workers to the (doubly-productive) manufacture of producers' goods, the community's stock of productive assets could be increased. The point is that, in so far as there is scope for different ways of deploying the surplus of basic goods, the prospects for an economy can be very different. The support of unproductive labour has a serious opportunity cost in growth possibilities foregone. Smith, it will be recalled, was vehement in his condemnation of the squandering of resources by individuals or governments, and emphatic in his advocacy of applying surplus income instead to building up the community's resources.

This takes us back to Adam Smith. One interpretation of 'productive labour' of which, we believe, Smith had an intuition, corresponds to the labour which in a Sraffa-type system is engaged in the production of basic goods. If we apply here the 'basic goods' criterion of productive labour, the 1,400 labour employed in the iron, coal, corn and transport sectors qualify as 'productive'. The remaining industrial workers, the 2,400 in the luxury sector, do not rate as productive in terms of basic goods production, but do so as producers of surplus value. By the broad definition total productive labour equals 3,800 units. The 1,000 servants fail on both productivity counts and fall into the unproductive category.

Smith evidently believed there was cause to judge labour 'productive' both by what we have called the 'surplus-value' criterion and by the 'basic goods' criterion. It would appear that Smith sought to take both criteria on board for the reason that both these properties of labour are of fundamental importance for the achievement of economic growth. Smith may be understood to designate as 'productive' all labour which produces a useful surplus, whether in terms of money or basic goods, a surplus which has the potential to advance the accumulation of capital. That surely makes sense.

3 ETHICAL ISSUES IN KEY ASPECTS OF ECONOMIC DEVELOPMENT: RATIONALITY AND JUSTICE

David Vazquez-Guzman

A group of Epicurean and Stoic philosophers began to debate with him. Some of them asked, 'What is this babbler trying to say?'

Acts 17:18, Luke, *c*.AD 66[1]

The aim of this chapter is to outline the ethical and philosophical underpinnings of two concepts in economics; namely, rationality and justice. Both the concept of rationality in decision-making and the powerful idea behind justice are important axioms in economics; for instance, that equality of distribution is preferred and that an agent needs to be rational in order to optimize. Examining the development of these concepts in historical context will bring out the way they have been influenced by various contrasting philosophical traditions such as the ancient Greek philosophical tradition and the more ancient Middle Eastern Jewish tradition of thought. This will help the reader to reflect on the suitability and relevance of these concepts in relation to decision-making and policy formulation. Reflecting on these issues is especially important today as contemporary discussions often go beyond the concepts of equilibrium and optimality, and enter into the gray area of ethics. As encouraged by other authors in this area,[2] this discussion will place economics within an ethical and philosophical framework.

To discuss the intellectual development of these concepts in depth we need to carry out an examination not from a theoretical or empirical perspective but from a methodological stand point. To gain a deeper understanding of rationality and justice we have to delve back into classical economics and how it was shaped by the Greek philosophical tradition, in particular through the application of logic and mathematics during the period of the Enlightenment. The arguments presented here will build on the works of influential contemporary scholars such as Amartya Sen, Margaret Schabas, Sheila Dow and Leonidas Montes who are interested in studying abstraction of ethical issues in economics.[3] Two schools of thought, British empiricism,[4] and Continental rationalism, both developed during the Enlightenment period and built on the ancient Greek tradition, have contributed to the adoption of these ideas in modern economics. For example, contemporary scholars such as John Rawls and Sen have often used these schools or approaches to develop their ideas. Rawls and Sen also draw on the writings of Immanuel Kant in their work. Regrettably, when using various key concepts in modern economics, we are often unaware that these are drawn on the knowledge derived from ancient texts; there is also a tendency to underestimate the influence that religion and belief systems played in their development. Of course, it is important to be aware that this kind of philosophical discussion might be sensitive to individuals as it touches upon personal beliefs. As already mentioned, the Enlightenment, and the development of ideas associated with it, had an important influence on the evolution of economics as a subject. However, it has recently been suggested that modern economics is not a solution to contemporary economic problems but instead is a part of the problem. This view suggests that economists need reflect on and question the concepts and assumptions on which current economics is based.[5] In this sense, it would be useful to investigate whether using ancient philosophies other than those based on the Greek tradition could cast new light onto this debate. This does not mean that the Greek tradition is irrelevant; in fact, it could be the cause of some problems,[6] and what I am suggesting is that other perspectives may provide valuable insights into current problems and issues.

This chapter begins by tracing the development of the concept of rationality in economics drawing on the ideas of the British empirical school and the Continental rationalist school. This is followed a discussion of equity and equality, but with a contrasting point of view. Finally, I shall draw the chapter together and put forward some concluding remarks.

The Concept of Rationality in Economics

Several seminal studies address the concept of rationality in economics.[7] They describe rationality or the rationale for human action from different angles and perspectives, but none tackles in depth the conceptual framework of how scientists make assertions about human actions. A traditional way of conceptualizing the decision-making process is to refer to the late eighteenth-century studies.[8] Humans, however, have been involved in making complex decisions for thousands of years. Although it might be difficult to trace back the roots of systematic thinking on decision-making into ancient times, searching for them nevertheless could still be helpful in challenging our 'westernized' thought processes and conclusions. It could provide new insights into the decision-making process in general and our understanding of the concept of rationality in particular. In the

Greek philosophical tradition, axioms are 'evident truths' that do not need to be proven. In modern economics, when discussing human preferences, one of the four axioms that underpin consumer choice is that decision-making has to be rational. In its simplest monotonic form this means that a consumer prefers more to less. Another notion suggests that rationality means that consumers are able to order their preferences. This concept suggests a binary relationship; one that is reflexive, transitive and complete.[9] The concept of rationality in contemporary economics is based on self-love and selfishness,[10] and these concepts have their roots in Continental rationalism and British empiricism.[11] Since these schools use as a basis different versions of the Greek tradition, learning about their relevant context(s) is useful in order to understand the key underlying reasons behind each school's choices.

As alluded earlier, economic thought was deeply influenced by the philosophical developments of the Enlightenment. This period contrasts sharply with what came to be known as the Scholastic period which preceded it. During the Scholastic period, there was an effort to reconcile medieval Catholic theology with philosophy. This proved impossible since there were numerous divisions amongst the ecclesiastical hierarchy as a result of the lack of a strong central authority to impose a solution, and there were even military conflicts related to it. The Protestant reformation during sixteenth century also undermined the Catholic Church's authority by providing a different philosophical approach.[12] Lastly, there were also debates being carried on by scientists and philosophers that were conducted outside of the Church; a process that was often the result of politics rather than formal religious intervention.

The British Tradition and Rationality: Hume and Human Nature

David Hume through numerous texts and publications developed a complete system of human nature, and he is a figure to follow because he had a major influence on Adam Smith, who is for many the father of modern economics. Hume's views were highly coloured and influenced by his pious mother and clergyman stepfather. His theory of human nature was not, however, an attempt to underpin or justify Christian views but to act as an alternative. Hume was greatly influenced by the Greek philosopher Phyrrho who had developed scepticism. And whose work he had discovered reading the manuscripts of Sextus Empiricus (*c.*AD 160–210) which had come to light towards the end of the fourteenth century. Hume discovered that there were two views of scepticism being discussed in these manuscripts. The first was academic scepticism, while the second was more radical and based on the work of Phyrrho, and which became known as Phyrrhonism.[13]

Hume uses the power of doubt as a guide in his criticism of religious doctrines. More specifically, his work was principally based on academic scepticism which preached that nothing could be known but that some opinions were more probable (such as our immediate senses) than others (such as miracles). Hume applied scepticism to throw doubt on some of the accepted religious facts of the age; for example, the biblical view of the creation of the world and the incidence of miracles. As a true sceptic, however, he also cast doubt on his own conclusions arguing that as individuals we are apt to fall in error, though he maintained this should not stop one from questioning. As he stated:

> Thus the sceptic still continues to reason and believe, even tho' he asserts, that he cannot defend his reason by reason; and by the same rule he must assent to the principle concerning the existence of body, tho' he cannot pretend by any arguments of philosophy to maintain its veracity.[14]

Using this approach, where the question itself is the centre of reasoning, Hume questioned a number of fundamental religious beliefs surrounding human behaviour. A particular belief he attacked was God as a creator, where he offered an alternative view of a 'self-existent' creation in his *Natural History of Religion*, published in 1757.[15] Then, with an alternative to the most important established institutional thought, that is the denial of any supreme intelligent power, he was confident to explain human nature in a different way. Traditional and institutional canonical teaching viewed egocentric self love and selfishness as sinful and as contrary to God's law. Hume, contrarily, building on the Greek philosophical tradition, saw egocentrism and self love as pervasive and a normal part of human behaviour and as such should be nurtured and harnessed for the good of mankind rather than despised and denigrated.[16]

It is through the development of these ideas that Hume's influence on the development of economic thought can be seen. His views much influenced Smith, a fellow philosopher and a friend.[17] Two passages from Smith in particular illustrate this influence. The first is 'We are not ready to suspect any person of being defective in selfishness',[18] and the second and perhaps more famous of the two is the following: 'it is not from the benevolence of the butcher, the brewer, or the baker that we expect our dinner, but from their regard to their own interest'.[19]

Hume does not see the motivation of self love as necessarily being benevolent. In the following passage from his *Treatise on Human Nature* (1738) he claims that:

> But it is certain, that self love, when it acts in liberty, instead of engaging us to honest actions, is the source of all injustice and violence; nor can a man ever correct those vices, without correcting and restraining the natural movements of that appetite.[20]

How self love can be shaped into a positive force for society is due to man continually adjusting his behaviour at the margin. Here Hume's process is similar to that put forward by Mandeville in his *Fable of the Bees* (1705). Hume puts forward that:

> It is self-love which is their [the laws of justice] real origin; and as the self-love of One person is naturally contrary to that of another, these several interested passions

are obliged to adjust themselves after such a manner as to concur in some system of conduct and behaviour. This system, therefore, comprehending the interest of each individual, is of course advantageous to the public; though it be not intended for that purpose by the inventors.[21]

By examining Hume's work and the influence the sceptic philosophical outlook had on him we can trace the impact his work had on Smith and how the concept of rationality was shaped by him,[22] and therefore we can say that the today's view in modern economics that individuals as naturally selfish comes from Hume's work based on Greek philosophy.

The Continental European View of Rationalism and Rationality: The Influence of Descartes

The ancient Greek influence can also be seen in the European philosophical tradition, but in a different way to the English. The work of Descartes is particularly enlightening on this topic. Like Hume, Descartes was influenced by religion, but unlike him, Descartes was brought up in the Catholic tradition and was educated at the Jesuit college of La Fleche. There he was exposed to, and absorbed, the works of Aquinas. He practised Jesuit meditation based on the work of Ignatius of Loyola in his *Spiritual Exercises* written in 1524, for he had founded the Jesuit order. In 1619, Descartes experienced a 'prophetic sign' of divine revelation in three of his dreams.[23] Later, in 1627 Cardinal Berulle exhorted him to devote his efforts to the reformation of philosophy; a task he carried out for the rest of his life. On his sojourn in Holland (where he had taken only the *Summa* of Aquinas and a Bible[24]), between 1628 and 1649 he wrote his famous *Discourse on the Method of Rightly Conducting Reason* (1637) and *Meditations on First Philosophy* (1641). We can see here that Descartes was deeply influenced by the Aristotelian philosophy which he had acquired through studying Aquinas's works. The transmission of Greek knowledge to Aquinas was through the work of Averroes, a very prominent Islamic philosopher.

Although certainly not a sceptic like Hume, Descartes also used a methodology in his work based on doubt. He did not trust human sentiments because, as he said, the senses were apt to deceive us. His Cartesian doubt, which can be seen as a 'faithful doubt', works in the following way:

[A]lthough the senses may sometimes deceive us about some minute or remote objects, yet there are many other facts as to which doubt is plainly impossible, although these are gathered from the same soured: e.g. that I am here, sitting by the fire, wearing a winter cloak, holding this paper in my hands, and so on. Again, these hands and my whole body – how can their existence be denied?[25]

In spite of his doubts or uncertainties he was sure that real truths existed and they could be assimilated depending on individuals' perceptions or the acquired knowledge about those truths. According to Descartes, even in dreams of the impossible, real and indubitable elements could exist. As he wrote:

> Suppose I am dreaming, and these particulars, that I open my eyes, shake my head, put out my hand, are incorrect; suppose even that I have no such hand, no such body; at any rate it has to be admitted that the things that appear in sleep are like painted representations, which cannot have been formed except in the likeness of real objects. So at least these general kinds of things, eyes, head, hands, body must not be imaginary but real objects.[26]

The importance he placed on doubt in his methodology is seen in the following passage where he used doubt to answer a fundamental philosophical question:

> I noticed that while I was trying to think everything false, it must needs be that I, who was thinking this, was something. And observing that this truth 'I am thinking, therefore I exist' was so solid and secure that the most extravagant suppositions of the skeptics could not overthrow it, I judged that I need not scruple to accept it as the first principle of philosophy that I was seeking.[27]

Doubt provided him with the proof of his own existence as he claims in his *Discourse*: 'from the mere fact that I thought of doubting the truth of other things, it followed quite evidently and certainly that I existed'.[28] He thought that if we doubt, we think, and if we think, we are; in Latin '*Cogito, ergo, sum*' – 'I think, therefore I am'. Cartesian doubt in science was followed by its four precepts to replace all dubitable knowledge: the scientific method, which is the basis for the beginning of the study of logic and other empirical sciences.

Descartes placed great store in the ability of mathematical logic to lead to indubitable certainty. He inherited this from the Greek philosophical tradition which claimed that to be a philosopher one had to be competent in mathematics.[29] The tradition says that, placed on the door of Plato's Academy were the words 'Let no one destitute of geometry enter my doors', so mathematical logic was central therefore to philosophy. Descartes emphasized its importance in his work introducing this concept into Western culture, as the following quote makes clear:

> Arithmetic, Geometry and other sciences of that kind which treat only of things that are very simple and very general without caring to ascertain whether they exist in nature or not, contain some measure of indubitable certainty ... For whether I am awake or asleep, two and three together always make five.[30]

That does not mean that he was uncritical of its use, as Scruton points out:

> Descartes even admits (see, for example, Principles, 1, 5, 6), that the evil genius might be deceiving me 'in those matters which seem to us supremely evident', such as mathematics – an admission that threatens his own solution to these skeptical problems.[31]

Nevertheless Descartes was emphatic that in the hierarchy of knowledge and science mathematical abstraction and logic ranked above all else.

Descartes also played a pivotal role in ascribing to the brain decision-making properties. For him the brain was central to all human activity. As he wrote: 'Although the human soul gives form to the whole body, its chief seat is in the brain; it is there alone that it performs not only intellection and imagination, but even sensation'.[32]

In this view he was in contrast with the British empiricists who ascribed an important role to sentiments in the decision-making process. In their view, sentiments were essentially a separate part of human essence.[33] For Descartes, and those who followed him in the Enlightenment, decision-making was a process that took place in the brain or mind and individuals reached decisions on the basis of applying the scientific method. This logical and deductive process had to be applied by a 'logical' and 'rational' individual; a view that was inherited from Cartesian thinking. Hence, for the Continental thinkers to be reasonable and logical was to be rational.

European Rationality and the Judeo-Christian Thought

The philosophers of the Enlightenment established their own account of the composition of human nature; a crucial concept which was independent of, and contrasted with, those that had been promulgated and developed by the established religious institutions. In particular they held views that were contrary to those of the Catholic Church at a time when criticism of the Church's view were considered heretical and blasphemous.[34]

Philosophers knew that in the Jewish and the early Christian traditions, the 'soul' was conceived of as the 'self'.[35] They also knew that Thomas Aquinas had established a 'mind-based' nature of humans. Aquinas took from Aristotle's philosophy the proof of the existence of the self in the mind, and a mind without the concept of "soul" as a separate entity. This was not the only Greek influence on human nature in his writings. In this context, the Greek debate about human nature, called the 'Thesis of the Substantiality of the Soul',[36] relied on the one hand, on the Platonic school which believed in the separate composition of human nature of soul and body (e.g. 'transcendentalism'). Plato's school resembles the spiritual nature of the Jewish tradition, and it was followed by Catholics through the work of Augustine in the fourth and fifth centuries, where this tradition had been widely recognized as 'gnostic'. Later, Aquinas, a fervent follower of Aristotle, developed a rather different concept of the soul than that of the first Christians. Eventually, Aquinas's rational concept of the soul was stated as the official Catholic version in the Council of Vienne in 1311.

In contrast to Aquinas's concept is that of the Judeo-Christian tradition. The Judeo-Christian inference was that every person's soul is its human's essence, both fully conscious and immortal. Added to this, there is an (instrumental) mind and body. For instance, in the question of 'The Most Important Commandment',[37] Jesus made it mandatory to love God with 'all the self'. Using hermeneutic analysis, this 'self' includes heart ('kardia': καρδια), which captures thoughts and feelings, and also includes soul or spirit ('psuche': ψυχη), which is the very nature of humans. And finally, an important part of the 'self' is mind or reason ('dianoia': διανοια). Paul, the apostle, used a similar definition of the self in the *First Letter to the Thessalonians,*[38] where he describes human nature. First, he mentioned 'spirit' ('pneuma': πνευμα). Next, 'soul' as dwelling in the heart ('psuche': ψυχη), and finally, body ('soma': σωμα).[39] In both of these systems, the soul is considered the same as in the Jewish tradition: as an immortal self, surrounding feelings and thoughts that the self is capable of controlling. Both Christians and Jews used interchangeably the concept of 'self' and the word 'soul' in the Scriptures. In fact, in the Greek and Hebrew languages, the words 'soul' and 'self' are used equivalently to define the concept of individuality. According to the Jewish tradition, the only difference between humans and animals is that humans are created in the image of God,[40] and also that humans are the only ones among all creatures able to have a 'soul'.

For Hume, individual custom and experience, rather than blind belief, was an important influence on his conception of human nature. Not surprisingly, Hume's conception of the self is in total opposition to that stated by the Jewish tradition, which includes the concept of 'soul' as a separate entity of reason or sentiments.[41] Hume's separation of the ideas on the self into two distinct kinds was as follows: first, as sentiments, like sensations, passions or emotions; and second, as ideas, such as memory and imagination. The difference was that in his system he supported the concept of personality without a transcendental essence, like that of a 'Christian' soul. For Hume, both, sentiments and ideas, are acquired in a complex way by experience. For instance, he said: 'We find by experience, that when an impression has been present with the mind, it again makes its appearance there as an idea';[42] and also:

> If we define a cause to be, an object precedent and contiguous to another, and so united with it in the imagination, that the idea of the one determines the mind to form the idea of the other, and the impression of the one to form a more lively idea of the other; we shall make still less difficulty of assenting to this opinion. Such an influence on the mind is in itself perfectly extraordinary and incomprehensible; nor can we be certain of its reality, but from experience and observation.[43]

The issue is that Hume's 'leap of faith' was to find his way of thinking in the belief that there is no proof of the 'self' or the 'existence' of the self itself.[44] He had difficulty in understanding the doctrine of miracles in Christianity. The examples that stand out in particular include the Israelites crossing the Red Sea in the Exodus, and, of course the resurrection of Jesus. After all, Hume was also a 'believer', not in miracles, but in 'scepticism'; as if the very nature of 'faith' in scepticism was rather different than religious faith (for instance Christians believing in Jesus as the awaited Messiah). There is no proof, nor a rationale, to use one or the other as a basis of thought than the mere power of one's own decisions.

Today, an agnostic view about facts and human behaviour prevails in economics, where everything needs to be 'credible' and logically connected. The credible part is problematic, because this secular concept refers to one's experience and to what others think, so leaving aside unprecedented events and ignoring issues where their nature is unknown. Custom and experience might bias the interpretation of facts because it is subject to the person's knowledge. From Hume's contribution, the Pyrrhonian view in economics tends to ignore incredible events, and any study that tries to make sense of them might be precluded or considered 'transcendental'. In spite of this, there is today research about making sense of this world outside of the credible.[45] On the other hand, 'consequentialist' Cartesian logic might also bias the supposed order where events should take place, also ignoring that new (and perhaps unimagined) sequences might occur. This today is explored in economics in chaos theory.[46]

The Idea of Justice and Equality in Economics

Today's concepts of justice and equality also have their roots in the ancient Greek philosophical tradition, and they have been influenced by Marx's historical materialism. This is particularly evident in the work of John Rawls and Amartya Sen, where the concepts of equality and justice are treated as equivalent.[47]

Rawls considered the concept of inequality as something embedded in the idea of 'justice as fairness', and his work draws heavily on the work of Locke, Rousseau and Kant.[48] However, he also draws more directly on the ancient Greek tradition, in particular that of Plato and Aristotle. From Plato he takes the idea that justice is 'the first virtue of social institutions'.[49] In *The Republic*, Plato (360 BC) conceived of a dual understanding of justice. For Plato there was not only the just individual but also the 'just' city that was organized according to laws made by 'just' individuals,[50] and he borrowed from Protagoras the elitism contained in his 'cosmopolitan' approach.[51]

In Sen's account, inequality might be considered a type of destitution, yet more than that, he uses the value of equality as a universal value judgement.[52] Sen's value judgement has the same Marxian basis as Rawls's justice,[53] the only difference is that Sen's justice does not use categorical imperatives, as Rawls's does, but formal arguments and mathematical rhetoric to convince the reader that inequality is bad in itself. Sen takes a reference to Rawls's work, and he argues that Rawl's exercise should be considered only as a 'device for moral reflection and political discussion'.[54] Moreover, Sen thinks that Rawls's approach should not be considered a practical solution to the problem of unfairness, because Sen's approach is trying to encompass a practical view of social phenomena, so it is supposed that Sen is going beyond Rawl's 'mental exercises'. In summary, these two authors are the main reference points for the issues of justice and equality in economics today, and both authors use the Greek tradition in their writings.

Commenting on the Greek inheritance, for Plato, an individual could be considered 'just' as long as he or she was guided by a vision of the 'Good' which was gained through the acquisition of knowledge.[55] For Plato, philosophers rather than plain workers were the most likely individuals able to attain that vision because of their continuous search for knowledge. Plato also believed that people also had to have other attributes to complement their being just. These included temperance, wisdom and courage. When these virtues were combined with justice an individual would become a 'harmonious' soul. For Plato a city that was ruled by virtuous peoples' laws would enjoy the best possible status and become a 'just' city. This approach served as a starting point to others in Greece.

The Greek philosopher Aristotle (384–322 BC) in his *Politics*[56] took a different view to that of Plato with regard to justice. He introduced three important ideas based on Protagoras's anthropocentric views. The first viewed justice as important in contributing to an individual's happiness (or *eudaimonia*) and according to the individual merits; this was probably one of the oldest accounts of desert justice.[57] The second ascribed justice to an individual's development and was one of the first scholars to take the concept of justice away from being handed down from a divine entity and placed in the hands of mankind,[58] so the concept became 'agnostic'. To Aristotle, the construction of the just city (*polis*) lay in the development of individuals. The third involved the participation of the individual in the judicial process without which the process was incomplete. For Aristotle, the political involvement of the individual in the process was necessary in preventing it from becoming a mere instrumental exercise.[59] Aristotle believed that the nature of justice was therefore perhaps the most important issue and that none of the other virtues would make sense without justice.[60] Building on this concept, Sen in his more recent writings on welfare has put forward views that draw on Aristotle's ideas.[61]

Another ancient account of justice can be found in the Jewish tradition which differs to the Greek tradition more on the grounds of its practical value than its philosophical or psychological treatment. This Jewish view sees inequality as a sort of opportunity. In this ideology, justice is rooted in the continued behaviour of individuals in accordance with the God-given Law (*Torah*): 'What stands out in the entire development of Jewish ethical formulations is the constant interpenetration of communal and individual obligations and concerns.'[62] Justice is not an end but a result. In this tradition, inequality is not viewed as a 'social ill', but as an opportunity. Every person can be entitled to receive more or less, according to their needs and as a sign of reward for his/her good behaviour. This idea of justice includes both resource-based and desert-based entitlements.

In the Jewish tradition the concept of inequality was linked to people's needs. The *Torah* (written approximately on 1200 B.D) tells the story of the Israelites' exodus from Egypt, and their time wandering in the desert where they were miraculously fed with *manna* (a kind of bread) from heaven. Here, the 'unequal' but fair distribution of necessities depending on people's needs was established. It is narrated that the Israelites were ordered to take just as much as they needed, nothing more, nothing less:

> The Israelites did as they were told; some gathered much, some little. And when they measured it by the *omer*, he who gathered much did not have too much, and he who gathered little did not have too little. Each one gathered as much as he needed.[63]

It is very important to clarify that 'good behaviour' was not only related to 'abstinence from bad things', as the Catholic tradition emphasizes, but to the pursuit of justice through the constant following of good works in the spirit of God's commandments.[64] In the Jewish tradition, justice is based on faith in the unique and supreme God,[65] which subsequently becomes both a necessary and a sufficient condition to inspire good behaviour. This was a *non-Kantian* 'categorical imperative'. Therefore, justice, a term that in Jewish literature is translated as 'righteousness', is the product of all the attitudes and actions of humans, which if there are good will produce 'God's justice',[66] otherwise, just 'human justice'.[67]

In line with the Jewish tradition, the attitude of the early Christians towards inequality was viewed as an opportunity to share worldly spoils with fellows. However, the Christian tradition of the first century narrowed (or extended) this view of justice to a simple command: the Golden Rule. This abstraction is credited to Jesus who is stated to have behaved with good attitudes towards his fellows as a reflection of loving God with all the self. [68] This rule was similar to the previous commandments of the Jewish law in the sense that it was given by a supreme authority (God), and it was also similar to the spirit of the law that was supposed to express positive actions to other fellows. For early Christians, this rule was essential to their daily life:

> Christian writers ...were downplaying another central element in Christian thought and morality, the emphasis on agapic love, [such] love seems to be a matter of motivationally active feeling rather than of being *rational*.[69]

Submission to this simple rule was supposed to bring justice and to produce equality in society. For instance, Paul (AD 57), reciting the story of the *manna* in the *Torah*, wrote in his letter to the Corinthians the following:

> Our desire is not that others might be relieved while you are hard pressed, but that there might be equality. At the present time *your plenty* will supply what they need, so that in turn their plenty will supply what you need. *Then there will be equality*.[70]

It was clear that sharing with others in need would produce equality.

Following the same inspiration, the responsibility of the head of the household in the Judeo-Christian tradition was described clearly in the ancient tradition of the *Torah*. The responsibility for the head was to provide for both his household and also for his extended family,[71] but with particular emphasis on his parents.[72] It was normally viewed that some individuals would receive less and others more, but the rich would have a responsibility to share more of what they had rather than the poor.[73] By following these commands, the existent inequality could be alleviated and good justice would be achieved. The early Christian tradition therefore inherited from the Jewish tradition a similar view towards justice and equality, which was a deed-based concept.

Usually this tradition is of no value for those that want to 'rationally' solve the present problem of inequality, because the rational person wants to elaborate either an endogenous way to incentivize every person to do something (e.g. the Kantian Rawls), or he/she wants to offer as an incentive an *a posteriori* solution through third party (government) intervention (e.g. the Aristotelian Sen). The philosopher might think that it is hard to achieve justice if this is an individual duty with a metaphysical incentive (e.g. a belief in God). Nevertheless, those wanting to emphasize the Judeo-Christian tradition criticize that no approach with a Greek base have achieved enough in real life. On the one hand individuals still exist and operate with a 'veil of ignorance', and on the other hand, it is clear that governmentis ineffective. There are methodological possibilities that the Jewish tradition might offer as asolution by convincing individuals of the necessity of solving this problem as one's duty, or to develop individual incentives to establish a mechanism of transfers from the rich to the poor. However, neither has been explored.

Conclusions

This chapter has attempted to provide a historical and philosophical underpinning of two concepts used in contemporary economics; namely, rationality and justice. Both are treated currently as being value free and neutral in their usage. By placing them in their philosophical context, this discussion provides us with a contradictory view. We find that both concepts are the result of deep philosophical and religious influences. Hence, it is argued that the 'modern' economic concept of rationality is no more objective than those put forward by the ancient Greek scholars or by the scholars of the Enlightenment period who drew on the Greek tradition to inform their thinking. The latter group of scholars were influenced greatly by the ancient Greek philosophers views towards religion and against the concept of God as a supreme being and how He was supposed to shape mankind's decision-making behaviour.

Similarly, the concept of justice, what we mean by it, how it relates to equality and inequality and how it is achieved has also been fashioned by philosophers and religious texts. Again, the role of God as a supreme being dictating what is right and the opposed anthropocentric views of Aristotle and Plato have played an important role in shaping our views. This is evident in the relatively contemporary works of Rawls and Sen. If these ancient texts still hold sway in crystallizing our concepts of them, it also might be fruitful to examine the texts of other ancient cultures to see what light they can throw on our understanding of human behaviour.

Also discussed is the value of Jewish and Judeo-Christian tradition in a more action-oriented sense when referring to justice, and in a more holistic view of human nature when referring to rationality. I suggest that policy recommendations could follow from its study, so throwing away the whole tradition because of the exogenous metaphysical reference, put forwards the need to do the same with those coming from the ancient Greece.

Acknowledgements

I appreciate discussions of these topics while in the UK with Sheila Dow and Prasanta K. Pattanaik. I thank Nicholas Perdikis and Kobil Ruziev for reading and commenting on the earlier drafts of the chapter, and also to Ulises Camb-pell for his valuable insights. I thank Willebaldo Martinez-Toyes for his support while at the Center of Social Researches of UACJ in Ciudad Juarez and Pedro Espinosa Tellez for his research assistantship. I acknowledge funding of CONA-CyT on previous stages of this research.

4 COMMODITY CONTROL: A MISSING ELEMENT IN KEYNES'S *GENERAL THEORY*

Dipak Ghosh and Victoria Chick[1]

Given observations by George Shackle and Victoria Chick that John Maynard Keynes's *General Theory* is like a play with many scenes,[2] it is only to be expected that *The General Theory* is but one act of the unfolding drama we have come to know as Keynesian economics. In *The General Theory*, the scene opens on a situation where not only labour but all other factors of production are unemployed simultaneously at a given time. For this reason, in general the mechanism of the Keynesian investment multiplier which we find in *The General Theory* operates mainly by varying the amount of production (and in consequence prices)[3] and reaches its conclusion at a point 'that is [still] *not* resource-constrained'.[4]

However, in 1938, only two years after the publication of *The General Theory*, Keynes brought back into the spotlight a problem he first broached in 1923 and came back to in 1926: the violent fluctuations of commodity prices.[5] In the early works the focus was on the debilitating effects of these fluctuations in both producers and users of primary products in manufacturing. In 1938, in keeping with emphasis on employment in *The General Theory*, the focus was slightly different: not only were these fluctuations disruptive to trade and to producers' incomes, but they could constrain the resources available to manufacturing and prove detrimental to output and employment in the industrialized countries. He proposed a buffer stock scheme to alleviate problems in the primary products sector which became known informally as Commod Control. ('Commod' was his generic term for the commodities that should come under his scheme.) He revisited the problem during the war years, further developing policies for improving the post-war system of production of and trade in commodities as an adjunct to shaping a post-war policy of full employment, along with – and connected to – his better known plans for reshaping the world's financial system.[6]

Here it is argued that Keynes's work concerned with stabilizing commodity prices and trade flows, which addressed the issue of resource constraints on output, can be seen as an additional element to the overall system we find in *The General Theory*.

Robert Skidelsky characterized the relationship between *The General Theory* and Keynes's other work as follows:

> The *General Theory* can be interpreted as a short-run theory of employment in a 'closed' economy, in which the stock of capital, physical and human, is taken as given. But Keynes had written a lot – notably in his *Tract on Monetary Reform* and *Treatise of Money* – about the problems of 'open' economies, particularly the problem of combining internal and external equilibrium. In the later book, and also in his pamphlet *The Means to Prosperity* (1933), he has sketched out plans for a world super-bank to expand world reserves, on which he drew in his war time proposals.[7]

The question of integration of ideas into the framework of *The General Theory* using different assumptions is hinted at in what Chick wrote:

> In terms of open systems ... [*The General Theory*] is a perfect example of how to handle a complex subject without resorting to reductionism, through the device of taking first one element of the overall system, then another, as the object of analysis, using the method of *ceteris paribus* to provide a closure for each partial system and later removing it.[8]

Viewed from such a perspective, it should not be surprising that Keynes would continue to consider reopening *The General Theory*, if and when necessary, to add yet more new elements.

There is continuity with *The General Theory* too, for his concern to reform commodity markets centred on the destructive power of excessive commodity price fluctuations, which brought *uncertainty* to both their producers and those who use them as raw materials in further production. This chapter reviews Keynes's proposals and briefly assess their relevance to policy for the current state of the global economy.

The Journey

After *The General Theory,* Keynes returned to his earlier investigation of commodity stocks and prices, emphasizing the link between the supply of primary products and output and employment in Britain.[9] His immediate concern was security of the supply of raw materials in the impending war, but he saw that his proposals also had peacetime relevance

> If only we could tackle the problems of peace with the same energy and whole-heartedness as we tackle those of war! Defence is old-established as a proper object for the state, whereas economic well-being is still a parvenu. Social action which is universally approved for the former purpose is still suspect when it comes to the latter ... I hope to show it is [possible] to combine the object of the Government's new Act [the Essential Commodities Reserves Act] with purposes useful even in peace.[10]

He was impressed by the violent fluctuations in commodity prices. He investigated the percentage by which 'the highest price in each of the last ten years exceeded the lowest price *in that year*' for rubber, cotton, wheat and lead. He found an average annual price range of 67 per cent.[11]

He explained the 'ill effect of these truly frightful fluctuations on trade stability'.[12] Even under more propitious conditions, those producing or using these commodities are put off holding stocks because of the high carrying costs; price fluctuations of this magnitude exacerbate the risk. Worse,

> In spite of the fact that the difficulty of rapidly altering the scale of output, especially where seasonal crops are concerned, leads to what appear to be very large stocks at the bottom of the market, nevertheless when the turn of the tide comes, stocks nearly always turn out to be insufficient, precisely for the reason that it is just as difficult rapidly to increase the scale of delivered output as it had been to diminish it. Prices rush up, uneconomic and excessive output is stimulated, and the seeds are sown of a subsequent collapse.[13]

This instability of supply and price can only damage continuity of output and employment in industries using these materials.

However, it was only in early 1942 that Keynes began to devote his attention to drawing up the details of arrangements for a 'commodity policy', arguing that such a policy was vital for maintaining 'good employment' in the industrialized countries as well as more stable incomes for primary producers.[14]

While in *The General Theory* the vagaries of the marginal efficiency of capital, i.e. expected profit, are held chiefly responsible for fluctuations in economic activity, in the 1938 article we find Keynes reverting to his concern that 'all sorts of chance causes' of fluctuations in the prices and supplies of the principal raw materials can 'lead to fluctuations in immediate demand'.[15] In this article we also find Keynes's observation that there exist 'two major groups of commodities which respond quite differently to the fluctuations of effective demand'.[16] (This observation connects him to the more familiar, later work of John Hicks and Nichloas Kaldor, as we shall see.) For one type of commodities 'prices [are] comparatively stable and fluctuations in demand [are] met by a centralised control of output and by organised arrangements for the withholding of stocks on the part of the producers themselves', and for the other type of commodities 'the producers themselves are not in a position to withhold their stocks and the scale of output is governed by price fluctuations'.[17] He called them administered and competitive prices, respectively.

Our claim that Keynes's thinking on commodity markets can be seen as a missing element in *The General Theory* is strengthened by this evaluation of the significance of the distinction: 'The fact that we have two major groups of commodities which respond quite differently to fluctuations in effective demand is of great importance to the general theory of the short period'.[18]

It is here, probably for the first time, that we get a glimpse of the literature on cost-based and demand-based theories of price determination. In 1943,[19] Michal Kalecki observed that *'[s]hort-term price changes* may be classified into two broad groups: those determined mainly by changes in cost of production and those determined mainly by changes in demand'.[20] While the changes in the prices of 'finished goods' are cost-determined, the changes in the prices of the industrial raw materials and primary foodstuffs are demand-determined. John Hicks described the cost-determined prices as 'fix-price' and the demand-determined prices as 'flex-price'.[21] These two types of price formation are caused by different conditions of supply.

Kalecki argued that, since supplies of 'finished' (manufactured or industrial) products are elastic 'as a result of existing reserves of productive capacity', any increase in demand for these products can be met by an increase in the volume of production without raising their prices.[22] Hicks pointed out that in the case of 'storables' (manufactured or industrial goods) the existence of stocks has a great deal to do with keeping prices fixed.[23] When there is excess demand for output, additional supply can be thrown on to the market to fill the gap between demand and supply. In the extreme case of products labelled by Hicks as 'non-storables', their supply is relatively inelastic in the short run because these products cannot be supplied out of stocks.

It is 'flow demand' and 'flow supply' that are equated at the price that is established. If, however, they are only equated at a high price (at a price that is high relative to 'normal cost of production') there is a signal for an increase in output; though the increase can materialize at a later date, that is to say, in the long run. If they are equated at a price that is low in relation to cost, output will (similarly) tend to decrease.[24]

Kalecki observed that any initial price rise for these products in response to an increase in demand may be exacerbated 'by the addition of a speculative element ... [and] this makes it even more difficult in the short period to catch up with demand'.[25]

The common characteristics of the products the prices of which are demand-determined are that they are all primary products, such as food, commercial crops, raw materials, energy. Their production is primarily land-based, as opposed to the industrial goods the production of which consists of the processing of basic materials produced by the primary sector and does not require land in any significant amount. The prices of these industrial goods are determined by their production cost.

It needs emphasizing that to call the cost-based prices 'fix-prices' does not mean that these prices never change. It is just that, in the short run, prices do not have to change whenever there is excess demand or excess supply in the market. They change chiefly in response to changes in the cost of production. The cost of production, in turn, depends on the prices of labour and raw materials. Any short-term disequilibrium in the market for these products is smoothed out by adjustments in stocks. Kaldor provides the following equation for the price (p) of industrial (fix-price) goods:

$$p = (1+\pi)wl$$

where π stands for the profit mark-up, w denotes the (money-) wage rate and l stands for labour required to produce one unit of output.[26] Thus, given the profit mark-up and labour productivity, the prices of industrial goods are dependent on the wage rate or price of labour.

However, the wage rate cannot be independent of the cost of living. As Kaldor put it:

> Whatever the supply of labor (or the potential supply of labor) in relation to demand, the price of labor in terms of food cannot fall below a certain minimum determined by the cost of subsistence, whether the cost is determined by custom or convention or by sheer biological needs.[27]

In other words, there is no such thing as a market-clearing wage rate without reference to the basic minimum cost of living. Today, in most countries, we are well above the subsistence wage, but the relationship continues except in really bad times: if and when the cost of living rises, labour will fight to preserve the real value of its wages, and if they are successful this gets translated into a rise in money-wages and hence the prices of industrial goods. Thus a rise in the prices of raw materials results in a general rise in prices rather than a change in relative prices.

Kaldor presented his analysis in a simple two-sector framework, consisting of agriculture (A) and industry (I). Production in sector A is predominantly land-based and subject to the law of diminishing returns; its supply in the short run is relatively inelastic. Prices for the products of this sector are, therefore, demand-determined or flex-price. Prices in sector I are based on the cost of production and a (given) profit mark-up or fix-price. Production in sector I depends on the former sector for its supply of primary products both as an input and as wage goods for labour. The rate of growth in the industrial sector depends not only on the supply to industry of raw materials but also on demand from the agricultural sector. Kaldor presents the interrelationship between the two sectors as follows.

$$O_I = (1/m)D_A$$

where O_I = the value of output of the industrial sector, D_A = demand for industrial products from the agricultural sector, and m = share of expenditure on agricultural products in total income of the industrial sector. He argues that the above relationship is the 'doctrine of the foreign trade multiplier as against the Keynesian savings-investment multiplier' and that the latter 'over longer periods is a far more important principle for explaining the growth and rhythm of industrial development'.[28] Insofar as primary products are mainly produced abroad (Keynes referred to them as Empire goods[29]) this is literally true, but the same principle holds when looking at changes in the level of output in a two-sector, closed-economy context, as Kaldor does. The Keynesian savings-investment multiplier, by contrast, deals with 'output as a whole'; only a few hints are offered as to how relative prices between consumption-goods and investment-goods might alter as the multiplier works itself out. In any case, Kaldor would argue, it is rooted in the short period.

Keynes's concern with commodity markets was of long standing. It started in 1923 with his article detailing how these markets contributed to the trade cycle, abetted by bank lending.[30] He then embarked on a substantial empirical study of the extent of stocks of a variety of commodities over several years[31] and in 1926 responded to the objection of the (US) Hoover administration to buffer stock schemes.[32] The US government saw a buffer stock scheme as giving a subsidy to producers of raw materials and foodstuffs. Keynes countered with the data on price volatility and irregularity of supplies. His understanding was that the purpose of such a scheme was not to increase producers' gains but to protect them from losses due only to the structure of the market and natural conditions of production of such goods. He commented, in a phrase resonant today, that for a government *not* to intervene in such a volatile market was '*laissez faire* gone crazy'.[33]

It is not surprising that by 1938 Keynes saw his policy of 'Commod Control' mainly in terms of its positive effects on employment. His stated aim was to secure 'a stimulus to our export industries, an increased control over the trade cycle, and an insurance against having to pay excessive prices for the primary products at a subsequent date'.[34] He proposed 'that the Government should offer storage for all Empire producers of specified raw materials, either free of warehouse charges and interest or for a nominal charge, provided they ship their surplus produce to approved warehouses in this country'.[35]

Keynes began to make plans for the post-World-War-II world in 1940. His early drafts of the Clearing Union conceived the International Clearing Union as one of a set of interlocking regimes governing money, investment, commodities and trade, though the monetary scheme was worked out in the most detail. 'However, at Roy Harrod's prodding Keynes did, on 20 January 1942, draft a memorandum on buffer stocks.'[36] That Keynes's 1938 paper is key is made clear in his letter to Harrod on 6 January, 1942 that '[I have] dragged out my 1938 article in this area'.[37] Ironically, he now criticized the 1938 piece for saying little about the trade cycle, the issue he first highlighted in connection with commodities markets in 1923.[38]

Policy, Negotiation, Defeat

The emphasis in Keynes's war-time proposals was on practical policy options, the devil and his detail. Keynes's thinking now took an international turn, as it was proposed to involve the Clearing Union in the finance of buffer stocks, and in any case the international focus suited the temper of the times.

The following quotation neatly summarizes the thinking which he pursued through many drafts (this comes from the sixth draft, which finally went to the War Cabinet Committee on Reconstruction Problems in 1943):

> Superimposed on the fortuitous short-period price swings affecting particular com-
> modities and particular groups of producers there is the fundamental malady of the
> trade cycle. Fortunately, the same technique of buffer stocks which has to be called
> into being to deal with the former is also capable of making a large contribution to the
> cure of the trade cycle itself. For the maintenance of good employment throughout
> the world, in industrial countries as well as in those producing primary commodities,
> this is of the first importance, sufficient by itself to justify the setting up of machinery
> for buffer stocks.[39]

Objections to his scheme came mainly from the Bank of England and the Ministry of Agriculture. The Bank of England 'condemned Keynes's mixture of private
trading and price control as a speculators' paradise'.[40] They suggested that the
only controls needed were those that discouraged speculators, and that 'these
could be operated as part of the control of credit'.[41] However, later in the same
exposition of Bank policy on commodity markets it is stated that the Bank proposed to require UK residents to show that they had a '"legitimate interest" in
the commodity in order to exclude pure speculation ... Keynes was consulted
and disagreed. He ... felt that there should be less regulation. A market needed
speculators'.[42] (Apparently, in contrast to his position in *The General Theory*,
Keynes now took the view that speculation was a stabilizing influence!)

No further mention of Keynes is made in this semi-official account of the
Bank's views. But his disagreement with the Bank went further than the role of
speculators: the Bank thought his scheme too *laissez faire* and favoured a complex system of long-term planning.[43]

The biggest thorn in Keynes's side was Sir Donald Fergusson at the Ministry
of Agriculture. He went even further than the Bank in his advocacy of planning.
In Keynes's interpretation he

> holds that every agricultural product ... ought to be planned internationally, every
> farmer being told ... what he is to grow ... [A] satisfactory price is to be guaranteed all
> round... Put down in black and white, this seems so balmy as not to be easily credible[44]

Keynes was never able to persuade him.

Despite the meticulous responses to other concerns raised, his scheme suffered a defeat perhaps more comprehensive than even his plan for a Clearing
Union. In fact the defeat was worse, for it came not only from the Americans
but from Keynes's own side.

Since Then

The importance of resource constraints resurfaced in the context of the harvest failure of 1972 and the oil crisis of 1973. These events provoked Hicks to observe that:

> The first of the things which is called in question by this most recent experience is
> the Keynesian identification of the limit to growth with Full Employment of Labour.

> What has now to be faced is the possibility that the limit might be set by something else ... Full Employment, at the high growth rates of the Bretton Woods period, cannot now be reached, since the supplies of primary products that would be needed to support it are not available.[45]

And in March 2013, there was discussion of the paucity of storage facilities for gas, leaving the country vulnerable to disruptions of supply and threatening rationing to industrial users should the cold weather continue.

The problem continues to resurface, but nothing has been done. A fate similar to Keynes's scheme befell the recommendations of the Brandt Commission in the 1980s.[46] As Kaldor observed, when the developing countries actually asked for a scheme for setting up international buffer stocks (through UNCTAD) they got a cool reception from the rest of the world.[47] In Kaldor's own words:

> Nobody seems to have understood that, while the proposal was promoted by the developing countries, its adoption was in vital interest of the 'developed' or industrialized countries, since it is a pre-condition for securing adequate long-term investment necessary for sustained industrial growth. [48]

The understanding that marked Keynes's work from as early as 1919,[49] that the prosperity of one country was dependent on the prosperity of others, was carried through into Keynes's commodity proposals and those of the Brandt Commission. The latter, indeed, concluded that

> Whatever their differences and however profound, there is a mutuality of interest between North and South. The fate of both is immediately connected. The search for solutions is not an act of benevolence but a condition of mutual survival.[50]

The reaction of the rich world seems to have been that what happened in poorer countries was not important to them.

Keynes, Kaldor and the members of the Brandt Commission all took it for granted that the non-industrialized or developing countries of the South would be the predominant suppliers of the primary products while the industrialized or developed countries of the North would be the predominant producers and exporters of manufactured products. The structure of world production and trade have now changed considerably. In particular, the developing countries have become far less dependent on primary products and there are more financial options to protect against price fluctuations. We need to update our world view. However, the examples given and more recent problems with commodity speculation and anxieties about food security suggest that it is too early to write off intervention in commodity markets as a quaint concern of a bygone age.

5 COST-DETERMINED AND DEMAND-DETERMINED PRICES: LESSONS FOR THE GLOBALIZED WORLD FROM DEVELOPMENT ECONOMICS

Dipak Ghosh and Kobil Ruziev[1]

While attempting to promote long-run economic growth, especially in the post-World War II period, labour-surplus underdeveloped economies discovered the limitations of Keynesian policy. This chapter revisits the nature of such limitations and argues that the globally integrated economies of the contemporary world, as it tries to solve the problem of unemployment in the post-Global Financial Crisis (GFC) period, can find valuable lessons from the experience of the developing countries.[2] The essay also shows that John Maynard Keynes himself was aware of the limitation of the strategy of demand management alone in tackling the problem of economic depression.

The chapter is organized as follows. The next section discusses the experience of the labour-surplus developing countries and the nature of constraints these countries encountered when attempting to generate employment for their surplus labour. A theoretical framework is then presented, which can be a basis of understanding Keynes's views with respect to such constraints as they were encountered by development economists. A discussion follows of policy implications of the theoretical framework and the Keynesian perspective on it. Finally, we discuss lessons present-day industrialized countries can draw from.

Developing Perspectives

Development economics as a subdiscipline of economics was born following the end of World War II, when the process of decolonization started. By this time the neoclassical orthodoxy was already firmly in place and it is not surprising that the majority of the development economists of the time 'tried to combine neoclassical and classical economics in an eclectic synthesis, and most refused to see existing societies as riven into classes and driven by their conflicts.'[3] Neoclassical development economists devoted their attention to the building of theoretical closed system general equilibrium models which tended to tell how the process of economic development and structural change should work, by making the assumptions needed to close their models, instead of studying the constraints an underdeveloped economy may have to encounter, in real life, in its attempt to industrialize.[4] It is no wonder that during the early 1980s in what has been described as 'an obituary of development economics' Albert Hirschman observed that:

> our subdiscipline had achieved its considerable lustre and excitement through the implicit idea that it could slay the dragon of backwardness virtually by itself or, at least, that its contribution to this task was central. We now know that this is not so.[5]

With reference to the above observation by Hirschman about the failure of neoclassical economics in addressing the problems of underdevelopment, Amartya Sen pointed out that this 'need not have caused great astonishment, since neoclassical economics did not apply terribly well anywhere else (either).'[6]

There, however, were exceptions; development economists such as Alexander Gerschenkron, Arthur Lewis and Hla Myint consciously returned to the classical economists for their inspiration.[7] Lewis's seminal article published in 1954 'is widely regarded as the single most influential contribution to the establishment of development economics as an academic discipline'.[8] Lewis built his model of the dual economy by drawing his inspiration from such classical authors as Adam Smith and Karl Marx. Lewis formulated his model with reference to countries containing surplus labour in the sense that the population is so large in comparison with capital and natural resources that in a large sector of the economy marginal productivity of labour is negligible, zero or even negative. The existence of this surplus labour implies that the supply of labour is unlimited at the 'subsistence' wage. This surplus labour exists in what Lewis describes as the 'subsistence sector', which according to him, does not use reproducible capital like its counterpart – 'the capitalist sector'. Average per capita output is, understandably, lower in the subsistence sector than in the capitalist sector. The process of economic development involves gradual transfer of surplus labour from the subsistence to the capitalist sector to accumulate capital to be reinvested in the capitalist sector to help transfer more surplus labour. This process continues until the labour surplus in the traditional sector disappears. For, when this situation is reached, transfer of labour from the traditional to the capitalist sector can only be achieved at a cost of output in the traditional sector.

It is important to understand that the concept of surplus labour in Lewis is not the same as the concept of 'disguised unemployment'.[9] The term disguised unemployment was first introduced by Joan Robinson to describe workers in industrialized economies who were compelled to accept less productive hand-to-mouth occupations as a result of being laid off due to lack of effective demand. In her own words:

> a decline in demand for the product of the general run of industries leads to a diversion of labour from occupations in which productivity is higher to others where it is lower. The cause of this diversion, a decline in effective demand, is exactly the same as the cause of unemployment in the ordinary sense, and it is natural to describe the adoption of inferior occupations by dismissed workers as *disguised unemployment*.[10]

Surplus labour in a dual economy, as described by Lewis, is different from the unemployed labour described in *The General Theory*. In the economy Keynes described, 'not only that labour is unlimited in supply, but also, and more fundamentally, that land and capital also are unlimited in supply – more fundamentally both in the short run sense'.[11] In this sense, the nature of the problem of employment generation in the capitalist sector of a dual economy is essentially different from that of job creation in an economy experiencing unemployment during economic recession or depression.

The basic features of Lewis's model of development in a dual economy have now been presented. Since this model has gone through a number of changes and interpretations in the hands of the neoclassical economists, losing its central message in the process, it is important to remind ourselves that, unlike the neoclassical development economists, Lewis's intention was not to build a well-behaved deterministic closed system theoretical model yielding an unique and stable equilibrium.[12] Lewis's model is an example of an open system where he discussed a number of reasons for which the process of transfer of surplus labour from the traditional sector to the capitalist sector might be prematurely halted. One such reason is the lack of availability of 'wage goods'.[13] In low income countries these are essentially food (food grains). Lewis observed:

> Now if the capitalist sector produces no food, its expansion increases the demand for food, raises the price of food in terms of capitalist products and so reduces profits. This is one of the senses in which industrialization is dependent upon agricultural improvement ...if we postulate that the capitalist sector is not producing food, we must either postulate that the subsistence sector is increasing its output, or else conclude that the expansion of the capitalist sector will be brought to an end through adverse terms of trade.[14]

The implication of this is that the ability to generate employment in the capitalist sector is constrained by the availability of food. And for this reason any attempt to generate employment by creating effective demand, as prescribed by Keynes for the mature industrialized countries, would fail to work for the developing economies. This is because, while attempting to generate employment in the capitalist sector, 'we encounter the bottleneck of supply of necessities which depends on the inelasticity of the agricultural production. Any increase in employment implies generation of additional incomes and thus, if no adequate increase in agricultural output is forthcoming, an inflationary increase in the prices of necessities will be unavoidable'.[15]

In fact immediately after the independence from the British rule, economists in India, who at first sought answers to the problems of economic development from Keynes's writings, came to a similar conclusion as Lewis about the inapplicability of Keynesian economics to the problems of economic development.[16] Rao observed that Keynes

> did not formulate the economic problem of underdeveloped countries, nor did he discuss the relevance to these countries of either the objective or the policy that he proposed for the more developed, i.e. the industrialized countries. The result has been a rather unintelligent application ... of what may be called Keynesian economics to the problem of underdeveloped countries.[17]

The author went on to argue that, in a country like India, in spite of the marginal propensity to consume and hence the size of the multiplier being very large, the tertiary and other increases in output, income and employment visualized by the multiplier process do not work. This is due to the fact that for developing countries the most important consumption goods happen to be food (food grains) and, in common with all other primary commodities, the supply curve of food grains is highly inelastic in the short run and can even be backward bending.

Let us try to elaborate a little more. According to Sen the opportunity for creation of wage employment, E, in a developing country depends on the availability of 'wage goods', M, and the real wage rate, w, and can be presented as follows:[18]

$$E = M/w$$

As we have seen above, the wage goods for a developing economy is mainly food (food grains). Indeed, Nicholas Kaldor calls food 'the wage good par excellence'.[19] The Soviet Union encountered a similar constraint during its early days of industrialization.[20] In a speech, at the July 1928 Plenum of the Communist Party Central Committee, Joseph Stalin underlined the need for availability of the agricultural surpluses for industrialization. He argued that since the Soviet Union could not follow the examples of the 'capitalist' countries, whose industrialization was shaped by resources mobilized from their colonies, it had only internal accumulation to fall back on for industrialization. The two sources of internal mobilization he mentioned were 'firstly, the working class, which creates value (for the advancement of the industry) ... and secondly, the peasantry'. Stalin observed that the peasantry

> not only pays the state the usual taxes, direct and indirect, it also overpays in the relatively high prices for manufactured goods – that is in the first place, and it is more or less underpaid in the prices for agricultural produce – that is in the second place

... This is an additional tax levied on the peasantry for the sake of promoting industry, which caters for the whole country, the peasantry included. It is something in
the nature of a 'tribute', of a super tax, which we are compelled to levy for the time
being in order to preserve and accelerate our present rate of industrial development,
in order to ensure an industry for the whole country[21]

To summarize, the central message of this section is as follows: the experience of
economic development shows that the success of the strategy of industrialization via transfer of labour from the agricultural sector to the industrial sector is
constrained by the availability of the supply of wage goods (which determines
the cost of living) produced in the agricultural sector. Since the supply of wage
goods is relatively inelastic in the short run, any rise in its demand causes its price
to rise and generates inflationary pressure, which may cause to slow down or even
halt the process of capital accumulation and hence, generation of employment
in the industrial sector. As Kaldor observed, 'the mechanism [of the multiplier]
operates by varying the amount of production in general. It leads to a situation
that is not resource-constrained'.[22] The resource constraint that the Indian and
the Soviet planners encountered was that of the supply of wage goods.

Cost-Based and Demand-Based Prices

The theoretical basis of our discussions so far can be found in Chapter 2 in this volume, which, for the purpose of brevity, we will not repeat here. In particular, this
concerns Michal Kalecki's and John Hicks's distinction between *cost-determined*
and *demand-determined* prices, and Kaldor's simple two-sector framework, which
uses these price systems to show how the rate of growth in the industrial sector
depends on that of the agricultural sector. More specifically, in Kaldor's two-sector
model, production in the agricultural sector is subject to the law of diminishing
returns and its supply in the short run is relatively inelastic. Production in the
industrial sector, on the other hand, depends on the former sector, implying the
rate of growth in the industrial sector depends on that of the agricultural sector.
Hence, the two-sector model, according to Kaldor, provides a doctrine of the foreign trade multiplier rather than the Keynesian savings-investment multiplier.

It is in this sense that Lewis, when discussing the scenario where the capitalist
sector produces no wage goods and has to depend on the subsistence sector for its
supply, observed that, 'it is not profitable to produce a growing volume of manufactures unless agricultural production is growing simultaneously'.[23] Kaldor wrote,

In some ways I think it may have been unfortunate that the very success of Keynes's ideas
in explaining unemployment in depression – essentially a short-period analysis – diverted
attention from the 'foreign trade multiplier' which over longer periods is a far more
important principle for explaining the growth and rhythm of industrial development.[24]

Before we leave this section, we must point out that although we have been treating wage goods as food (food grain) in our discussion so far, an appeal to Engels's law would tell us that the wage goods are really a basket of goods for individual consumption by households. Such a basket of goods for the Organization for Economic Cooperation and Development (OECD) countries consists of food, beverages and tobacco, transport services and rent. The first four items of this basket are produced by the primary sector or the 'agricultural sector' in Kaldor's two-sector model.

The Policy Implication and a Keynsian Perspective

The interdependence between the primary (agricultural) sector and the industrial sector was the nature of the problem addressed by the Brandt Commission in the 1980s.[25] Talking about the commodity situation in the 1970s – the harvest failures of 1972, the oil crisis of 1973 and the shortage of industrial raw materials around the same time – Hicks reflected on the Keynesian identification of the limit to growth with full employment of labour.[26] He argued that 'full employment at the high growth rates of the Bretton Woods period could not be reached as *the supplies of primary products needed to support it were no longer easily available*'.[27]

From Keynes's writings, however, one can detect the link between the role of the supply of primary products and export demand as well as employment. But, it was only after 1941 that Keynes devoted his attention to drawing up the details of arrangements for a 'commodity policy', arguing that such a policy was vital for maintaining 'good employment' in the industrialized countries. A short glimpse of Keynes's views over the period is presented below.

In an essay published in 1930 on the economic pessimism in the United Kingdom at that time, Keynes wrote:

> We are being afflicted with a new disease of which some readers may not yet have heard the name, but of which they will hear a great deal in the years to come – namely, technological unemployment. This means unemployment due to our discovery of means of economising the use of labour outrunning the pace at which we can find new use of labour.[28]

Keynes, however, was convinced that 'this is only a temporary phase of maladjustment' and a solution to this problem of unemployment caused by labour saving technical progress would be found. He went on to add:

> assuming no important wars and no important increase in population, the economic problem may be solved, or at least within sight of solution, within a hundred years. This means that the economic problem is not – if we look into the future – the permanent problem of the human race.[29]

As was also discussed in detail in Chapter 2, in Keynes's 1938 work we come across the mention of the impact of fluctuations in the prices of the principal raw materials which can lead to fluctuations in immediate demand. So he proposed 'that, the

Government should offer storage for all Empire producers of specified raw materials, either free of warehouse charges and interest or for a nominal charge, provided they ship their surplus produce to approved warehouses to this country.'[30]

Keynes's plan for the post-World War II world-wide price stabilization included setting up of an international agency for stabilizing commodity prices by means of buffer stocks of as many commodities as possible.[31] It is worth noticing Keynes's recognition that labour-saving technical progress is not the only cause of long-term unemployment in the industrialized countries and that constraints associated with the foreign trade multiplier also play an important role. Keynes's proposal to the Bretton Woods conference for setting up of an international Commodity Control Agency, which would set up buffer stocks for all the main commodities, for stabilizing commodity price and to be financed by a truly international currency was rejected as was the recommendations of the Brandt Commission in the 1980s. Kaldor also observed that when the developing countries actually asked for a scheme for setting up international buffer stocks, they got a cool reception from the rest of the world.[32]

As was also noted in Chapter 2, it has long been taken for granted that the developing countries of the South will remain predominantly suppliers of the primary products, which Keynes referred to as 'Empire produce',[33] while the developed countries of the North will remain the predominant producers and exporters of manufactured products. However, since the world has now changed considerably, we need to update our world view. In the next section we will look at the implication of our analysis for the policymakers in the industrialized countries.

Lessons for a Globalized World

A number of predominantly commodity-producing countries of the earlier period are now enjoying a rather healthy rate of industrialization, thus becoming manufacturers and exporters of manufactured goods as well as beginning to consume commodities, which they used to export, themselves. This implies that the primary goods supply constraint is no longer relevant for the industrialized countries of the days of Keynes, Kaldor and the Brandt Commission; rather, it is becoming relevant for the entire global economy. In other words, since the supply of wage goods or foodstuff, which are produced mainly in the agricultural sector, is relatively inelastic in the short run, any rise in its demand generates inflationary pressure and causes a slow-down or even a halt in employment generation in the industrial sector. The implication is that it might be difficult to sustain economic growth, especially in industrialized economies, in the wake of deteriorating terms of trade between the capitalist and agricultural sectors. This, coupled with dwindling carbohydrate reserves and the absence of viable alternative energy sources, indicates that in the globalized world we live in today slow economic growth and persistent price increases are a more likely outcome.

The recent movement in commodity prices already provides some evidence for this hypothesis. The trend in commodity prices for the last two decades of the twentieth century had been relatively stable, with the exception of temporary and mild swings associated with business cycles. Since the turn of the new century, however, prices of all major commodities such as food grains, energy and raw materials have been increasing dramatically, partly due to speculative activity. Using the Kaleckian pricing framework, some studies found evidence for the link between the global growth in industrial production and the movement between prices of primary commodities and that of finished goods for the economies of the industrialized countries in general, and the US economy in particular.[34] Another study, using various econometric models of estimation, also found evidence for the positive relationship between growth in industrial output of individual countries and overall demand for primary commodities, which, the study argues, triggers price increases affecting all industrialized countries.[35]

It is important to note that compared to the previous booms in commodity prices, the current upsurge has been notable for its broad coverage and duration.[36] Figure 5.1 shows monthly price indices for food and beverages and fuel for the 1993–2013 period. Food and beverages include, among other things, cereal, meat, vegetable oil, tea, coffee and cocoa; and fuel includes crude oil, natural gas and coal.

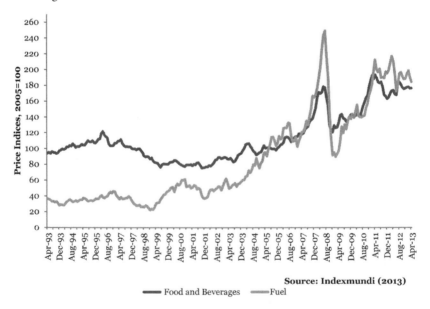

Source: Indexmundi (2013)

━━ Food and Beverages ━━ Fuel

Figure 5.1: Monthly price indices for food and beverages and fuel, 1993–2003.

As can be seen from Figure 5.1, both the level as well as the volatility of price indices for food commodities and fuel products have increased considerably since the early 2000s. More specifically, the food and beverages price index went up from around 80 in mid-2001 to a peak value of around 180 in mid-2008. This raised concerns not only about inflation and growth but also global food security, especially in relation to less developed countries such as Bangladesh, Ghana, Malawi, Guatemala, Tajikistan, etc. with significant proportion of poor populations who spend most of their income (around 70 per cent) on food. After falling briefly to around 130 at the end of 2008, the food and beverage price index started rising again from 2009, renewing concerns about the impact of high and volatile food prices on food security and inflation.

There are a number of factors that contribute to the recent upsurge and volatility of the price of food commodities. First, a sustained economic growth observed in recent years in large developing economies such as the economic powerhouses China and India, combined with the economic revival of the former Communist Bloc countries emerging from their deep economic depression in the 1990s, boosted demand for food commodities, including through diet diversification which led to higher demand for meat products and hence also for animal feed. Since some of these countries were once major commodity exporters and are now gaining momentum to compete with the industrialized countries for the consumption of these products, increases in the demand for commodities are outpacing increases in its supply. Second, policies promoting the use of agricultural commodities in the production of biofuels also need a mention. Third, rising fuel and fertilizer prices put upward pressure on production and transportation costs of food products. Fourth, the depreciation of the US dollar pushed commodity prices through the following channels: (i) since most commodities are priced in US dollars, depreciation of the dollar makes commodities less expensive for consumers in other countries of the world, thereby increasing their demand; (ii) depreciation of the US dollar reduces returns on dollar-denominated financial assets and increases the risk of inflationary pressure in the United States, thereby increasing investors' demand for commodities as alternative assets; (iii) lower interest rates also make it more attractive to borrow, thereby fuelling demand and speculation in commodity and other asset markets; and (iv) depreciation of the dollar leads to monetary easing in other countries, especially in economies whose currencies are pegged to the US dollar, again boosting demand for commodities and other assets.[37] Last but not least, all these factors also resulted in low levels of stock of food commodities, making commodity prices more volatile. Since the trend in most of these underlying factors is unlikely to change any time soon, industry experts argue that food prices will continue to remain high in the near future.[38]

Keynes's proposal for shaping the post-War world in Bretton Woods in 1944 involved setting up an International Clearing Union – an international central bank and an international agency for stabilizing commodity prices, which he named the International Commodity Control. While the proposal for this second organization was never seriously considered at the international level, his proposal for the clearing union came into existence only in a much emasculated form.[39] However, with the collapse of the Bretton-Woods system of exchange rates in 1973, any hope for the long run stability of the dollar price of individual commodities also evaporated; this is despite the fact that most commodities are still being priced in US dollars. In an article surveying the developments of the monetary and fiscal policy in the OECDcountries since 1985, Jean-Philippe Cotis, a former chief economist at the OECD, observed that '[r]ecent developments in oil and commodity prices may ultimately provide a safer test to disentangle whether progress [in these countries] has stemmed from better policy frameworks or from sheer luck'.[40]

On the basis of the arguments put forward in this chapter, let us now revisit Keynes's suggestion at the Bretton Woods Conference – that of having a truly international currency under the supervision of a truly global central bank as well as an agreement for controlling the supply of commodities. The time has also come to remind ourselves of the Brandt Commission's recommendations regarding the international organizations and negotiations: 'negotiations should look for joint gains, rather than slowly wresting uncertain "concessions". The starting point has to be some perceptions of mutual interest in change'.[41] And in doing that, we have to keep in mind that the old division of the world between the predominantly industrialized North and predominantly primary-producing South of the 1980s has now changed.

6 KALECKI AND THE SAVINGS CONSTRAINT ON ECONOMIC DEVELOPMENT

Jan Toporowski

Kalecki's Vision of Economic Development

Dipak Ghosh was one of the few economists who took Michal Kalecki to heart. This chapter rehearses arguments that would have been familiar to Dipak.[1] Nevertheless, many of those arguments have been forgotten in development economics and therefore deserve revival in this tribute to one of Kalecki's thoughtful followers. The first part of this essay presents a general outline of Kalecki's development economics. The second part focuses on a key principle of Kalecki's development economics that he took over from his macroeconomic analysis, the view that developing economies are not constrained by prior savings.

Kalecki was made aware of the political economy of development during his formative years as an economist, in the 1920s. He observed the political debates in Poland at that time around the works of Rudolf Hilferding, Rosa Luxemburg and Henryk Grossman, all of whom accorded an important role to developing countries in their analyses of capitalism. Luxemburg, in particular in her book *The Accumulation of Capital* which Kalecki knew well, examined critically the impact of capitalism on traditional economies. In his decade of work at the United Nations, from 1945 to 1955, Kalecki analysed in detail the problems of developing countries and started his consultancy work for some of their governments, notably Israel and Mexico. Following his return to Poland in 1955, he was active in seminars and research projects on developing countries, and advised the governments of India and Cuba. This work was brought to an abrupt halt in 1968, when his Polish collaborators in these projects came under political attack.[2] By then development economics was on its way back to those traditional ideas and policies that stressed the importance of the nineteenth-century virtues of thrift and saving.

Kalecki's first published intervention in development economics was a review of Mihail Manoilescu's *Die Nationalen Produktivkrafte und der Assenhandel* (published in English as *The Theory of Protection and International Trade,* 1931).[3] Manoilescu had put forward an early version of the import-substitution argument in favour of developing country protectionism. Because developing country productivity in industry is higher than in agriculture, even if that industrial productivity may be lower than in industrialized countries, improvements in efficiency can be obtained by expanding industry behind protective tariff barriers. The resulting overall improvement in productivity may result in a higher output available to an economy than might have been obtained from relying on low productivity agricultural exports to pay for industrial imports. Kalecki criticized one possible neoclassical objection to this theory, namely that developing countries experience capital scarcity, and that market forces would tend 'naturally' to equalize the marginal productivity of capital or labour in industry or agriculture. According to Kalecki, such capital scarcity was not binding in agricultural countries, since rural unemployment or underemployment allowed investment to be undertaken unconstrained by 'the supply of new saving' up to the point of full employment. At the same time, he criticized the notion that protection for new industries was a sufficient condition for economic development: 'To represent free trade as the *only* obstacle to the economic progress of backward countries is to divert attention from such urgent social problems as land reform and others'.[4]

The critical issue for developing countries was how such investment could be organized. When Kalecki returned to this question, as a government adviser to Israel in 1950, he considered two possible alternatives for countries such as Israel with minimal indigenous investment goods capacity. In this situation, countries could rely on foreign direct investment, or on government-organized investments. The first possibility he considered to be of dubious benefit, because it was unlikely to be on a sufficient scale or attracted to industries that could supply the domestic market, and hence limit inflationary pressures in them. State-organized investments should therefore be undertaken with a view to maximizing the exports needed to finance the import of industrial machinery, developing domestic investment capacity and minimizing domestic inflation. Private sector investment was to be regulated to ensure that it did not absorb scarce foreign exchange in ventures that were not high on the government's development priorities.[5]

Kalecki went on to expand on these themes in his subsequent work on economic development. In the first place, he examined the political and social formation in which economic development could take place. He had no illusions about the existence in developing countries of some 'naturally' entrepreneurial capitalist class. Instead he highlighted those features of economic and social backwardness that served as obstacles to industrial development, in a way that was later taken up by the 'structuralist' school of development economists. Key to opening up the possibilities for such development was political leadership and land reform. Land reform was critical because upon it depended the ability of the agricultural sector to supply food to a growing industrial sector whose workers still had a large income elasticity of demand for foodstuffs. Otherwise, real wages fell, or food imports rose, alleviated perhaps by food grants from the agricultural surpluses of the industrialized countries. Without land reform, the financial accumulation from higher agricultural production or prices would be absorbed by rural debt service or rents, which would then finance luxury consumption rather than being invested in the expansion of agricultural production.

Kalecki had little faith in the ability of foreign companies to overcome the foreign exchange constraint by means of foreign direct investment. He considered that such investment was very expensive in terms of the amount of profit that foreign companies repatriated, openly or covertly, through transfer pricing. He gave one of the earliest expositions of the effects of such pricing practices.[6] He considered that official loans usually came with political strings and requirements for favourable terms for companies from countries granting such loans. However, he favoured long-term trade agreements between countries. These he felt allowed governments to plan more securely with assured markets abroad.

A key political requirement for economic development, according to Kalecki, was the installation in power of an 'intermediate régime'. This was a government based on the 'lower-middle class', the urban professional classes and small businessmen who have an interest in economic development and are willing to push through crucial land reforms. But they may not necessarily be in favour of socialism, may be bought off by big business and foreign companies.[7] This is perhaps the most troublesome of Kalecki's political concepts.[8] He had in mind the Nasser's government in Egypt. But that, like many of the intermediate regimes of Latin America was, initially at least, based on an alliance of military leaders and trade unions. In India, Jawaharlal Nehru was remarkably cautious in challenging the power of the big landowners who delivered the Congress votes in the rural areas.

With an intermediate regime in place, the key to economic development was planning industrialization. Kalecki considered this to be a financial problem, even though he did not consider developing countries to be subject to a saving constraint, because the financing of investment determined whether the investment drive would be sustainable, or would dissipate into inflation and luxury consumption. Given low wages in developing countries, any substantial investment effort would result in higher demand for 'necessities'. If the supply of such necessities did not increase, then the resulting inflation would reduce real wages, so that the workers themselves would be largely financing the investment drive. At the same time, without land reform, the additional incomes of the food producers would be absorbed by higher rents and debt repayments, increasing demand for luxury goods among merchants, moneylenders and landowners. Formal finance for domestic investment could always be obtained through domestic loans. But if it became necessary to finance investment out of taxes, then Kalecki favoured taxes on profits and higher incomes, because this would have least impact on lower income groups, and may even reduce inflationary pressure by reducing luxury consumption. Capital imports (foreign credits) can ease the foreign exchange constraint, and indeed may support general government spending programmes by allowing the import of specialist health equipment, as well as investment goods.[9] However, foreign credits came in different forms and were frequently politically motivated. The best form of loan was one repayable in finished goods rather than in foreign currency.[10]

The Saving Constraint

The analytical foundation of Kalecki's 'structuralist' vision of economic development was in his reflux theory of saving, investment and profits. In an industrialized capitalist economy, a government financial deficit expands the sales revenue of firms without increasing their costs, so that their profits and savings rise. Similarly, if firms undertake additional investment, using their own savings or bank credit, then this new expenditure ends up as additional profits for firms. In a developing economy, government expenditure and investment 'leaks' out of the system into incomes of non-productive social groups (landowners, merchants and moneylenders). But the key leakage occurs through foreign trade, as a result of the large increase in imports of capital equipment, raw materials and finished goods that is attendant upon an investment boom in a developing country. This in turn drains the scarce foreign exchange reserves of such a country.

For Kalecki, therefore, there was no 'saving' constraint on economic development. Investment, he always insisted, 'finances itself ... If investment is financed out of the liquid reserves of the entrepreneurs concerned, the process will result in a shift of (bank) deposits from these entrepreneurs to other capitalists. If investment is financed by short-term bank credit, the savings accruing in the form of deposits will be available for absorption of the issue of debentures and shares by the investing entrepreneurs. Thus the latter are able to repay the bank credits involved. Finally, if investment is financed by long-term bank credit, the saving, being the counterpart of the higher investment, will swell the deposits, or will be used for repayment of bank credits'.[11]

The two constraints on this have already been mentioned. They are inflation, due to an inelastic supply of food, and a shortage of foreign currency to allow imports to reinforce domestic supplies of consumer and investment. Although Kalecki noted the widespread use of the term 'forced savings' for a decline in real wages due to inflation, he did not in any way indicate that this was a means of 'financing' investment.[12] All that was needed for 'saving' to match investment was basic bank intermediaries and the existence of capitalists with money, or with access to credit.

It is useful to compare Kalecki's view with that of John Maynard Keynes in this regard. In his *General Theory* Keynes asserted the equality between saving and investment as arising from the identity between income and expenditure.[13] A more sophisticated follower of Keynes has argued that the determination of saving by investment arises because of the evolution of the banking system to the point where that system can advance loans without having to acquire deposits.[14] By contrast, Kalecki derived the determination of saving by investment from Karl Marx's scheme of reproduction, in volume 2 of *Capital*. With the standard Kaleckian starting assumption of a closed economy whose workers do not save, and capitalists do not consume, then investment will always be equal to saving, or capitalists' profits.[15] Indeed, a similar argument is implicit in Keynes's *Treatise on Money* in his famous 'widow's cruise' analogy although Keynes confined himself there, like Marx, to the realization that capitalists' consumption adds to profits, rather than diminishing it, as the advocates of thrift have traditionally argued.[16]

Thus for Kalecki the constraint on investment in developing countries, came not from any limited amount of available saving, but from the possibility of inflation, which would distribute the saving counterpart of investment to non-entrepreneurial classes (retailers and landowners), and the drain on foreign currency as an investment boom results in increased imports. The inflationary redistribution of saving could be partially overcome by financing public sector investment with taxes on those non-entrepreneurial classes, and further taxes on luxury imported goods. But neither of these constraints constituted any effective 'saving constraint'.

These foreign exchange and domestic considerations made Kalecki sceptical of the benefits of installing the most capital-intensive (labour-productive) variants of particular investment projects. These had been advocated by Maurice Dobb and Amartya Sen, subject to a constraint of maintaining the level of real wages. In Kalecki's view, the choice of different variants in particular industries was not wide, while inflating capital requirements increased demand for wage good necessities or imports at a time when such demand was already likely to be high.[17]

Conclusion

Kalecki was absolutely adamant that investment creates its saving counterpart by transferring the financial resources of investing capitalists to capitalists in general. Visiting Warsaw in May 1958, John K. Galbraith found Kalecki fulminating against the notion that savings are a constraint on investment in developing countries, a notion that Kalecki attributed to Roy Harrod. Kalecki retaliated by contributing to Harrod's *festschrift* a revised version of his 1963 essay entitled 'Problems of Financing Economic Development in a Mixed Economy' in which he concluded that supplies, rather than unspent income, are what matters in removing constraints on development:

> The key to 'financing' a more rapid growth is the removal of obstacles to the expansion of agriculture, such as feudal land-ownership and domination of peasants by money lenders and peasants ... Foreign credits contribute to the economic surplus and thus they reduce *pro tanto* the need for domestic savings' through increasing 'the supply of necessities' and 'by raising the *volume* of home supplies without creating new incomes'.[18]

However, by then it was too late. The reversion of economic theory to its pre-Keynesian (strictly speaking pre-Hobson) fetishism of thrift had already started, and nowhere more strongly than in development economics. The standard approach from the 1970s onwards attributed economic backwardness to 'saving gaps' rather than social backwardness and inequality.[19] Nevertheless, following his death, Kalecki's work was continued by a small but significant group of economists who had worked or studied with him. Notable among them were Joan Robinson, Thomas Balogh, Eprime Eshag, and more recently Julio Lopez-Gallardo, Ignacy Sachs, Bruce McFarlane and Dipak Ghosh.

7 A RE-EVALUATION OF BANKING SECTOR REFORMS IN TRANSITION ECONOMICS: INTENTIONS AND UNINTENDED CONSEQUENCES

Kobil Ruziev and Sheila Dow

Transformation of the centrally planned economies (CPEs) into market economies implied embarking on a wide range of reforms in every aspect of economic life. In particular, since money and banks served different purposes under central planning compared to a market economy, these institutions too required fundamental restructuring. When transforming their banking sectors most transition economies (TEs) followed policy recommendations, known in the literature as the 'Washington consensus on banking transition', associated mainly with the International Monetary Fund (IMF) and the World Bank.[1]

Unfortunately, the implementation of these policies failed to deliver the expected results in a consistent manner. Price liberalization led to hyperinflation in most TEs, which in turn damaged the public's trust in money and banks. As a result, the prospects for banking development were set back. The newly-created banking sector failed to fill the gap left by the monobank system, resulting in a credit crunch, an inter-enterprise payments crisis and the development of inefficient money surrogates and barter transactions, which had direct implications for production and output. Similarly, gradual removal of controls over capital account transactions, combined with the aggressive entry of foreign banks to gain market share, fuelled the inflow of foreign capital into these economies. But, the sudden reversal of these flows caused problems in banking sectors of most TEs in the late 1990s and more recently following the Global Financial Crisis (GFC).

The purpose of this chapter is to offer an explanation for these outcomes from an institutional perspective. We start by describing briefly the essence of the problems in the organization of the monetary and banking sector under central planning to which reforms were addressed. This is followed by an account of the policy proposals initiated by the international financial institutions (IFIs) to transform the monobank sector into effective market-based financial intermediaries. Then we examine the nature and source of the unintended consequences of liberalization policies. Lessons will also be dawn for economic thinking and policy recommendations for TEs in light of the current GFC. Although the chapter discusses banking system transformation in TEs, it particularly focuses on economies of the former Soviet Union (FSU).

Reforming the Banking Sector in CPEs: The Nature of the Problem

The organization and functions of money and banks were fundamentally different in CPEs compared to market economies. Socialist money circulation was composed of two separate and semi-independent circuits, cash (coins and notes in circulation) and non-cash money (bank deposits) respectively, each with its own characteristics and peculiarities. While cash money served as a medium of exchange, non-cash money was used only for accounting purposes, such as financing and resource transfer to different sectors of the economy. Cash money and non-cash money were not freely interchangeable. Non-cash money was exchanged for cash money only through payroll withdrawals, and sundry transfer payments such as pensions and social security benefits to the household sector. In addition to being only partially convertible into cash money, non-cash money was not freely convertible into goods and services.[2] If enterprises were entitled to buy goods according to their input plans but were short of a means of payment, non-cash money would be supplied by the banking sector. On the other hand, enterprises could not spend their extra non-cash money holdings if they did not have an authorization to buy. Nevertheless, since some manoeuvring was possible within administratively set plan targets, enterprises would convert their redundant non-cash balances into inventory.[3] Furthermore, if any retail businesses had surplus cash money by the end of business, they were required by law to deposit it with the banking system. In short, what was called money under central planning did not represent universalized title to goods and services and its role in the economic process was reduced to the function of a '*numeraire*'.

Banks were designed to facilitate the process of planning and production. The monobank system did not distinguish between central banking and commercial banking and its role was limited to the organization of the payments system and pumping short-term credits to the enterprise sector to facilitate inter-enterprise trade. Since all enterprises held their accounts with banks, banks controlled their financial flows, monitored their performance and supplied all necessary information to the authorities.

The enterprise sector depended heavily upon short-term bank credit to finance their working capital. For example, as Table 7.1 shows, in the FSU in the main sectors of the economy such as industry, agriculture and trade, more than 50 per cent of enterprise working capital was financed by bank credit. Distribution of credit was according to instructions from the planners and without any reference to the creditworthiness of the recipient firms or any risk assessment. Moreover, long-term financing for the start-up capital of new enterprises, or new investment expansions in existing ones, was provided from the state budget as non-repayable grants.

Table 7.1: Sources of enterprise working capital financing in the FSU in 1980.

	National economy	Industry	Agriculture	Trade
Own resources	24.0	33.0	22.8	28.0
Bank credits	46.3	50.2	55.7	56.6
Other	29.7	16.8	21.5	15.4
Total	100.0	100.0	100.0	100.0

Source: Geraschenko and Lavrushin (1982, p. 20)

Although bank credit was the main source of external finance for enterprises, the monobank did not intermediate between savers and investors as banks do in market economies. Notions such as market-determined interest rates, the cost of funds, collateral and creditworthiness were irrelevant to the banking practice of centrally planned economies. An inevitable feature of this system was that the enterprise sector did not face market-type financial constraints, leading to the inefficient allocation of resources, giving rise to the so-called phenomenon of the soft budget constraints.[4] Therefore, inevitably, along with the other fundamental macroeconomic reforms, the process of transition to a market economy also necessitated a fundamental restructuring of the banking sector.

Another particularity of banking under central planning was the separation of corporate banking from retail (or household) banking. As a rule, three big banks specialized in individual sectors, such as industry, agriculture and foreign trade provided corporate banking services. The provision of retail banking services to households was the primary function of the state savings bank. The general public's confidence in this bank was high because it was the only financial institution that offered depositors financial gain and readily exchanged deposits for cash money at a one-to-one ratio on demand. Indeed, the pre-transition ratio of total bank deposits to GDP was about 70 per cent in the FSU and even higher in Eastern European countries.[5] For households, these deposits would appear to perform the functions of money (unlike corporate bank deposits), being universalized title to goods and services. However, a substantial part of household wealth was in fact forced saving, known in the literature as the 'monetary overhang' – the result of a higher rate of growth in household financial assets compared to that in available goods and services over the years. Household sector financial assets accumulated in this way were estimated to be no less than half of household deposits in the FSU.[6] The monetary overhang represented suppressed inflation, which was contained by administratively-set prices, and was seen as a potential source of macroeconomic imbalance.

Policy Recommendations and Intended Outcomes

The transformation of the banking sector was one of the building blocks of the grand plan of macroeconomic transformation in CPEs which comprised 'the Holy Trinity' of liberalization, stabilization and privatization.[7] When transforming their banking sectors, most transition countries followed policy recommendations associated predominantly with the IMF and the World Bank. These recommendations called for price liberalization, abolition of the distinction between cash money and non-cash money, the establishment of a two-tier banking sector (i.e. the separation of commercial banking from central banking), liberalization of interest rates, restructuring and privatization of commercial banks, entry of new private banks, domestic and foreign, regulated by minimum capital and licensing requirements, provision of effective prudential regulation, and sequential liberalization of controls over current and capital account transactions.[8]

It was intended that these reforms would help to achieve a number of goals that were fundamental in successful transformation of the monobank system into a market-based two-tier banking sector. First, it was anticipated that the liberalization of administratively-set prices (which did not represent relative scarcities), combined with the monetary overhang would lead to a jump in the price level. However, since the price jump was expected to be only a one-off event, it was thought to be natural because setting market-determined prices was paramount for providing the right signals to market participants; these signals were to be the driving force of production and determining force of consumption.

Second, it was argued that, with the abolition of the separation between cash money and non-cash money, money would become universalized title to goods and services; this in turn would help monetization of the economy and hence the process of wealth formation, and facilitate financial intermediation.

Third, the establishment of a two-tier banking system and liberalization of interest rates were seen as necessary for building an efficient market-based banking sector that was capable of imposing financial discipline and hardening the infamous soft budget constraints on the enterprise sector.

Fourth, privatization of state-owned commercial banks, entry of new private banks, and provision of effective prudential regulation were expected to increase competition in banking services and facilitate banking development by increasing the interest paid on deposits and reducing the cost of lending to enterprises. In particular, involving foreign banks in the bank privatization process was also encouraged. It was argued that entry of foreign banks would increase competition, reduce cost of lending, and open up access to international financial markets. And more importantly, by bringing new technologies, risk management methodologies, and new products and services, they would generate positive externalities vital to the development of the overall banking sector.[9]

And fifth, achieving current account convertibility and abandoning controls on long-term inward capital flows were expected to stimulate the inflow of long-term foreign direct investments. Sequential liberalization of capital controls over medium and short-term capital flows, to be implemented only after establishing a sound supervisory and regulatory system, was thought to be desirable as free movement of capital would ensure internationally efficient allocation of financial resources in favour of TEs, thereby removing financing constraints on economic growth in these economies.[10]

All in all, the reform policies were intended to get rid of macroeconomic imbalances such as monetary overhang and repressed inflation, help monetization of the economy and wealth formation, facilitate financial deepening, and establish a market-based banking sector capable of filling the gap left by the monobank sector and imposing hard budget constraints on the enterprise sector which would guarantee more efficient use of resources.

Given the nature of the CPEs' macroeconomic problems, as well as the way banks operate in market economies, the policy recommendations and expected outcomes offered under the Washington Consensus on banking transition seemed to be logical and make perfect sense, albeit only in the long run, judging by the slow and time-consuming process of the banking sector development experienced by the market economies themselves.[11] Regrettably, these recommendations failed to address a number of important issues such as (i) the enterprise sector's heavy reliance on bank credit (ii) the opportunity of maintaining, and building upon, the existing public trust in banks (iii) the time-consuming nature of the institution-building process and (iv) the possibility of sudden reversals of international capital inflows, which are all of paramount importance in successful transformation of the banking sector. In other words, although the Washington Consensus on banking transition correctly identified major weaknesses in banking under central planning and attempted to explain what to expect from implementing the suggested policy recommendations, it did not appropriately address how to use the existing institutional settings and experience to best effect.

Moreover, all the former CPEs were assumed to be a homogenous group, and hence the policy advocates saw no reason to differentiate policy advice in the transformation of their banking sectors, as if the heterogeneity of initial conditions across TEs did not matter. In fact, the whole transition package itself was inspired by the 'success' of the stabilization policies implemented in some of the Latin American countries which were structurally and fundamentally different from the CPEs.[12] As a result, the implementation of the recommendations developed within the context of this universal framework resulted in a number of serious unintended consequences. As Abalkin observed in the context of Russia,

> Lacking both the appropriate experience and the specialists familiar (not merely by hearsay) with Russia's realities, the IMF has followed the path of using universal models with certain corrections. A serious contradiction arose between universalism, which was elevated to the rank of an unshakable principle, and the necessity for a nonstandard, creative approach to solving a problem of a qualitatively new type.[13]

In the following section, we will discuss the main unintended consequences of the banking sector reforms common to most of the TEs, and explain why they happened and why the degree and intensity of the problems were substantially different between the Eastern European and FSU countries.

Reforms and Unintended Consequences

Macroeconomic Chaos and Collapse of Trust in Money and Banks

It was implicitly, and perhaps naively, assumed that price liberalization would not affect the general public's trust in banks and the restructured banking sector would not face any problem in filling the gap left by the monobank in meeting the credit needs of enterprises. In fact, the nature of discussions on banking reform in the early 1990s suggests that policy advisors were more concerned with making the banking sector create *less* credit, not the other way around. Since, as we have seen, the working capital of the enterprise sector depended heavily upon bank credit under central planning, the possibility of a credit shortage threatened the sustainability of inter-enterprise payments and thus the scope for production, output and employment to avoid social and economic shocks.

Policy recommendations offered under the Washington Consensus were formed on the basis of the general equilibrium framework; hence it has been suggested that in order to get the system working properly it was necessary that reforms started with the immediate elimination of such macroeconomic imbalances as repressed inflation and monetary overhang.[14] Following these recommendations most transition countries immediately liberalized prices of almost all goods and services.[15] Price reforms were especially spontaneous in Russia, and were also followed, somewhat reluctantly, by all other members of the FSU because of their membership of the rouble zone; any member country not following suit would import inflation from the rest of the rouble zone. As expected, price liberalization led to hyperinflation in almost all transition economies. However, the unprecedented level of this inflation and its persistence in most TEs was unexpected and thus turned out to be the first unintended consequence of this policy. Table 7.2 compares the annual inflation rates in selected TEs in the 1990s to the average inflation rate for the pre-GFC crisis period of 2000–2006. As can be seen from the table, the annual inflation figures in the Commonwealth of Independent States (CIS) jumped from around 100 per cent in 1991 to about 1060 per cent in 1992. It increased further in the following two years: to about 1860 per cent in 1993 and over 2650 per cent in 1994 respectively. Even after the introduction of national currencies, inflation remained high in the CIS; inflation was moderated only after 1999. The Baltic States were more successful in managing to curb inflation. They responded to this shock by setting their sights firmly on macro-stabilization policies. After the introduction of their national currencies in 1992–3, they arranged currency-board type institutions to combat inflation; Estonia pegged her currency to the Deutsche Mark, Latvia to a basket of currencies, and Lithuania to the US dollar. As a result, inflation was reduced to two digit figures by 1994 and to single digit figures by 1998.

Although the experience of Bulgaria and Romania was not as bad as for the CIS countries, high inflation persisted in these countries until the late 1990s. Although inflation was also persistent in the Czech Republic, Hungary and Poland, these countries experienced the mildest inflationary shock amongst all TEs. The highest rate of inflation recorded since 1991 was about 70 per cent in Poland, 52 per cent in the Czech Republic, and 35 per cent in Hungary (all in 1991).

Table 7.2: Inflation in selected transition economies

	1991	1993	1995	1997	1999	2000–6*
CIS region	*110.4*	*1860.4*	*350.3*	*34.5*	*48.2*	*14.3*
Armenia	274.0	1822.0	175.8	14.0	0.7	2.7
Azerbaijan	107.0	1129.0	412.0	3.5	-8.5	4.7
Belarus	94.1	1190.2	709.3	63.8	293.8	48.0
Georgia	79.0	3125.4	162.7	7.1	19.2	6.1
Kazakhstan	78.8	1662.0	176.3	17.4	8.3	8.1
Kyrgyz Rep	85.0	772.4	43.5	23.4	35.9	6.4
Moldova	98.0	1184.0	30.2	11.8	39.3	13.5
Russia	92.7	875.0	197.7	14.7	86.1	15.0
Tajikistan	112.0	2195.0	609.0	88.0	27.6	17.6
Turkmeni-stan	103.0	3102.0	1005.3	83.7	24.2	8.8
Ukraine	91.0	4734.0	377.0	15.9	22.7	11.1
Uzbekistan	109.7	534.2	304.6	70.9	29.1	29.0
Baltic States	*202.5*	*203.1*	*31.2*	*9.5*	*2.2*	*2.9*
Estonia	210.5	89.8	29.0	11.2	3.3	3.7
Latvia	172.2	109.2	25.0	8.4	2.4	3.6
Lithuania	224.7	410.4	39.6	8.9	0.8	1.3
SEE region	*251.9*	*164.6*	*47.2*	*618.4*	*23.3*	*13.6*
Bulgaria	333.5	73.0	62.0	1082.0	0.7	6.3
Romania	170.2	256.1	32.3	154.8	45.8	20.9
CEE region	*52.4*	*26.2*	*21.7*	*13.9*	*6.5*	*4.2*
Czech Rep	52.0	20.8	9.1	8.5	2.1	2.5
Hungary	35.0	22.5	28.2	18.3	10.0	6.2
Poland	70.3	35.3	27.8	14.9	7.3	3.8

* simple average
Source: EBRD (EBRD) (Various Years)

The high rate of inflation that persisted in most of the TEs in the 1990s played the role of a catalyst in the development of further unintended consequences.

It wiped out the real value of financial wealth and thus severely shattered the general public's trust in deposit taking institutions. This was especially the case for the countries of the FSU. This in turn hampered the banking sector's ability to attract deposits. Because inflation eroded the real value of business deposits and simultaneously increased the nominal value of payments under contractual obligations, it also made enterprises more and more dependent upon external finance, thus putting strain on inter-enterprise payments. Since banks were experiencing a crisis of their own at this time, enterprises had to resort to alternative ways of financing their working capital, which gave rise to the phenomenon known in the literature as barterization of transactions.

This phenomenon, which included not only pure barter transactions, but also transactions in promissory notes and mutual debt write-offs, was observed in almost all of the twenty plus transition economies in the 1990s.[16] However, it was most severe in Russia and Ukraine where, at its peak in 1998, barter accounted for more than 50 per cent of all industrial transactions. According to the survey data provided by the Russian Economic Barometer, the number of Russian respondents citing shortage of working capital as the main reason for barterization increased from 47 per cent in 1994 to 61 per cent in 1998.[17] Moreover, enterprise managers noted that both their own liquidity and that of their business partners were equally an important reason for resorting to non-monetary transactions.[18]

As banks struggled to gain the general public's confidence, their ability to create credit declined and economies became more and more reliant upon cash transactions. The pattern of change was similar during transition for all members of the FSU: reliance on cash transactions increased initially and the importance of banking subsequently decreased.[19] The existence of trust in money and financial institutions is vital in a free enterprise system. In fact, the entire financial superstructure in market economies is built upon the notion of confidence. As a rule, commercial banks hold their reserves with the central bank, whereas non-bank financial intermediaries (NBFIs) hold their reserves with commercial banks. As shown in Figure 7.1, the whole financial system can be seen as an inverted pyramid built upon confidence in outside money, held as reserves in the central bank by commercial banks. If confidence in outside money falls, then there is a danger that the entire inverted pyramid of the private financial sector may collapse.[20]

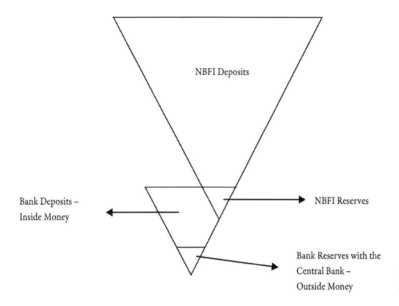

Figure 7.1:Outside money, inside money and the financial superstructure.

On the other hand, if agents do not have confidence in inside money, the size of the inverted pyramid (which can be seen as a proxy for financial deepening) in Figure 7.1 will not expand regardless of the level of return promised on the liabilities of banks and NBFIs. Therefore, raising the real rate of interest paid on deposits is not a sufficient tool to attract idle savings into the formal financial system to boost financial intermediation. Policies directed towards building confidence in inside money, and its issuer – the private financial sector, play an important role too. In addition, if saving in inside money is a new 'culture' for agents, then, naturally the confidence-building period may take even longer. Another issue that highlights the peculiarity of banking is that losing and regaining the general public's trust in inside as well as outside money are not necessarily symmetric processes: trust may be lost very quickly, but it may take years to restore it.

It is beyond the scope of this chapter to survey the experience of individual countries. However, we would like to touch briefly upon how the general public's trust was hit repeatedly in Russia, one of the biggest TEs, and draw our conclusions on this unique experience.

Russia's experience with reforms and how this affected the general public's trust in deposit-taking institutions is quite remarkable. The household sector's confidence in domestic currency as well as domestic financial institutions was hit several times between 1991 and 2000.[21] Unprompted decentralization of the economic process by the ad hoc mass privatization and price liberalization was followed by hyperinflation; the annual rate of inflation was about 1500 per cent in 1992 and almost 900 per cent in 1993. It was during this period that the general public's trust in banks was hit the hardest. During this period the economy experienced a shortage of cash (notes and coins) in circulation, which also led to a temporary freeze on deposit withdrawals from the state-owned banks. Since no measures were taken to protect the real value of financial assets, hyperinflation wiped out the real value of the household sector's bank deposits very quickly. As a result, confidence in the banking sector plunged to a record low; households attempted to protect their purchasing power in non-rouble and non-deposit forms.

Hyperinflation quickly eroded the working capital of the enterprise sector too, making businesses heavily reliant on external financing, specifically on bank credit. With their deposit base shrinking, commercial banks were not in a position to meet the enterprise sector's demand for credit. As a result, enterprises started having difficulties in financing their working capital. In order to prevent the looming payment crisis, the authorities were forced to grant centralized and directed credit to banks. Nonetheless, with the banks' intermediary role steadily declining, these policies did not prove entirely successful. As a result non-payments and inter-enterprise indebtedness started rising. It is recorded that by the end of 1994 only 3 per cent of working capital was financed through own capital, 7 per cent through loans, and 90 per cent through accounts payable and other liabilities.[22]

As a result of liberal entry rules and weak regulation, numerous non-bank financial institutions entered the banking market in the early 1990s. Unfortunately, most of these NBFIs were fraudulent Ponzi-pyramid schemes, which could stay in business as long as their contractual outflows did not exceed contractual inflows. They offered unrealistically high rates of interest on deposits and would have collapsed soon under normal macroeconomic conditions. However, by engaging in speculative activities, especially in the foreign exchange market, they were able to extend their lifecycle. In mid-1995, the monetary authorities formally replaced the floating exchange rate regime with a managed regime, as an anchor to curb inflation. These policies seriously limited the ability of Ponzi-pyramid schemes to fund their contractual outflows in the foreign exchange market, which accelerated their downfall. Since these schemes stayed afloat longer than expected, even very cautious households were caught up in them.[23]

Ironically, although the authorities' attempt to curb inflation brought an end to unsound NBFIs, it also contributed to the creation of another type of Ponzi-pyramid scheme, this time initiated by the fiscal authorities. To coordinate anti-inflationary policies, the fiscal authorities decided to issue short-term government bonds (GKOs) so that the private sector would finance the continuing fiscal deficit.[24] Unfortunately, however, with the economy still contracting, and with record low world prices for oil, tax revenues failed to increase by any significant amount (tax avoidance and evasion were also widespread), resulting in the government's inability to meet its obligations. As a result, the government announced default on its obligations on 17 August 1998. Since GKOs had paid a high positive real return and in the environment of increased uncertainty and high risk associated with lending to businesses, these bonds had proved to be very popular among banks. The moratorium on the government's debt obligations shook the banking sector severely; hundreds of banks collapsed again and as a result the general public's trust hit a new low.

Another drawback of the stabilization policies introduced in 1995 was that low risk, high return GKOs 'crowded out' bank credit, the volume of which was already low, from the enterprise sector and further worsened the non-payment problem, resulting in a payments crisis. At its peak in 1998, non-monetary transactions such as mutual write-offs, promissory notes and pure barter transactions constituted more than 50 per cent of industrial transactions in Russia. After the crisis of 1998, annual rate of inflation was finally controlled and was reduced to about 20 per cent. The steady rise of oil prices also contributed towards macroeconomic stabilization. As a result, since 1999 the economy's reliance on cash money began to decline and the importance of banking started to rise slowly.

Although the Russian experience was not typical of many TEs, development of events in Russia affected the speed of progress in most of the FSU countries. Furthermore, most TEs pursued initial reforms almost in the same manner and faced similar consequences: hyperinflation, collapse of confidence in banks, a credit crunch and payments crisis.

Heterogeneity of Initial Conditions, Removal of Capital Controls and Subsequent Developments

Most TEs shared a broad spectrum of problems in transforming their financial sectors, started the process of transition with comparable reform strategies and faced similar consequences. Nonetheless, the degree of initial shock and the recovery that followed differed substantially depending on the initial conditions and subsequent experiences in terms of pace and sequencing of reforms. In terms of initial conditions, the economies of the FSU and Eastern Europe were different in a number of areas. Countries in Eastern Europe had fewer than fifty years of central planning experience, whereas countries of the FSU had more than seventy years of central planning experience.[25] In addition, most of the countries of the FSU had no experience of independent nationhood over the last couple of centuries, which meant that the transition process in these economies involved not only the development of markets but also the development of the state.[26]

In the FSU, private ownership of property was not tolerated and the entire economic process, from production to distribution, was centrally planned and managed at ministerial level. In contrast, the former republic of Yugoslavia (FRY) had long been known as the most decentralized of all communist economies. In the FRY, tolerance of limited private ownership and decentralization resulted in self-management of the process of production at the enterprise level. Hungary and Poland made a move towards this type of economic management well before the dramatic political changes of the late 1980s (by 1968 and 1981 respectively). Even within the Eastern European countries, there were differences; Bulgaria and Romania were less fortunate, inheriting a Stalinist type of centralized economy.[27] In a nutshell, since Eastern European countries were more decentralized and their economies were more productive compared to their counterparts in the FSU, the degree of price distortion and monetary overhang was less severe. Arguably, these factors partly explain why inflation was milder and its impact less severe in countries like Hungary, Poland and the Czech Republic.

In terms of the preparation of banks for a free enterprise system, again, the countries of Eastern Europe started the process earlier. The FRY had a market-type two-tier banking sector since 1965, and Hungary and Poland since 1987 and 1988 respectively. In Hungary, where partial reforms were initiated in the late 1960s, the first bank with foreign participation was established in 1979. This was the Central European Bank Ltd, a joint venture with six international banks and the National Bank of Hungary (NBH). In 1986 Citibank Budapest was established as a joint venture with Citibank, which held 80 per cent of the bank's capital, and NBH.[28] By and large, by the second half of the 1980s, most Eastern European countries had established two-tier banking systems. Member countries of the FSU effectively underwent this process only in the early 1990s.[29]

In terms of the pace and sequencing of reforms, most of the TEs also reduced barriers to capital account transactions at quite an early stage. In particular, the possibility of joining the European Union (EU), where free movement of capital is a legal requirement, provided an added incentive for carrying out fast and consistent liberalization reforms in Eastern European countries. In particular, most of the Eastern European economies attempted to restructure their banking sectors by offering their state-owned banks to strategic foreign investors. Since these countries had comparatively high per capita income, had inherited less severe macroeconomic distortions, and were located nearest to the market economies of the EU, they were attractive for foreign bank entry. Following the example of Hungary, soon Poland, the Czech Republic, Bulgaria, Romania and the Baltic States also sold their largest banks to strategic foreign investors.

The share of foreign-owned bank assets in total banking sector assets rose from virtually zero in the late 1980s to more than half a decade later in most Eastern European countries; by 2005, they accounted for around 85 per cent of banking sector assets in Central Eastern Europe and over 60 per cent in South Eastern Europe.[30] Leading up to the GFC, the share of foreign-owned bank assets in total bank assets in Eastern Europe as a whole was estimated to be more than five times higher than that in Western Europe.[31] In contrast, with the exception of the Baltic countries, foreign banks do not have significant presence in the FSU countries. For example, in Russia, foreign banks accounted for less than 20 per cent of banking sector assets in 2010.[32]

Before the crisis, this general trend of increasing foreign ownership of banks was viewed in a positive light as a driver of economic growth in the region although the previous studies had already suggested that economic and financial problems in the home country of parent banks can result in economically and statistically significant reduction in commercial lending by foreign-owned banks in host countries.[33] Arguably foreign banks brought market expertise and efficient corporate governance, assisted with payments system modernization, and increased competition and efficiency. Moreover, the dominance of foreign banks, coupled with the relaxation of capital controls, is thought to have helped these economies to gain access to international financial markets, thereby easing liquidity constraints and hence facilitating economic growth. In its annual transition report in 2006, the EBRD noted that in terms of its impact on growth, the 'provision of financial services, irrespective of the channels through which they are provided, is more important' and that 'the total amount of finance that matters more than its composition.'[34]

Subsequently, starting from the early 2000s, bank credit to the private sector increased significantly in most transition countries, reaching peak levels in 2005–7.[35] In Eastern European counties, the trend was driven mostly by foreign-owned banks which had easy access to cheap funds from parent banks eager to expand their market share in the region. In the FSU countries, where foreign bank presence is not significant, domestically-owned banks borrowed directly from the international financial markets. In countries such as Kazakhstan and Russia, international wholesale credit markets became a significant source of funding to support domestic credit expansion.

However, these developments had several undesirable consequences, some more fundamental than others. First, the credit boom was not directed at financing production as it eluded the enterprise sector. According to the Business Environment and Enterprise Performance Survey data as reported in Table 7.3 (generated by the World Bank and EBRD), only around 10 per cent of the surveyed enterprises in TEs were able to obtain bank credit to finance their working capital needs in 2005 compared to over 50 per cent in the pre-transition period (see Table 7.1). Bank financing of fixed capital expansion was similarly low although it was marginally better in Eastern European countries.

Table 7.3: Enterprise financing sources in TEs in 2005.

		Central Europe and Baltic States	South East Europe Region	Commonwealth of Independent States
Working Capital	Internal Finance	68.0	73.2	77.3
	Borrowing from Banks	10.1	12.9	10.1
	Equity	6.9	1.0	2.0
	Trade Credit	6.2	5.6	4.0
	Other	8.8	7.3	6.6
Fixed Capital	Internal Finance	62.4	70.8	77.2
	Borrowing from Banks	14.3	17.7	11.6
	Equity	6.5	0.9	1.9
	Trade Credit	1.9	2.4	1.8
	Other	14.9	8.2	7.5

Source: EBRD (2006, p. 48)

Second, contrary to expectations, foreign banks in Eastern European countries were more actively involved in lending to households, which traditionally requires relatively less sophistication and expertise compared to lending to businesses. For the 2000–5 period, the growth rate of household loans was higher than that of enterprise loans throughout the transition region and accounted for more than half of total credit to the private sector in some countries.[36] A significant proportion of these loans in turn were directed towards mortgage financing in the real estate and construction sectors which became important drivers of economic growth. As a result, the construction sector's share in gross value added rose in most countries; in countries such as Estonia, Lithuania, Kazakhstan and Romania, it increased almost twice between 2000 and 2007.[37] Because of the heightened interest in investing in the sector, real estate prices increased dramatically, also partly due to speculation.

When sub-prime borrowers started to default on their mortgage obligations systematically in the US in the first half of 2007, values of these mortgages as well as all other assets derived from them went down, resulting in huge losses for investors internationally. In response, international investors increased their perception of risk on other emerging market assets too. As a result, external loans to both foreign as well as domestically-owned banks, which were of paramount importance in supporting the unprecedented credit growth in the region, suddenly dried up and the cost of available ones increased dramatically. Hungary in Eastern Europe and Kazakhstan in the FSU were affected particularly badly from the housing market crisis.[38] The bursting of the credit bubble also led to reduction in economic growth in TEs, with countries in the Central and South-East Europe and the Baltic regions suffering the most.

Third, a foreign-currency-driven lending boom was a feature of the banking systems in the majority of TEs throughout the 2001–8 period.[39] Dependence on foreign borrowing, including for speculative currency carry trade purposes, exposed the banking sectors of these countries to significant foreign exchange risk.[40] At the end of 2009, more than half of loans and deposits in most TEs were denominated in foreign currency; the Czech Republic, Russia and Poland were the only three countries where local currency loans and deposits exceeded 60 per cent.[41] Borrowing in foreign currencies was attractive to households and enterprises as traditionally high domestic nominal interest rates coupled with decreasing inflation rates and appreciating domestic currencies in TEs made it more expensive to borrow in domestic currencies. Although individual banks passed on foreign exchange risk to borrowers in this way, the systemic risk did not disappear as the repayment source of these loans, i.e. enterprise and house-hold earnings, was in domestic currency. When the tide of capital flows reversed following the onset of the GFC, exchange rates of these economies came under pressure leading to significant depreciation of domestic currencies (e.g. over 20 per cent in countries like Russia and Kazakhstan), making it difficult for house-holds and corporations to repay foreign currency loans.

Last but not least, the availability of cheap foreign-currency-denominated loans from international financial markets reduced banks' reliance on the domestic deposit base in their capacity to create credit, thereby delaying the process of build-ing trust in outside as well as inside money.[42] It also increased the vulnerability of TEs to external financial shocks as the GFC was transmitted to these economies by multinational banks mostly through the financial flows channel. Although both internationally-borrowing domestic banks and foreign-owned banks cut their lending in response to the crisis, empirical studies have shown that foreign-owned banks reduced their lending earlier and faster.[43] Moreover, it was also found that, in countries where most of the lending was in local currency and funded from the domestic deposit base, the reduction in the supply of credit was less severe.[44]

Concluding Remarks

In summary, following the policy recommendations of IFIs, all TEs abolished the distinction between cash money and non-cash money and gradually modernized their payments systems, starting with corporate banking and then extending the process to retail banking. They established two-tier banking sectors, liberalized interest rates, restructured their commercial banks and gradually removed capi-tal controls. Under normal circumstances, these policies would have improved the general public's trust in banks and facilitated banking sector development. However, the impact of these developments was overshadowed by the ill-thought-out and uncoordinated policies pursued in the early 1990s. The shock-therapy type of policy recommendations promoted under the Washington Consensus and pursued in most TEs in the early 1990s resulted in unexpected and unin-tended consequences, such as persistent inflation, macroeconomic chaos, and the general public's loss of trust in money and banks, which had clear implica-tions for credit creation, and thus for production, output and employment.

Although the removal of capital controls increased capital inflow to TEs and eased financing constraints on economic growth, internationally-borrowed funds eluded the enterprise sector as they were used mostly to finance household consumption and construction development. Excessive reliance on international borrowing, especially leading up to the GFC, not only increased the exposure of the banking sectors of these economies to sudden reversal of capital flows and hence foreign currency risk, but also made them more vulnerable to external financial shocks. Furthermore, while access to international financial markets allowed banks to increase the supply of credit to the economy, it reduced their reliance on the domestic deposit base to create credit, which, although time-consuming to build upon, is a more stable source of credit growth as confirmed by empirical studies. Table 7.4 summarizes key aspects of our discussion on policy recommendations, intentions and unintended consequences.

In general, our analysis shows that, particularly for the FSU countries, the introduction of gradual changes would have been more suitable for guaranteeing a smoother transition from the monobank system to the market-based two-tier system; policies should have been designed to build upon existing trust in money and banks and to take into account the existing institutional settings and initial conditions.

Table 7.4: Brief summary of policy recommendations, intentions and unintended consequences.

Policy Recommendations	Intended Outcomes	Unintended Consequences
Liberalize prices	One-off increase in price level	Macroeconomic chaos and persistent hyperinflation with consequences on trust building in outside as well as inside money
Abolish the separation between non-cash and cash money	Improves monetization and wealth formation and facilitates financial intermediation	Hyperinflation wipes out the value of savings; importance of banking declines and reliance on cash transactions increase
Establish two-tier banking sector	Commercial banking: leads to efficient allocation of resources, imposition of financial discipline on enterprises, and hardening soft budget constraints	General public loses trust in banks which then fail to fill the gap left by the monobank, leading to credit shortages, proliferation inter-enterprise non-payments and subsequent development of barterization of transactions
	Central banking: provides effective prudential regulation and supervision of the activities of commercial banks	Banking sector troubles are also partly due to weak and ineffective supervision and prudential regulation, which in turn is explained by time consuming nature of building up competent and adequately trained human capital

Policy Recommendations	Intended Outcomes	Unintended Consequences
Privatize state-owned banks, involving foreign banks if possible; encourage entry of new private banks	Improves competition which should lead to higher return on deposits and lower cost of lending to enterprises	Lax regulation and supervision leads to propagation of inadequately capitalized private banks and spread of Ponzi pyramid schemes in some countries (e.g. Russia and Albania); contrary to expectations, foreign banks prefer lending to household sector which requires less sophistication and expertise
After achieving macro economic stability, gradually liberalize capital account transactions	Represents optimizing household and firm decisions that support internationally efficient resource allocations; removes financing constraints on economic growth	Instead of basing their credit creation capacity on domestic deposit base, banks increasingly rely on international markets as a source of credit expansion with implications to the sector's exposure to foreign exchange risk; speculative demand for international loans to seek profit from currency carry trade is also in the rise; sudden reversal of capital flows increased the vulnerability of TEs to external financial shocks

The experience of TEs shows that policy recommendations based upon a perception of a problem which is much more simplistic than the real problem are bound to result in unintended and undesirable consequences. But does this mean less policy prescription? Not necessarily. The implication is that we cannot rely on particular economic dogmas as if they were universal truths. Economics is a social science; like its subject matter, it evolves over time. With it, our approach to tackling contemporary economic problems must also change. Since we have shown here that policy based on neoclassical theory did not have the intended outcome for TEs, the time is ripe to move away from the fictional assumptions of neoclassical orthodoxy such as perfect information and perfect knowledge, which ensure the smooth functioning of markets. We should move towards a more realist approach where we recognize the importance of history and experience, and appreciate both the complexity of economic systems and the time-consuming nature of institutional development. The result would be that we would be more realistic about our policy recommendations, and more cautious about the expected outcomes.

8 DYNAMICS OF RISK, CONCENTRATION AND EFFIENCY IN BANKING SECTORS OF TRANSITION ECONOMIES

Khurshid Djalilov and Jens Hölscher

The presence of a sound banking sector is important for ensuring smooth and efficient running of a market-based economy as banks play a crucial role in channelling funds from lenders to borrowers with productive investment projects. Over the last two decades the financial systems of the former Soviet Union (FSU) as well as countries in central and eastern Europe (CEE) have undergone substantial reforms, the impact which on the overall economy is now established in the literature.[1]

The aim of this chapter is to compare risk-taking behaviour, concentration, as well as efficiency in the banking sectors of two groups of countries. The first includes the early transition economies, which have now progressed sufficiently to become members of the European Union (EU), while the second are late transition countries, that is, countries in the FSU. Countries in group one are: the Czech Republic, Estonia, Hungary, Latvia, Lithuania and Poland, and those in group two are: Armenia, Azerbaijan, Belarus, Georgia, Kazakhstan, Kyrgyz Republic, Moldova, Tajikistan, Ukraine and Uzbekistan.

We start by reviewing the existing literature, which is followed by describing the methodology and the data source. Then we discuss the results and conclude.

Review of the Existing Studies

Why the Former Soviet Republics?

Over the last twenty-five years, a plethora of studies have focussed on the transition of countries from CEE from a system of central planning to a market economy. However, the majority of the FSU countries have been largely ignored due to the paucity of reliable information and these countries are substantially different from the early transition countries in CEE. There are many reasons for this. Firstly, the FSU countries were controlled by the communist regime for more than seventy years. This resulted in the lack of a national collective memory of any other form of economic organization or institutions in these countries and no experience of managing a domestic market economy prior to the collapse of the Soviet Union in 1991. During the Gorbachev era in the late 1980s, when reforms to establish a market economy took place in the Baltic states of the FSU and in several countries in CEE, the other countries of the FSU did not follow suit. The latter group of countries provide a sharp contrast to countries such as Hungary, Poland and the former Czechoslovakia, and even to the Baltic states of the FSU, which only had a system of central planning for the period following the Second World War until the 1990s. This historical legacy has a huge impact on how quickly a market economy can be established and emphasizes the importance of historical backgrounds and initial conditions at the beginning of transition on the direction and speed of financial sector development and its impact on economic growth.

Second, many FSU countries are rich in mineral and energy resources which has implications on economic growth but also potential internal conflicts associated with the problem of resource allocation. Third, some FSU countries, especially those located in central Asia, are geographically very extensive and political instability in neighbouring countries such as Afghanistan can be contagious. For these countries, maintaining economic growth and ensuring financial stability are vital to retain social cohesion and sustained development.

Table 8.1 summarizes a selection of relevant indicators to show that late transition countries are different from early ones. Particularly, we use six questions in developing these indicators: (1) a country was under socialism for more than sixty-five years; (2) a country is rich in mineral resources; (3) a country is not an EU member; (4) absence of market economy before World War II (WWII); (5) the European Bank for Reconstruction and Development's (EBRD) Banking Reform Index is low; and (6) the EBRD's Competition Policy Index is low.

Table 8.1: Indicators distinguishing early and late transition countries.

| | More than 65 years under socialism (1) | Rich in mineral resources (2) | Non-EU member state (3) | Absence of market economy before WWII (4) | Low EBRD index (2010) | | Total (7) |
					Banking Reform (5)	Competition policy (6)	
			Late Transition				
Armenia	1	0	1	1	1	1	5
Azerbaijan	1	1	1	1	1	1	6
Belorus	1	0	1	1	1	1	5
Georgia	1	0	1	1	1	1	5
Kazakhstan	1	1	1	1	1	1	6
Kyrgyz Republic	1	1	1	1	1	1	6
Moldova	0	0	1	1	1	1	4
Tajikistan	1	0	1	1	1	1	5
Ukraine	1	1	1	1	1	1	6
Uzbekistan	1	1	1	1	1	1	6

	More than 65 years under socialism (1)	Rich in mineral resources (2)	Non-EU member state (3)	Absence of market economy before WWII (4)	Low EBRD index (2010)		Total (7)
					Banking Reform (5)	Competition policy (6)	
Early Transition							
Czech Republic	0	0	0	0	*	*	0
Estonia	0	0	0	0	0	0	0
Hungary	0	0	0	0	0	0	0
Latvia	0	0	0	0	0	0	0
Lithuania	0	0	0	0	0	0	0
Poland	0	0	0	0	0	0	0

*Authors' calculations

A. If the answers to the questions of the columns 1-4 are 'yes', then the score is equal to 1, otherwise 0. B. If EBRD indices are equal or less than 3.0 then the score is 1, otherwise 0. C. * –EBRD indices are absent for Czech Republic.

A country has a score of 1 if the answers to the questions in columns 1–4 are 'yes', otherwise 0. The EBRD regularly assesses the transition process from a planned to a market economy in the former socialist countries and the indices range from 1 to 4, where 1 represents no or little change from a centrally planned economy and 4 represents a standard typical of an industrialized market economy. The scores in columns 5–6 are equal to 1 if the relevant EBRD's index is equal to or less than 3, and they take the value of 0 otherwise.

All of the early transition countries joined the camp of socialism during and after WWII. However, the majority of the FSU countries were part of the Soviet Union before WWII and were under socialism for more than sixty-five years. None of the late transition countries is a member of the EU and did not have experience of running a modern market economy prior to the collapse of the Soviet Union in 1991. Additionally, all of the late transition countries have equal or lower than 3.0 scores for the relevant EBRD's indices. Thus, although all transition economies started the reform process from similar initial conditions, late and early transition countries now seem to be structurally different. In this sense, it would be interesting to compare various financial indicators such as efficiency, market concentration, and risk taking behaviour in the banking sectors of these countries.

Bank Efficiency

Some studies show that new banks are not as efficient as long established ones and that older banks are found to be more profitable.[2] Contrary to the earlier studies, some find that foreign banks are on average most efficient and that new banks are more efficient than long established ones in Croatia for the period 1995–2000.[3] Other studies on banking efficiency in transition countries show that banks with majority foreign ownership are more efficient than privately-owned and state-owned banks.[4] However, another study finds foreign banks to have higher profit, but lower cost efficiency.[5] Moreover, the efficiency gap between foreign, domestic and state banks is also shrinking over time. Finally, another study on banking efficiency finds evidence that reforms have a positive impact on bank efficiency.[6]

Market Concentration

The existing literature assumes that high levels of concentration favours companies' collusive behaviour, which ultimately weakens competition in the market and supports the view of a negative link between concentration and competition. However, there are two dominant views on the impact of competition on banks' risk-taking behaviour: 'competition-fragility' and 'competition-stability'. Some studies show that greater competition lowers the franchise value of banks, which increases their incentives to take higher risks.[7] By focusing on the deposit market another study concludes that higher levels of competition increases banks' risk of failure.[8] Thus, these results confirm the competition-fragility view. However, a contrasting result is also found that supports the competition-stability view, suggesting that greater competition may contribute to banking sector stability. For example, it has been argued that the loan rates are lower under higher competition which may reduce incentives to allocate resources to riskier projects taking into account moral hazard and adverse selection problems.[9] However, some scholars claim that previous researchers ignore the fact that lower rates (under higher competition) reduce bank revenues from performing loans.[10] Taking this into account they find a U-shaped relationship between competition and the risk of failure for banks, that is, greater competition increases the risk of bank failure in very competitive markets, while decreasing the risk of failure in highly concentrated markets.[11]

Risk-Taking Behaviour

Several studies address risk-taking behaviour of banks but most focus on developed and developing countries.[12] However, banks behave differently under different institutional settings which implies that the results obtained for developed and developing countries may not apply to the transition ones.[13] Furthermore, whilst various aspects of banking-sector developments in CEE countries have been studied extensively over the last decades, studies on risk taking behaviour by banks in the FSU countries is still limited.[14] Existing studies find no indication of excessive risk-taking by specific ownership or size categories of banks.[15] Additionally, some conclude that banks with market power in CEE tend to take on lower credit risk. Therefore, this study provides an opportunity to fill this gap in the literature.[16]

Method and Data

Efficiency is obtained by estimating a profit function while the variables concentration and risk are obtained by construction, which will be explained in more detail in the following sections.

Efficiency

Numerous studies have focused on measuring firm efficiency in different sectors in a number of countries. Most of the studies use a production function in measuring efficiency. Although many different methods have been used, most are based on the transformation function, particularly those that describe a production technology at a firm level. The aim is to maximize value given available technology, prices and other relevant constraints. Assuming a common set of constraints, the efficiency is measured as the distance between individual production units and the best practice frontier. Different methods are used to measure the frontier; two most popular approaches are parametric and non-parametric modelling. Data Envelopment Analysis (DEA) is a non-parametric approach using linear programming, while econometric models estimate deterministic or stochastic frontier (SF) which is a parametric approach. Both allow estimation of firm level efficiency.

In this chapter we employ the SF estimation technique as DEA does not take account of measurement errors and other types of statistical noise, and assumes that all deviations from the frontier are due to technical inefficiency. Further, profit efficiency is superior to revenue and cost efficiencies as the first simultaneously considers both revenue maximization and cost minimization so this is the approach used in this study. The profit efficiency of the bank measures how well profits are maximized with respect to a benchmark, or industry best practice. Following the existing literature, an intermediation approach is used to identify input–output variables for the banks in our estimations. The choice of variables is described in Table 8.2.[17]

Table 8.2: Input-output variables used for SF.

Variables	Description
Total profit	Dependent variable and equals to Net Profit after Tax
	Output
Total loans ($y1$)	Gross loans
Total interest bearing funds ($y2$)	Funds banks allocate in other financial institutions' interest bearing accounts
	Input Prices
Total interest expenses ($w1$)	Expenses of banks for attracting funds (i.e. cost of capital)
Overheads ($w2$)	Administrative and labour expenses (i.e. cost of labour)
	Control
GDP per capita	This is calculated at constant US dollars (2005) and taken from World Bank Development Indicators (2013)

Source: The bank specific variables are taken from the financial statements of the banks (Bankscope).

The specifying equation to estimate efficiency levels is a widely used translog functional form for the profit function, which takes the following form:

$Ln(Total\ Profit/w_2)=\alpha_0 + \Sigma_j\,\alpha_j\,ln\,(y_j)_{it} + \frac{1}{2}\,\Sigma_j\,\Sigma_k\,\alpha_{jk}\,ln\,(y_j)_{it}\,ln\,(y_k)_{it} + \beta_1$ $ln(w_1/w_2)_{it}\ +$

$+ \frac{1}{2}\,\beta_{11}\,ln\,(w_1/w_2)_{it}\,ln\,(w_1/w_2)_{it} + \Sigma_j\,\vartheta_j\,ln\,(y_j)_{it}\,ln\,(w_1/w_2)_{it} + \gamma_t\,ln(control)$ $_t+ v_{it} - u_{it}\ (1)$

where i and t index the bank and year respectively, and $\alpha_{jk} = \alpha_{kj}$. There are two outputs (y); *total loans* and *total interest bearing funds*, and two input prices (w), namely, *total interest expenses* and *overheads* (Table 8.2). The profit function is normalized using the input price (overheads) to ensure price homogeneity, following the literature.[18] The model has a control variable (GDP per capita) to account for cross-country heterogeneity.

Equation (1) contains two error terms, v_{it} and u_{it}; v_{it} accounts for statistical noise with a symmetric distribution, whereas u_{it} has a non-negative distribution and reflects bank level inefficiency. There are many assumptions regarding the distribution of u_{it} and we follow the existing literature for parameterization of time effects, where the inefficiency term (u_{it}) is modelled as a truncated-normal random variable multiplied by a specific function of time.[19]

Concentration

The existing literature uses various variables to account for concentration and competition in a banking sector. Considering a heterogeneous nature of the banks in our sample, we use the Herfindahl-Hirschman Index (HHI) as a concentration variable in our analyses following the existing studies.[20] The index is equal to the squared sum of each banks' market share and thus a higher value implies a higher level of concentration.

Bank Risk-Taking

Recent studies use different risk measurements for a banking sector (e.g. credit risk, default risk, etc.). Following these studies, we use a Z score as the measure of bank risk as it is monotonically associated with a measure of a bank's probability of failure.[21] The Z score is expressed as return on assets (ROA) plus the equity–asset ratio (EAR) divided by the standard deviation of return on assets. Since the Z score indicates the distance to insolvency, a higher value of the score implies that a bank is less risky.[22] This represents a more universal measure of bank risk-taking behaviour and has been extensively used in the literature of finance and banking. As the Z score is highly skewed, we use the natural logarithm form.[23] Return on assets is calculated as net income divided by total assets and is taken from the bank financial statements retrieved using the Bankscope database.

Data

The sample includes only those banks which have at least three years of financial statements in Bankscope for the period 2000–12. Thus, 254 banks are included in the sample.

Discussions

The results for the technical efficiency, which are presented in Table 8.3, show that two groups of the transition countries do not differ hugely across the research period. However, the variation in technical efficiency is higher for banks in the late transition countries. In addition, there is no suggestion that the efficiency has improved in the early transition countries although the variation is higher for the late transition countries.

Table 8.3: Estimates of competition, risk and efficiency.

	Late transition countries				
	Competition and risk			Technical efficiency (te)	
Year	HHI	Z score	Banks	scores	Banks
2000	0.55	16.30	42	0.48	33
2001	0.54	20.73	46	0.47	40
2002	0.42	13.36	49	0.45	43
2003	0.47	11.05	60	0.45	52
2004	0.43	12.12	70	0.45	66
2005	0.33	10.31	85	0.45	80
2006	0.31	10.27	89	0.44	84
2007	0.32	11.76	102	0.44	93
2008	0.28	17.98	112	0.42	89
2009	0.30	18.52	119	0.45	76
2010	0.30	17.50	124	0.41	96
2011	0.26	16.91	128	0.41	94
2012	0.29	13.20	108	0.41	93
	Early transition countries				
	Competition and risk			Technical efficiency (te)	
Year	HHI	Z Score	Banks	scores	Banks
2000	0.34	12.84	39	0.43	36
2001	0.34	12.46	47	0.43	42
2002	0.32	12.81	51	0.46	46
2003	0.30	11.71	58	0.44	55
2004	0.25	13.22	79	0.44	72
2005	0.25	12.23	84	0.42	78
2006	0.24	12.92	92	0.41	84
2007	0.24	11.61	90	0.41	85
2008	0.25	10.71	90	0.43	74
2009	0.24	12.29	103	0.42	63
2010	0.24	13.93	107	0.42	67
2011	0.22	13.27	104	0.42	72
2012	0.22	14.88	96	0.42	76

*Authors' calculations

HHI is relatively higher in the group of late transition economies indicating a more concentrated market in these countries. However, HHI has significantly decreased in the group of late transition economies with a HHI score of 0.55 in

2000 and 0.29 in 2012. This indicates that the competition in the banking sector improved over the period 2000–2012.

The volatility of the Z score is higher in the group of late transition economies, but banks in the group of the early transition countries take more risks as their Z scores are lower (Table 8.3). Particularly, the scores for the early and late transition economies in 2000 were 16.30 and 12.84 respectively. However, in 2012, the Z score increased to 14.88 in late transition countries, while it decreased to 13.20 in early transition countries. This implies that early transition economies became more cautious about taking higher risks, which may be due to the recent global financial crisis. In contrast, late transition economies seem to be taking higher risks more recently. This is consistent with economic theory implying that late transition economies are improving their skills of risk assessment.

Concluding Remarks

This chapter has aimed to analyse the dynamics of the efficiency, concentration- and risk in the banking sectors of early and late transition economies. Efficiency scores were constructed using the SF estimating method; measures of risk and concentrationwere constructed using a Z score and an HHI index respectively. The results for the technical efficiency in Table 8.3 show that bank efficiency, concentration, and risk-taking behaviour in the two contrasting groups of transition countries do not differ significantly across the research periods. However, the variation is higher in the banking sectors of late transition countries. HHI is relatively higher in late transition economies indicating a more concentrated market in these countries. The volatility of the Z score is higher in late transition economies, but banks in early transition countries seem to be taking more risks as their Z scores are lower (Table 8.3). Additionally, banks in more competitive banking sectors tend to take higher risks to survive and flourish. Moreover, more advanced and less concentrated (more competitive) markets have better risk assessment expertise and are able to take higher level of risk.

In general, the banking sectors in both groups of transition countries seem to have become less concentrated and to have increased the level of risk-taking towards the end of the research period (Table 8.3). However, the late transition countries slightly decreased their level of risk-taking over the period 2008–12. Perhaps, this is due to early transition countries becoming more integrated to global financial markets, and being hit more by the recent global financial crisis. This could explain why they have been more cautious about taking risks over periods of financial and economic instability. Moreover, stronger integration to the world economy, particularly, to more advanced countries help countries improve efficiency in banking sectors. For example, the accession of China into the World Trade Organization (WTO) speeded up the banking sector reforms in China.[24] Similarly, to some extent, the EU membership helps early transition countries improve efficiency of their banking sectors.[25]

Overall, the results are consistent with economic theory which suggests that banks tend to take higher level of risks in more advanced and competitive markets. Moreover, they have better expertise in risk assessment compared to that of late transition countries. Therefore, even though the levels of risk-taking in both groups of transition countries are gradually increasing, it is higher in early transition countries as the latter has higher levels of competition.

9 FICTIONS OF TRANSITION: ON THE ROLE OF CENTRAL BANKS IN POST-SOCIALIST TRANSFORMATIONS

Daniela Gabor

Doctoral students are famously, and necessarily, lost at the beginning of their research process. Confusion breeds the urge to explore and (de/re)construct. Dipak Ghosh, one of the supervisors of my thesis on the central bank of Romania after the collapse of communism in 1989, nurtured that urge well. Socratic in spirit, most of our conversations focused on one question: how could the industrial structures inherited from central planning function in a capitalist logic of organizing production? Dipak was well-versed in 'Sovietology' and 'Transitology' – the Western academic scholarship on the economics of, and transition from, central planning. He invited me to engage with the pervasive claims that state-owned enterprise (SOEs) could undermine the (macro) stability and competitiveness of the emergent capitalism(s).[1] This claim appeared particularly appropriate for Romania, viewed, with few exceptions,[2] as *the* basket-case among its Eastern European peers for its journey from 'hypercentralized' socialism[3] to 'incoherent cocktail capitalism' resulting from chaotic economic and institutional reforms after 1990.[4]

I, in turn, wondered whether the central bank institutions and monetary policies put in place after the fall of communism in Romania had not, in practice, diminished the chances that large industrial companies could 'catch-up' with Western competitors. This question emerged from reading the report of the first Romanian Commission for Transition,[5] a national initiative set up in 1990 to think carefully about the core policies that should guide transformation. The Commission proposed that industrial upgrading should be the basis for catching up with capitalist Europe, through an ambitious set of measures that would promote capital investment in existing strategic industrial sectors, neglected during the 1980s, to rebuild technological capabilities of the Romanian industry. Alongside price controls for strategic intermediary inputs and careful exchange rate management, the Commission stressed that relationship banking[6] would be crucial to support investment. Banks, private- and state-owned, would develop profit-driven relationships with private and state-owned industries, allowing governments to channel subsidized credit with the objective of improving external competitiveness. Put differently, Romanian officials outlined an agenda for moving to the mode of coordinated capitalism *a la* Germany.[7] Yet one year later, in 1991, when the International Monetary Fund (IMF) became officially involved in designing the Romanian transition, the definition of the transition 'challenge' changed dramatically: state-owned enterprises were no longer conceived as the potential national champions of a Romanian coordinated capitalism, but, along 'Sovietology' lines, as the 'dinosaurs' of a by-gone era that threatened the path to liberal market capitalism.[8]

Was the IMF correct in dismissing the Commission's ambitions? Such conflicting representations could not be reconciled by hypothesis testing, since standard empirical approaches are ill suited for analysing profound structural changes (and data gaps). The more apposite question, rather, focused on the macroeconomic *conditions* – the monetary policy regimes and financial system features – under which complex organizations in the state-owned industrial sector could survive and eventually become competitive. In other words, I was interested in providing a conceptualization of central banking in 'transition' built on post-Keynesian concerns with the role of money in a monetary economy of production, and on structuralist/dependency school concerns with the articulation between industrial policies, financial institutions and monetary policy.[9]

The task of persuasion, it became rapidly obvious from my conversations with Dipak, required a departure from the typical (dis)equilibrium approaches dominating Sovietology studies, to different epistemological and ontological positions that highlighted (i) the importance of ideas[10] and hegemonic fictions – myths and stereotypes about socialist production (re)produced by Sovietologists and Transitologists and (ii) the importance of a closer theoretical engagement between the political economy of central banking and theories of industrial organization.

From this two-pronged standpoint, the central bank is no longer simply conceived as the neutral carrier of a particular theory of monetary policy, as scholars typically do, but rather as a key institution of the national political economy whose ideas (about state-owned enterprises), practices and leverage in negotiations with external and domestic actors can play a (the?) crucial role in shaping 'transition'. That is, the cloak of neutrality that central banks enjoy – weaved from the supposed objectivity of models, theories and practices of intervention – renders their ideational stand even more important. When considering central banks as strategic actors in the argumentative terrain where political struggles over economic reform take place, it matters analytically whether central banks embrace closely or critically with hegemonic fictions about state-owned companies. In the former case, industrial restructuring means industrial downsizing that is achieved, among other measures, through monetary and exchange rate policies that curtail practices of relationship lending, while in the latter, industrial restructuring is a distinct, admittedly complex, possibility that requires coordinated monetary and industrial policies.

The former case leads to a regime of central-bank led financialization. The term refers to practices and ideas focused on transforming the socialist legacy of relational banking into arm's-length relations between finance and industry. By linking soft-budget constraints to aggregate demand pressures and thus macroeconomic (in)stability, central banks implement tight monetary policies and exchange rate flexibility that curtail the possibilities for banks to generate profits from traditional lending to business. The central bank uses instances of government support for state-owned companies as an *institutional alibi* to explain the failures of its policies as failures of the state (and of industrial policies).

The main goal of this chapter is to bring central bank politics into 'Transitology' accounts, particularly where it concerns the relationship between the financial system and industrial restructuring. It is divided in three parts: (i) fictions of state and markets infusing post-socialist debates on economic reforms; (ii) industrial restructuring as the 'war' on state-owned 'dinosaurs' and (iii) central-bank led financialization.

From 'Sovietology' to 'Transitology': Fictions of the State and Market

the role and prospects of SOEs were underestimated – often with colourful images of dinosaurs producing obsolete goods for the region's bloated industrial sectors ... there was no coherent policy towards them, except to privatise as rapidly as possible or simply to make them fold by cutting off finance, so little thought went into trying consciously to modify their behaviour before privatization. This trap was 'state desertion' sometimes going further to involve explicit tax and other discrimination against SOEs vis-à-vis private firms.

Portes, 1995.

the soft budget constraint ... has been a workhorse for those involved in studying and formulating policy for post-socialist economies. There has hardly been a report on transition – by the World Bank, EBRDor other agencies in the last decade in which expressions of 'soft' and hard budget constraint have not appeared prominently

Kornai et al., 2003.[11]

When the Berlin Wall fell in 1989, Sovietologists, many taken by surprise, instantly became 'Transitologists', scholars whose considerable expertise was called upon to provide insights useful for policy. While the name changed, the premise stayed the same: a celebratory narrative of liberal market mechanisms.[12] This narrative dismissed state-owned companies as irremediably inefficient at micro-level and dangerous to stability at macro-level, as the quotes above suggest. Instead, it invoked the image of the flexible specialization model dominating the literature on industrial organization at the time, a model based on developing incentives to attract foreign manufacturers into greenfield investments, while neglecting the older industrial regions into 'the new rust belts' of the formerly planned countries.[13]

Yet the hegemonic narrative of the 'dinosaur' state-owned companies was not constructed in the mainstream industrial organization literature, even if the latter provided an alternative appealing to policymakers. Rather, Micheal Burawoy and Janos Lukacs[14] argued that the metaphor could be traced back to a methodological error committed by Sovietologist economists (and by orthodox Marxists): to juxtapose the 'empirical reality of one society with the ideal type of another', that is, to contrast the empirical reality of the soviet economy (large scale, vertically integrated enterprises in the industrial sector) with the 'fiction' of atomistic competition in perfect capitalist markets.

Paradoxically, the early debates on central planning explicitly engaged with the realities of capitalism. Theorists of (central) planning argued that socialism could perfectly imitate the 'fiction' of capitalist competitive markets, but ultimately, that the economic case for socialism relied on the 'realities' of capitalism, that is, on its tendencies to concentration and centralization.[15] The moving force behind capitalism – technological progress – required economies and efficiencies that could only be achieved through large-scale production. Since capitalism inevitably gravitated towards monopoly,[16] the task of the socialist planner was to plan state monopoly better than private capital. This conclusion unsettled Austrian economists. While sharing Lange's suspicion of monopolies, Austrians maintained that socialist monopoly would fail to generate incentives to innovate.[17] In contrast, in unfettered capitalism, innovation would arise from the *possibility* of market entry. The market retained (if in abstract) its disciplining role even in monopoly capitalism.

The 'Sovietology' economics of the 1980s ignored both Lange's warning that socialism ought to be judged against monopoly capitalism and the Austrian engagement with 'despotic' monopoly. In the (dis)equilibrium models that measured the distance from the Walrasian market-clearing point,[18] reality mattered little since the socialist firm was assumed to work as the competitive firm (of general equilibrium models), while planners fulfilled the allocative functions of the market. In turn, Janos Kornai's[19] shortage approach rejected the neoclassical treatment of state-owned firms as profit maximizers operating under a hard budget constraint. Rather, it constructed the state-owned Soviet firm in direct contrast with the neoclassical firm operating in perfect competition.[20] The latter is driven by profit, constrained by demand and essentially disciplined by market competition into efficiency. By contrast, the former operates under soft-budget constraints since resources are allocated through bargaining, while prices have no signalling role. Without binding constraints, state-owned firms inevitably fail the test of efficiency and lack incentives to innovate.

Yet this powerful juxtaposition of the heavy 'dinosaur' and the slender atomistic firm is misleading. It obscures important questions of the context in which firms operate, including the possibility (however unlikely) that socialist enterprises could be efficient and innovative, and conversely, that capitalist companies may not, at least not without considerable support from the state. The starting point for this argument is to recognize that socialist and capitalist firms share a fundamental characteristic: complex organizations operating in an environment marked by uncertainty. From this standpoint, the important question becomes how do firms cope with uncertainty?

Capitalist firms typically rely on planning and on the state to address uncertainty. As early as 1967, Galbraith[21] argued that capitalist firms best manage uncertainty by eliminating the market. He observed that technological progress required commitments of time and capital that could only be made by large companies. Yet the large-scale, technology-intensive capitalist firm must reduce uncertainty in order to be commercially viable, for the market is too unreliable to generate spontaneously either sophisticated technological inputs or consumer preferences. Thus, Galbraith argued, monopolies engage systematically in planning to eliminate the market both by controlling strategic supply factors and by creating demand, ideas later explored by scholars interested in the simultaneous globalization and disintegration of production.[22] Furthermore, the state plays an important role in shielding firms, including monopolies, from the vagaries of technological progress (and from market uncertainties), by funding high-risk innovation that would not otherwise be undertaken by the private sector.[23]

The predicament of socialist firms was different: supply uncertainties, since the logic of the plan inevitably engendered shortages.[24] This, for Sovietologists, implied that 'micro-efficiency is neither possible nor indeed desirable given the logic and needs of the system'.[25] Without micro-efficiency, the system of incentives governing the planned system created a 'lack of any flexible response capability'.[26] But this may not necessarily be the case. Rather, Burawoy and Luckas[27] discovered during their participant observation study of the Hungarian planned system, state-owned enterprises could become – admittedly surprising – flexible organization in their efforts to cope with supply uncertainties. Managers navigated supply uncertainties through substitutions, queuing for inputs and outputs and most importantly, by accumulating bargaining power in negotiations for investment resources with the central planners.

Important for the argument here, Burawoy and Lukacs compared the division of an American multinational and a Hungarian socialist enterprise. The Hungarian firm, they found, was under continuous pressure to innovate, reorganize production and introduce modern machinery. Workers, rather than the planners reviled by Sovietologist economists, played the active role in this process. In contrast, the capitalist division did not go beyond the plans set for it by headquarters, had poorly planned production and wasted more than the socialist firm. Paradoxically, they argued, the complex organization of the capitalist multinational meant that its division would have fitted better Kornai's theories of the shortage economy than the socialist firm, whose dynamism and efficiency would have taken by surprise any Sovietologist economist, had they taken the trouble to go interdisciplinary and engage with critical sociological accounts of socialist industry.

Alas, they didn't.

'Fighting the Dinosaurs': A (Central) Banking Task

In transition studies, 'unintended consequences' have become a powerful explanatory tool.[28] Persistent high (or hyper) inflation, exchange rate volatility, unemployment, unprecedented de-industrialization, twin banking and currency crises are all to be found on the list of 'surprises' that followed the implementation, in varying degrees, of the Washington Consensus Holly Trinity: liberalization, privatization and stabilization. Policymakers, in particular international organizations with little experience of the region, advised or imposed 'blue-prints' ill-fitted to the distinctive institutional and structural characteristics of planned economies, thus severely underestimating the potential outcomes. To a greater (Romania, Bulgaria, former Soviet Union) or lesser (Poland, Hungary, the Czech Republic, Slovenia) extent, unintended consequences spared no country.

Was this a collective knowledge failure? It would certainly be convenient to think so, since ignorance is far less problematic than deliberate action. But what if instead ignorance is used as a strategic ploy to mask specific political intentions? Consider the Autumn 1991 issue of the highly ranked *Journal of Economic Perspectives*, dedicated to 'Economic Transition in the Soviet Union and Eastern Europe'. Its highly influential contributors ranged from the father of 'financial repression' theories Ronald McKinnon[29] to Stanley Fisher of the MIT, Karen Brooks of the World Bank and Thomas Wolf of the IMF. The special issue can thus be considered *the* platform for exposing the prevailing wisdom – the transition paradigm – of that time.

Contributions in the special issue are remarkable for two reasons. First, contrary to standard 'ignorance' accounts, contributors pay close attention to the institutional details of centrally planned economies to argue that Soviet countries across had proven remarkably resilient to partial attempts at reform, so that radical measures were necessary.[30] This was not the highly theoretical, a-institutional approach that later critiques attributed to Big Bang advocates.[31] Second, the 'dinosaur' state-owned enterprises emerge as the critical concern,[32] portrayed as 'bizarre' entities unlikely to ever abandon 'soft-budget constraints'[33] since social commitments would pressure governments into maintaining their preferential treatment. To counteract such possibilities, contributors called for a war on institutions of the planned economy, a 'disruption ... on a historically unprecedented scale ... a successful reform program must be trenchantly negative, at least in the initial stages. It must aim at destroying institutions and overcoming the logic of the command economy. The economic space must be cleared to allow new institutions to arise from and support the autonomous, self-interested agents'.[34] In other words, the specific political preference for a world of general equilibrium demanded a concerted attack on 'dinosaurs'. Supporters understood well, and predicted accurately, the outcomes of this cry for war: large-scale economic disruption.

Both the central bank and the banking sector would prove crucial to the war on state-owned companies. Thus, framing reform through soft-budget constraints, rather than active industrial restructuring, had two important implications. It first established that industrial restructuring would mean industrial downsizing, since 'over-industrialized' formerly planned economies had to get rid of the 'dinosaurs'.[35] Second, it confronted policymakers with a challenge. Given that even the most enthusiastic 'big bang' privatization would take longer than its advocates wished for, who would enforce hard-budget constraint on state-enterprises, and how? The obvious candidate was the banking sector: banks would assess creditworthiness and only lend to those firms who could prove viable in a market-based system.

However, assigning banks the task of hardening budget constraint raised a new set of problems. Most banks were also state-owned. Even if banks were private, mainstream finance scholarship had pointed out that relationship banking – banks developing close relationships with borrowers to overcome problems of asymmetric information – inevitably engendered soft-budget constraints.[36] Harbouring such doubts, 'transition' scholars went as far as to suggest that state-owned relationship banking could never harden budget constraints. Indeed, McKinnon predictably worried that state-owned banks would fail to impose hard budget constraints since the legacy of socialism in the banking sector meant a 'passive system of credit' subordinated to the central plan.[37] Banks had little experience of lending to profit-driven firms. Therefore, he recommended that liberalized firms – both state-owned and private – should be prevented from accessing bank loans in the first stages of transition. Firms would instead be forced to prove their ability to survive under capitalism by tapping non-bank funding (capital markets) or relying on their own resources. While neither international institutions nor domestic policymakers took this radical suggestion seriously, McKinnon's contribution laid the building blocks for a profound distrust of relationship banking in Central and Eastern Europe, distrust readily apparent in research and policy papers produced by the international organizations involved in shaping 'transition'.[38]

It cannot be denied that state-owned companies and state-owned banks often developed relationships based on corrupt practices, and that such relationships would translate into deteriorated loan portfolios for banks. This is a well-known and well-documented account across formerly planned economies. But relationship banking is neither always 'corrupt' nor exclusive to state-owned entities. Indeed, strategic interactions between private corporations and private banks prevail in coordinated types of capitalism and are often a key ingredient in the competitiveness of those economies.[39] For example, a version of such coordination occurred in Romania after 2006, when foreign-owned banks introduced loan externalization. This practice allowed foreign companies with activity in Romania to benefit from a loan extended by a parent bank based on existing relationships in other jurisdictions and to take advantage of lower costs of funding for the originating bank (and hence for the borrower). Transnational banks in turn could bypass regulatory constraints in the host country. Yet no scholar has deemed such practices of private (foreign) banks as corrupt.

This neoliberal distrust was instrumental in creating a central bank-led financialization moment, where central banks dedicated their energies to severing the link between (state-owned) banks and industrial companies.

Battling Over Ideas: Central Banking in Transition

Central banks became rapidly involved in reshaping post-socialist financial systems. The approach depended on how central banks understood money and the relationship between finance and industrial restructuring.

Economic ideas do not travel unadulterated across borders, from Western academia and international policy bodies into coherent policy packages.[40] Rather, national policy actors often translate and adapt hegemonic ideas in order to reconcile pressing and potentially conflicting political demands. But the political role of ideas can go even further: policy actors may embrace new economic ideas to legitimize policies formulated *a priori* either under conditions of profound uncertainty that do not fit neatly into available economic theories, or when they are confronted with policy outcomes that undermine their theoretical position,[41] outcomes that need explanation. In any of these scenarios, the internationally hegemonic ideas can only be anchored domestically through political processes. Put differently, and less controversially since the postcrash debates, economics is always and everywhere political economy.[42]

Consider the ideational repertoire available to an (often newly established) central bank in Eastern Europe around 1990. To start with, theories of central banking express no preference for either the institutional make-up of the financial system that central banks oversee, or for the specific relationships between the financial system and the 'real' economy. In standard (general equilibrium) models, the financial system is typically treated as a 'system of arbitrage equations' without analytically relevant institutional form. Crisis is the only instance where institutional form matters. Historically, central banks assumed the lender of last resort for the banking sector, lending to banks a la Bagehot.[43] In order to continue to perform traditional activities of maturity transformation and credit intermediation, commercial banks require central bank support during crises, when the distinction between liquidity and solvency becomes blurry.

In the formerly planned context, a central bank sympathetic to post-Keynesian or institutionalist ideas about money as a social phenomenon, crucial for economic activity in both the short and the long-run, would have asked how to mediate the profound uncertainties of transition, particularly prevailing in the relationship between banks and state enterprises. Indeed, SOEs saw uncertainties multiply rapidly beyond the supply uncertainties of the central planning era. On the demand side, SOEs lost export markets, faced greater competition from Western companies and falling domestic demand. Perhaps more importantly, the rapid dismantling of the central plan forced SOEs into capitalist relations of production. Since Karl Marx and John Maynard Keynes, institutional accounts emphasize the role of money as a vital institution of capitalism, where production is about realizing gains and converting output into money values. In a monetary economy of production, money is no longer the veil over atomistic firms, but the oil that runs the machine, particularly one dominated by large-scale monopolies. When translated to the transition context, where market funding (equity or long-term debt) was simply not available, this implies that both (privatized) SOEs and newly established private companies could finance either from retained earnings – highly volatile given demand contractions – or bank loans. Put differently, access to bank loans became critical for both state and new private companies, while in turn, access to central bank lending became critical for (state-owned) banks if they were to become instrumental in the journey to capitalist competitiveness, however difficult.[44]

That central banks would adopt such policies is not that far fetched. Several in Eastern Europe did so. For instance policy makers in the Czech Republic and Poland, usually depicted as tough shock therapists with a highly independent central bank, acknowledged that monetary policies would directly, and substantially, affect industrial restructuring. The Czech central bank coordinated its liquidity policies with the government's industrial strategies, as did the central banks of Hungary and Poland.[45] Poland is a particularly interesting example: during 1994–7 it became the poster case for post-socialist success. Its then minister of finance explained success as follows:

> contrary to the opinion of many observers, what really mattered was the efficiency of policy and not the dose of gradualism or radicalism ... [W]e strongly opposed the approach that claimed that the best industrial policy is not having one at all. We in the

government have actively and deliberately supported the restructuring of Polish enterprises.[46]

Furthermore, a post-Keynesian central bank would have interpreted rapid increases in money supply as an endogenous consequence of higher demand for loans, triggered by higher working capital needs arising from higher input prices and mark-up pricing. Mark-up pricing reflected the logic of central planning, where industries and countries were carefully located along production chains corresponding to their resource endowments. Accordingly, import plans reflected domestic demand for unavailable raw materials and fuels, finished products not manufactured at home (mainly investment goods) and intermediary products unavailable domestically in the quantities demanded. Except for a few resource intensive countries, domestically produced raw inputs were reserved for internal use. Furthermore, international trade within the socialist block was based on production requirements rather than considerations of competitiveness.[47] Limited diversification to preserve economies of scale implied limited scope for substitution of intermediary inputs, reducing the scope for devaluation strategies aimed at correcting current account deficits.

Indeed, the complex network of established relationships between large, vertically-integrated firms dominating industrial sectors across Eastern Europe and the former Soviet Union meant that price increases would quickly spread throughout the system as both demand and production costs depended on companies up and downstream in the production chain. Because cost–push pressures were essential for pricing, the post-Keynesian attention to mark-up pricing could have played a crucial role in containing inflationary pressures. Put differently, where the industrial sector was highly dependent on imports for production and exports for revenue, cost–push pressures would intimately be linked to developments in exchange rates. Since nominal devaluations immediately passed through into prices, the stability mandate would have required central banks to spend their energy on ensuring that exchange rate devaluations did not generate inflationary spirals. The Zloty Stabilization Fund allowed the Polish central bank to do so.[48] Yet the IMF refused to endorse international efforts to create stabilization funds for other countries in the region, instead pushing for full convertibility and fully floating exchange rate regimes.[49]

That few central banks embraced endogenous money has to be understood against the hegemony of monetarism and 'dinosaur SOEs' ideas in Western academia and international policy bodies, particularly the International Monetary Fund (IMF), the latter closely involved in designing transition across most countries of the Eastern European/former Soviet Union block. Consider the following quote from two IMF economists that took part in various mission to transition countries:

> There were few monetarists in transitional economies, at least in the beginning ... The idea that prices were related to money was often not intuitive. Rather, the price formation process was viewed as a complex process that involved many technical elements and many factors outside the authorities' control, especially external factors. In fact, tight monetary policy was precisely designed to make the traditional cost-plus-mark up pricing policy impossible. This meant that the same situation IMF economists would see as inflationary would often be viewed as too tight a monetary policy setting by the local authorities'.[50]

This quote suggests that the struggle over stabilization policies was a struggle over ideas about money, price theories and central banking. IMF teams were well aware of the (post-Keynesian) ideas that informed policymakers – both in government and in central banks – across Eastern Europe, and sought to change both those ideas (often by the full force of conditionality) and the practices of mark-up pricing prevailing in the state-owned sector. Again, rather than unintended consequences, this was part of a deliberate, carefully orchestrated, strategy to change radically the nature and operations of the 'dinosaur' industries inherited from the planned period.

Crucial to enlisting central banks into a 'dinosaur' narrative was to shift the debate onto monetarist terrain by arguing that the legacy of the plan contained the seeds of an extended period of high inflation because formerly planned economies had accumulated substantial excess demand.[51] Put differently, the IMF warned central banks that the only way to achieve their new mandate of price stability was to recognize the existence of excess demand. The IMF first argued that formerly planned economies were characterized by chronic shortages and rationing that led to the accumulation of forced savings (monetary overhang) that would increase inflationary pressures.[52] Second, and more important, the legacy of interactions between state-owned companies and state-owned banks meant that soft-budget constraints would continue to prevail unless banks were prevented from granting soft-credits.[53] State ownership in the banking sector combined with extensive information asymmetries meant that banks could not implement a market-driven process of credit allocation, nor that they should be allowed to continue their strategic interactions with state-owned companies. Monetary and fiscal restraint had to accompany price liberalization and ensure that state-owned companies became profit-maximizers.[54] In other words, the IMF held, a tight credit policy would not affect output, but merely redistribute the monetary overhang. Through tight monetary policies, central banks would discipline (state-owned) banks into disciplining state-owned companies.

Central Bank-Led Financialization: The Silent War

[We are] a state-owned enterprise that succeeded in both increasing production and mobilizing demand. Whatever we have achieved through restructuring production, banks are destroying, through extremely high interest rates and a very slow payment mechanism ... While the essence of restructuring, money, is at banks' discretion, there is a silent war going on (Gabor 2010a: 46).

The metaphor of war invoked above by the director of a Romanian state-owned company in 1993 can be traced back to the agenda set out in the *Journal of Economic Perspectives* special issue discussed earlier. In there, Ericson had called for the destruction of institutions inherited from the central plan, including state-owned companies. The Romanian company was experiencing first hand the power of that hegemonic idea only two years later. In that war, the potential for the state-owned company to become competitive – demonstrated, the quote suggests, by coping with the uncertainties of transition – did not matter. Instead, state-owned banks became agents of institutional destruction, as Ericson and McKinnon envisaged, through the liquidity policies of the central bank.

Since the global financial crisis in 2008, it is widely accepted that increasing the cost and limiting the availability of funding for banks may worsen a crisis and tip countries into recession.[55] This is the story of the early transition recessions. IMF programmes in Eastern Europe sought to tighten monetary policy and downplayed the importance of the exchange rate pass through[56] for price stability. IMF conditionality imposed tight constraints on the lender of last resort function, restricting access to loans and/or imposing high interest rates.

Thus, central banks attempted to prevent commercial banks from meeting the demand for loans by limiting access to reserves. Both central banks and the IMF expected a mere redistribution of the monetary overhang without a liquidity crunch.

Yet, just like in Latin American countries, IMF staff recognized that one crucial ingredient of the output collapse in Eastern Europe had been a sharp fall in real credit available to enterprises.[57] Put differently, central bank monetary policies guided by IMF monetary targets did generate severe liquidity shortages[58] while the neglect of exchange rate stability fed inflationary spirals, often leading to stagflation.[59] Pressured by the macroeconomic policy stance into the task of 'disciplining' state-owned companies, commercial banks – both state-owned and private – found it difficult to cover funding gaps and to engage in that most traditional of banking activities, maturity transformation.

Consider the example of Romania captured in the quote above. Throughout 1991 and 1992, the IMF conditionality sought to curb state banks' access to central bank reserves, with the explicit objective of changing the relationship between state-owned banks and state-owned companies. In that, the IMF programmes were successful. State-owned banks dominating the banking sector at the time often refused to allow state-owned companies immediate access to their deposits because that would have left them with a funding gap that could not be met from either the interbank market or central bank reserves. In effect, the reluctance of the central bank to fulfil its lender of last resort function had broader monetary implications, undermining a crucial moneyness attribute of bank deposits as means of payment.

With delays in access to their bank deposits and working capital needs increasing rapidly due to exchange rate depreciations, state-owned companies were in turn forced to delay payments to suppliers by weeks and even months.[60] Attempts to severe the link between state-owned companies and (state-owned) banks – via the central bank's credit policies – confirmed the prediction of post-Keynesian monetary theorists that the industrial sector could not function without access to bank credit when forced into capitalist relations of production. The widespread credit crunches produced severe industrial contractions throughout most formerly-planned economies and a spontaneous emergence of alternative payment mechanisms either through barters or inter-company arrears (credit). As the working capital needs of companies were pushed up by price liberalization, the increase in demand for credit was frustrated by the tight monetary/credit policy. In the absence of credit, the complex networks of vertically-integrated chains of production and trade laid the basis for spontaneously emerging networks of credit liaisons, what post-Keynesians would recognize as the transition equivalent of a money endogenizing process. Whereas in a market-based system a policy of bank credit rationing would drive unsatisfied borrowers willing to pay higher rates to other financial institutions, in the post-socialist context it resulted in intercompany credits. In turn, companies responded to payment blockages by resorting to inter-enterprise arrears, taking advantage of the existing relationships in supply chains and political connections. Such behaviour confirmed the prediction of old institutionalist theories. These warned that the policies of rapid privatization ignored the institutional legacies and path-dependence confronting policies seeking to effect rapid transformation.[61] Companies generated credit relations built on existing supplier networks when monetary policy sought to constrain relational banking.

How did the IMF and central banks engage with the empirical realities of credit and liquidity shortages? Testimony to their enduring interpretative flexibility, neoliberal narratives attributed the rapidly growing inter-company arrears and overdue loans to pervasive soft-budget constraints. Without access to credit, SOEs only managed to survive because vested interests supported them. These in turn required stronger doses of monetary medicine (tightening of monetary conditions) and structural reform (privatization).

Thus, framing the monetary challenge through the concept of 'soft budget constraints' had two important consequences. It first narrowed the space for

activist industrial policies. Confronted with reluctant central banks, governments of a more interventionist disposition found it more difficult to design
and finance industrial policies that could have carefully identified both state-
owned and private companies with potential competitiveness in international
markets, as 'transition' economies outside the IMF's influence did (Vietnam or
China). With limited space for industrial policies, it was powerful industrial
actors with political connections that would typically get access to short-lived
populist measures that governments described as industrial policy. Thus, for
central banks and the IMF, it was easy to re-frame the failures of monetary
policy to effectively support industrial restructuring or to deliver price stability as the failures of governments populated by rent-seekers and subjugated to
vested interests. The 'soft budget constraint' became a convenient institutional
alibi for central banks that could not deliver price stability either for ideational
reasons – refusing to recognize the crucial role that exchange rates played for
price dynamics – or for material reasons, since few central banks had the foreign
exchange reserves necessary to prevent the exchange rate from depreciating rapidly and the IMF refused to support stabilization funds.

Second, the soft-budget constraint narrative was effective in energizing institutional change. Indeed, despite different starting points and diverse policies for
financial development, formerly planned economies ended up, by early 2000s,
with very similar institutional features of the financial sector:[62] commercial
banks, increasingly foreign-owned, lending primarily to governments through
short-term debt instruments. Companies, private and the few remaining state-
owned, met working capital needs from retained earnings. Highly illiquid,
volatile stock markets left foreign direct investment as the main source of long-
term capital investment. This is precisely what Transitologists concerned with
soft budget constraints demanded at the beginning of transition: a rapid erosion of relationship banking. Through a process in which central banks' liquidity
policies played a crucial role, banking systems across Eastern Europe became
increasingly financialized, moving into short-term pursuit of profit from market-based activities at the expense of (potentially equally profitable) long-term
relationships with productive activity.[63]

Conclusion

Conventional studies of central banking and monetary policies pay little attention to questions of politics or political economy. For some, central banking
should be inherently apolitical, and can only remain so if scholarly attention
remains focused on models, monetary theories and how these may or may not
be successful in addressing the 'real' problems that an economy faces.

Yet, this contribution has argued, bringing in the politics of central banking can shed new light on how we understand and theorize the trajectory of financial systems in formerly planned economies. Rather than price stability *per se*, central banking in transition has primarily concerned itself with institutional change, seeking to reorder the institutional legacy of the plan and to ensure that the banks, state-owned and private, implement the mainstream understanding of that institutional change.

10 THE POLITICAL ECONOMY OF FINANCIAL REFORMS IN AUTHORITARIAN TRANSITION ECONOMIES: A COMPARATIVE STUDY OF KAZAKHSTAN AND UZBEKISTAN

Alexandr Akimov

Ever since the collapse of the Eastern Communist bloc in the late 1980s and early 1990s, and the declared transition by its former members towards western-style democracy and market institutions, a significant research effort has been directed towards studying the experiences of these 'transition economies'. After more than two decades since the onset of transition, these countries now show great diversity in outcome of their reforms. Some, mainly in Eastern Europe, established (or reinstated) democratic traditions and market institutions similar to those found in Western Europe. In contrast, in the countries of the former Soviet Union there exists a number of highly autocratic regimes whose political and market institutions are still qualitatively inferior to those found in Western and Eastern Europe. The level of economic development also varies significantly and, does not necessarily correlate with the development of Western-style institutions. The aim of this chapter is to examine why these developments took place by conducting a comparative case study of the experiences of Kazakhstan and Uzbekistan.

Gerard Roland[1] framed a political economy approach to economic reform in transition economies in terms of the scope, speed and sequencing of reforms, or more broadly, the choice between gradualism vs shock therapy. He coined the phrase 'political economy of transition' and discussed *ex-ante* and *ex-post* political constraints for reform acceptability and reform reversibility respectively, and the ways to overcome these constraints.[2] The framework has proved to be valid and useful in the analysis of many transition countries, particularly in Eastern and South Eastern Europe. It implicitly assumes that the general population, which has the ability to influence the decisions of their policymakers through the democratic electoral processes, strives for development and economic growth.

However, the approach does not seem to be particularly useful in the analysis of reforms (or lack thereof) in countries, where post-communist regimes turned authoritarian. For example, by the end of the 1990s, all Central Asian regimes of the former Soviet Union (FSU) could be classified as such albeit with varying degrees of authoritarianism.[3]

The implementation of any reform programme in authoritarian countries in either the real sector or the financial sector depends critically on the political will of national leaders. The financial system in any country thus cannot be analysed comprehensively in an institutional 'vacuum' without detailed consideration of the political environment, economic progress and other institutional issues specific to authoritarian regimes.

This chapter will, therefore, examine financial and economic reforms in two neighbouring post-communist Central Asian countries, Uzbekistan and Kazakhstan. These countries share a common Soviet heritage and have close cultural, linguistic and religious ties; yet, their approach to economic reform has been different. As a consequence, the outcomes of their reforms programmes varied. This difference is especially noticeable in the aftermath of the global financial crisis (GFC). Critically assessed are the approaches to reform of these countries from a political economy of authoritarianism perspective.

The rest of the chapter consists of four main sections. First the background to the chapter is presented, then the sequence of political, economic and financial developments in Uzbekistan and Kazakhstan respectively over the last two and half decades is explained. This background will assist in analysis of the political and economic development strategies in both countries under the framework of the political economy of authoritarianism. Finally, a summary and the principal conclusions of the chapter will be presented.

Political and Economic Developments in Uzbekistan from the Time of Independence to Post GFC

The political and economic environment in Uzbekistan in the late 1980s largely reflected the general trends in the late stage of the USSR's lifecycle. Islam Karimov was appointed as the Head of the Communist Party of the Uzbek Soviet Socialist Republic (UzSSR) in 1989. He did not support Mikhail Gorbachev's policy initiatives of rapid liberalization and restructuring and opposed the dissolution of the Soviet Union. For example, he supported the 1991 Soviet referendum to maintain a unified country and was also sympathetic to the so-called 'August coup', which attempted to reverse the eventual break-up of the USSR.

However, when the coup failed, he reacted decisively to a changed political landscape and Uzbekistan proclaimed its independence. Faced with the imminent collapse of the Soviet Union, the political elite in Uzbekistan began to consolidate its power. At first, the Uzbek branch of the Soviet Communist party changed its name to the Peoples Democratic Party of Uzbekistan (PDPU) and confirmed Karimov as its leader. The secret service and police forces were both nationalized and subordinated to Karimov.

Four days after the resignation of Gorbachev as the Soviet President on 25 December 1991, a referendum and presidential election took place in Uzbekistan. The referendum confirmed the already de facto independence of Uzbekistan. In the presidential elections, in which two candidates competed, Karimov won with an overwhelming majority of 86 per cent over the opposition candidate Muhammad Solih from the *Erk* (Freedom) Party. Another popular movement, the *Birlik* (Unity) Party, had been refused registration and was, therefore, unable to nominate its candidate for the election.

The structure of the economy in the UzSSR was dominated by agriculture, which contributed 40 per cent to the Republic's net material product; whereas the shares of industry, construction and services were 33 per cent, 14 per cent and 13 per cent respectively.[4] Following its independence in 1991, Uzbekistan had to deal with several economic problems, such as rapid inflation and declining economic growth as well as proceed with reforms. From the outset, the Uzbek government confirmed its commitment to build a democratic state with a market-economy. Since 1993, the country's leadership started to brand their policies as their 'own way of progress and revival'.[5] In practice, this meant a more gradual approach to the implementation of the reforms.

Three broad stages can be identified in Uzbekistan's economic development since independence. The first stage, which extended over 1992–6 was described by Pomfret[6] as 'the Uzbek paradox'. The second stage between 1997 and 1999 can be termed 'reform reversals'. The final stage covers the period from 2000 and can be called 'regime maturity and minor adjustments'.

Early Years of Independence, 1991–1996

In 1992 Uzbekistan obtained its national symbols. It became a member of the UN and other international organizations, and adopted its first Constitution. The Constitution confirmed Uzbekistan as a secular state and it enshrined the rule of law, freedom of conscience and religion, press freedom and democracy. A three-tiered power structure was established, including executive, legislative and judicial power branches. However, the executive branch, headed by the president, was granted superior powers over both the legislature and the judiciary. The parliament, which was built on the foundations of the Supreme Council inherited from Soviet times, was dominated by the PDPU members and functioned until December 1994, when the first post-independence parliamentary elections were held under the new Constitution. All influential opposition groups were repressed, including the two most powerful opposition parties, *Birlik* and *Erk*. The Vice-President, Shukurullo Mirsaidov, a representative of the influential 'Tashkent clan', was arrested on 'abuse of power' charges after an attempt to overthrow Karimov.[7]

In the first post-independence parliamentary elections, the PDPU continued to enjoy dominance by securing 189 seats in the 250-seat parliament. Since the only other political party, Vatan Taraqqiyoti (Progress of Motherland), was also pro-government, Karimov was ensured full support for all his actions for a second term. The new parliament immediately called a referendum in March 1995 aiming to extend the president's first term in office until 2000. According to official statistics, 99 per cent of those who participated in the referendum voted for the extension. In the same year, under pressure from the international community, Karimov announced a policy of tolerance towards opposition parties and movements. In practice, a number of new 'petty' parties were created, which occasionally criticized the government on minor social and communal matters.

Despite the lack of political choice and rather forceful nature of the referendum, which affected its credibility, Karimov enjoyed broad popularity among citizens. The general public credited Karimov for maintaining peace and stability, restraining organized crime, and providing a social safety net and support. The referendum was a pivotal point in Uzbekistan's political landscape as it resulted in Karimov achieving his complete dominance in Uzbekistan's power hierarchy.

Economic policies in the early independence years were primarily concerned with price liberalization, the control of inflation and the privatization of the public sector. They did however attempt to maintain a reasonable level of social protection.[8] From the outset, the Uzbek government was reluctant to follow 'big-bang' or 'shock therapy' reforms which had been introduced first in Poland and then implemented in Russia and Kazakhstan. However, Uzbekistan had to follow the price-liberalization programme introduced in Russia since it remained in the rouble zone. To avoid possible social unrest, prices for some essential goods, like basic foodstuffs, utilities and transport, remained subsidized (though regularly adjusted for inflation). As a result, inflation reached three- and four-digit levels over the 1992–5 period. With no macro-economic instruments to counteract inflation, the Uzbek leadership decided to introduce a national currency; first temporary, in November 1993 and then permanent in July 1994. Through a range of monetary and fiscal measures, inflation started to fall from the second half of 1994. The government introduced a managed floating exchange rate regime and also relaxed private access to foreign currency.

The privatization policy in Uzbekistan was initially very gradual and was planned to proceed in three stages. The first stage took place between 1992 and 1993 and was largely successful. All housing as well as small businesses, primarily in the services sector, were privatized. During the second stage, which was named 'mass privatization', the remaining small enterprises, most of the medium and some of the larger enterprises were scheduled for privatization.[9] The third stage took place from 1996 with an attempt to de-nationalize most of the remaining large enterprises but this also had very limited success. The government retained control over land and natural resources.

The reforms in the banking sector started in 1991, when a two-tier banking sector was established. Former branches of the Gosbank and specialized banks of the Soviet Union evolved smoothly into Uzbekistan's Central Bank and commercial banks. A stock exchange was founded in 1994 mainly to support privatization efforts and several legislative enactments were adopted to regulate the stock market.[10]

To counteract shortages of consumer goods, the Uzbek leadership initially pursued a relatively open foreign trade policy for imports. However, to prevent an outflow of locally produced goods, export tariffs and several import quotas and licenses were introduced as from November 1992.[11] Moreover, Uzbekistan's major exports of cotton, some non-ferrous metals and fertilizers remained under the state's control. These export tax revenues were used to subsidize the sale of some essential consumer goods imported from abroad.[12]

To counter the high level of budget deficit, reforms were undertaken in the taxation system with the introduction of various indirect taxes and a revision of income tax rates. Tax collection was improved and social programmes were revised to improve their efficiency. This combination of measures helped to reduce the budget deficit between 1994 and 1995.[13]

The Uzbek economy fared comparatively well in the early 1990s. The largest fall of GDP, −11.2 per cent, occurred in 1992. Between 1993 and 1995, the decline slowed and in 1996, GDP growth resumed. The savings rate dropped dramatically to a low 3.7 per cent in 1992, but then went on to recover. An active public investment policy served as a 'cushion' for output decline in the early 1990s and investment improved to 25–30 per cent of GDP during the period 1995–6. Foreign direct investment, however, never really took off; the highest figure for the period was a mere 0.6 per cent of GDP in 1994. Table 10.1 presents a selection of economic indicators for the period 1992–9 to illustrate these macroeconomic developments.

Although Uzbekistan was a slow reformer, an important feature of the reforms was their efficient implementation. As a result, Uzbekistan's quality of governance could be favourably compared not only to other CIS countries, but also to several Eastern European countries.

Table 10.1: Selected economic indicators, 1992–9

Indicator	1992	1993	1994	1995	1996	1997	1998	1999
GDP growth[*], %	-11.2	-2.3	-5.2	-0.9	1.7	5.2	4.3	4.3
GDP per capita[†]	578	553	514	500	499	515	528	543
GDP per capita[‡]	1343	1310	1243	1233	1257	1328	1371	1435
Domestic savings/GDP	3.7	17.8	14.5	27.1	22.7	18.7	16.5	17.3
Investments/ GDP	19.8	14.6	18.3	27.3	29.2	21.7	20.9	17.5
FDI/GDP (%)	0.0	0.4	0.6	-0.2	0.0	1.1	0.9	0.7
Inflation (GDP deflator, %)	712	1079	1239	371	82	66.1	39.0	44.1
Budget deficit (% of GDP)	-18.4	-10.4	-6.1	-4.1	-7.3	-2.4	-3.0	-2.6

[*] 1989–2000 for GDP growth
[†] Constant, year 2000 USD
[‡] PPP method; in USD
Source: European Bank for Reconstruction and Development (EBRD) (1997, 1999); World
 Bank (2014). *Control Tightening, and Reform Reversals, 1996–9*

With the suppression of the official opposition, unregistered Islamic radical movements started to gain some support. One such group, the Islamic Movement of
Uzbekistan (IMU), organized a number of violent attacks in various Uzbek regions
in 1999. These attacks were used as a justification for the widespread oppression of
members of various independent Islamic networks and their families.[14]

In 1999 and 2000, the second post-independent parliamentary and presidential elections took place. In the 1999 parliamentary elections, representatives
of five pro-government parties were elected. Many elected deputies were bureaucrats who used administrative power to secure success in their campaigns. In
January 2000, presidential elections were conducted with two candidates running for the presidency. Karimov was nominated by the newly established
Fidokorlar (Devotees) Party. The other candidate, Abdulhafiz Jalolov, the leader
of the PDPU, was little known to the general public. Unsurprisingly, Karimov
received 93.9 per cent of all votes.[15]

As a result of internal and external shocks in 1996–8, economic policies in
Uzbekistan changed dramatically towards the end of the 1990s. In response to poor
cotton and grain harvests, a drop in price for major exports, and the 1998 Russian
financial crisis, the Uzbek government softened monetary policy and introduced
foreign currency rationing. The authorities announced a switch to an import substitution policy by directing large credits to import substitution projects.[16]

The rationing of foreign exchange improved the current account and trade balances on the one hand, but encouraged 'rent-seeking' activities by bureaucrats on the
other. The overvalued local currency damaged the competitiveness of local exporters
and created imbalances in the economy. The privatization programme also stalled.[17]

The reform reversals, however, did not adversely affect the economy, which
continued to grow during the period 1997–9. Inflation gradually fell to an

annual level of 50 per cent between 1998 and 1999. The budget deficit was also kept under control despite the continuous funding of social programmes.[18]

In the financial sector, the government introduced a number of important reforms, such as improving the payments system, implementing international accounting standards, establishing a new banking regulatory framework in line with Basel requirements, and launching of the stock exchange. Simultaneously, the government consolidated the banking system in its control (with over 70 per cent of banking assets held by state-owned banks) and kept control over lending and the deposit rates offered by the banks.[19]

The Establishment of a Political Regime and 'Ad Hoc' Economic Developments, 2000–7

In 2002, the government initiated a further constitutional reform by (i) extending the presidential term of office from five to seven years, and (ii) creating a bi-cameral parliament. Both initiatives were approved through a referendum with 91 per cent and 93 per cent of votes respectively. In 2004, the new bi-cameral parliament was elected. The new parliament remained under presidential control: the senate members were directly or indirectly appointed by the president, whereas the legislative chamber had only deputies from pro-presidential parties, including the newly-created Liberal Democratic Party (LDP), which secured the majority of votes. Opposition parties yet again failed to obtain registration and hence could not participate in the elections.

Little has changed in the political landscape of Uzbekistan since then. Parliamentary elections in 2009 followed a very similar scenario. The same pro-government parties participated in the elections with the LDP winning the elections with just over a third of all seats. However, it mattered little for the formation of the government. The Cabinet, including the prime minister, was appointed by the president. The prime minister at the time of this study, Shavkat Mirziyoyev, does not represent the parliamentary majority but has remained in office since 2003. Leaders of political parties or even parties themselves are little known to the voters.

In terms of ad hoc policies, in 1999, the Uzbek parliament announced a set of liberalization measures including the reduction of state intervention, the strengthening of legal protection for enterprises from such intervention, and the liberalization of the foreign exchange market. However, these reforms have remained largely unfulfilled. The privatization of large enterprises has not advanced due to government's reluctance to give up its majority stake holding in those enterprises. Agriculture remained largely un-reformed. The trade regime remained restrictive with some tariffs actually rising to support import substitution policies.[20] From 2001 utility prices, including electricity and urban water, were gradually liberalized to cost recovery levels. Payment collection was enhanced by compulsory deduction of all utility payments from workers' wage payments.

Multiple exchange rates were unified and convertibility for current account transactions was declared at the end of 2003. However, it did not last long as the system of multiple exchange rates gradually returned. Fiscal and monetary policy remained tight, resulting in the reduction of public debt and levels of inflation. However, some observers noted deterioration in the quality of official statistics, pointing at an increasing divergence between official and alternative estimates of consumer price inflation.[21] Reforms in the financial sector largely stalled. The population's trust in the banking sector remained low due to difficulties faced by customers in accessing cash from their bank accounts as well as the tax collection responsibilities banks were required to fulfil on behalf of the government. Furthermore, the, announced privatizations in the banking sector did not go ahead and state-owned banks continued to dominate the sector.[22]

Economic growth gradually picked up in 2004 and 2005 thanks to strong agricultural harvests, as well as a robust performance of the export sector. However, foreign direct investment remained scarce due to the unfavourable business environment. Growing numbers of migrants started to flow from Uzbekistan to Russia and Kazakhstan for seasonal work remitting their incomes to support their families' at home.[23] Table 10.2 provides a snapshot of the economy by presenting selected economic indicators for the period 1997–2007.

Table 10.2: Main economic indicators in Uzbekistan, 1997–2007.

Indicator	1997	1998	1999	2000	2001	2002	2003	2004	2005	2006	2007
GDP growth, %[*]	5.2	4.3	4.3	3.8	4.2	4.0	4.2	7.7	7	7.3	9.5
GDP per capita[*]	411	422	436	446	459	471	486	517	547	580	626
GDP per capita[†]	1506	1545	1594	1632	1679	1725	1777	1892	2001	2121	2290
Domestic savings/GDP	25.3	27.7	24.9	26.0	27.2	22.0	26.3	29.0	29.1	24.8	17.2
Investments /GDP	28.2	28.1	25.1	22.1	26.5	20.8	19.1	20.7	17.9	18	20.9
FDI/ GDP (%)	1.1	0.9	0.7	0.5	0.7	0.7	0.8	1.5	1.3	1.0	3.2
Inflation (GDP deflator, %)	66.1	39.0	44.1	47.3	45.2	45.4	26.7	15.7	21.4	21.5	24.0
Budget deficit (% of GDP)	-2.4	-3.0	-2.6	-2.2	-1.3	-1.9	0.1	1.2	2.8	6.8	5.4

[*] Constant, year 2005 USD
[†] PPP method; in USD
Source: EBRD (2002, 2005, 2007, 2010); World Bank (2014)

Politics and Economy in the Post-GFC Period of 2008–13

The most recent presidential elections were conducted in 2007. Karimov received 88.1 per cent of the votes, whereas three other carefully pre-selected candidates received around 3 per cent each.[24] Since Uzbekistan's Constitution only allows a president to remain in office for two terms, it is unclear on what grounds Karimov was allowed to run. No explanation was offered to the public by election officials and the country's leadership. The presidential term was reduced back down to five years through amendments to the constitution in 2011. The next elections are due in early 2015 and it is very unlikely that Karimov will voluntarily step down. Instead, it is likely that he will continually seek re-election until either natural forces take their toll or he is overthrown by a coup from within his own circle. The second scenario looks unlikely at this stage as Karimov retains a tight grip on power.

The Uzbek economy weathered the storm of the Global Financial Crisis (GFC) very well, and GDP has continued to grow at the very healthy rate of over 8 per cent (see, Table 10.3). Due to a tight fiscal policy, the budget remained in surplus throughout the period. Government projects kept investment rates steady, and savings rebounded from the large decline in 2008–9. Restrictive government trade policy and low level of integration of the Uzbek financial system blocked the negative influences arising from the global trade and capital markets. However, the crisis had some impact on Uzbekistan due to reductions in remittances coming from Russia and Kazakhstan.[25] Remittances from Russia fell from $3,007 million in 2008 to $2,071 in 2009. However, remittances rebounded strongly in 2010.[26] Strong measures from the Uzbek government to counteract the negative effects arising from the GFC, included a fiscal stimulus, bank recapitalization and administrative price controls for staple products. These measures allowed Uzbekistan to maintain its strong economic growth rate.

Table 10.3: Main economic indicators in Uzbekistan, 2008–12.

Indicator	2008	2009	2010	2011	2012	change 1990–2012
GDP growth, %	9	8.1	8.5	8.3	8.2	124.4%
GDP per capita*	671	713	752	793	846	54.6%
GDP per capita†	2456	2611	2754	2903	3095	54.6%
Domestic savings/GDP	13.5	8.2	27.7	24.9	20.9	–
Investments /GDP	25.3	26.1	24.5	23.1	22.8	–
FDI/ GDP (%)	2.5	2.6	4.1	3.2	2.1	–
Inflation (GDP deflator, %)	19.9	20.8	19.6	15.1	14.8	–
Budget deficit (% of GDP)	10.7	2.8	4.9	9.0	3.0	–

* Constant, year 2005 USD
† PPP method; in USD
Source: EBRD (2010, 2012); World Bank (2014)

All in all, looking back at the period since independence, it is clear that the Uzbek leadership was able to establish a repressive model of political and economic management. The regime has retained its legitimacy within the country thanks to the relative success of its economic policies in maintaining growth.

The Political and Economic Environment in Kazakhstan from Pre-Independence to Just After the GFC

As for Kazakhstan, the late 1980s was a period of growing nationalistic self-consciousness among ethnic Kazakhs. Nursultan Nazarbaev, an ethnic Kazakh, replaced an ethnic Russian, Gennadiy Kolbin, as a leader of the Kazakh Soviet Socialist Republic (KSSR) in May 1989. With a good command of the Kazakh language and knowledge of Kazakh traditions as well as a good employment record in the Russian-dominated industrial sector, he was able to calm down nationalistic tensions in both the Russian-dominated north and the Kazakh-dominated south.

Nazarbaev gradually built power by becoming the chairman of the Supreme Council in 1989 and the President of the KSSR in 1990. He enjoyed a good relationship with Gorbachev and supported him in his efforts to maintain the Soviet Union as a united country. Following the establishment of the Commonwealth of Independent States by Russia, Ukraine and Belarus, which effectively dissolved the Soviet Union, Kazakhstan proclaimed its independence on 16 December 1991.[27]

In common with all Soviet republics at the end of the 1980s, Kazakhstan experienced a slowdown in growth, which turned negative in the early 1990s. Agriculture, industry, construction, transport and communications dominated the economic structure of pre-reform Kazakhstan, accounting for 42 per cent, 21 per cent, 16 per cent and 10 per cent respectively in 1990.[28]

The Early Years of Reforms, 1992–4

Upon independence, Nazarbaev announced his commitment to political and economic reform.[29] The early years of independence can be characterized by the relative freedom of expression in the political arena. Although Nazarbaev enjoyed the widespread support of the general population, the establishment of a strong presidential republic did not begin until 1995. The first Constitution was passed almost unanimously in January 1993 by the deputies of the Supreme Council which significantly strengthened the executive branch of power.

Despite securing much stronger powers under the Constitution, he continued to strive for further legislative changes in his favour, but faced opposition from the deputies, including the parliamentary speaker. Under pressure from the presidential office and the state-controlled media, the parliament was dissolved towards the end of 1993, granting the president powers to executively enact laws until a new parliament was elected. In March 1994, the new parliament was elected albeit with considerable worries concerning the fairness of the election process.[30]

In terms of economic reforms, Kazakhstan began its own reform programme in 1991. In January 1992, most prices were liberalized. The newly founded Kazakh State Property Committee started work on a programme of privatization. However, reforms remained largely segmented until 1993, when the national currency, the tenge, was introduced. The National Privatization Programme for 1993–5 embarked on the mass privatization of medium-sized enterprises. Large enterprises were privatized on a 'case-by-case' basis using tenders. By the end of 1994, new legislation was enacted on foreign direct investment, permitting the repatriation of profits. Substantial trade liberalization was achieved by the first half of 1995, following the abolition of all export quotas and the elimination of most export and import licences.[31]

In the financial system, policymakers had to deal with the problem of rapidly growing poorly capitalized and managed banks, and the resultant problem of non-performing loans (NPLs).[32] As a consequence, a number of key laws aimed at dealing with NPLs and strengthening prudential regulation and supervision were adopted.[33]

Political Consolidation and the Acceleration of Economic Reforms, 1995–7

In 1995, following a complaint, the Constitutional Court declared the 1994 parliamentary elections invalid and the parliament was dissolved.[34] Nazarbaev then stepped in to call a referendum to extend his term in office until 2000 and won over 95 per cent of the votes. Shortly after, the new Constitution of 1995, which granted Nazarbaev much greater presidential powers, was approved in another referendum with around 90 per cent of votes in favour. In December 1995, a new and smaller bi-cameral parliament was elected.[35] These changes ensured that no more threats to the president's power would come from the legislative and judicial branches of the state. This meant that in the future challenges could only come from the executive branch and the president's inner circle.

In 1994, a wealthy businessman, Akezhan Kazhegeldin, became Kazakhstan's prime minister. In his initial three years in charge of the Cabinet, he earned a reputation as a strong reformer and he exercised considerable independence in his economic policies. In addition, he clashed with Nazarbaev's daughter, Dariga, and his son-in-law, Rahat Aliev. Consequently, Nazarbaev dismissed Kazhegeldin, accusing him of failing to address social issues.[36] Shortly after the dismissal, Kazhegeldin openly challenged Nazarbaev's peculiar stance on the inappropriateness of a Western democracy for Kazakhstan, and expressed his intention to run for presidential office in 2000. This did not arise as Nazarbaev called for an early election in 1999, and ensured that Kazhegeldin could not run for office by bringing charges against him based on administrative violation. With no real competition, Nazarbaev easily won the elections with nearly 80 per cent of the votes cast in his favour. The same year, a new parliament was elected which was dominated by the newly created pro-presidential parties such as *Otan* (Motherland), the Civil party and the Agrarian party.[37] In 2000, the Constitutional Act of the First President of Kazakhstan was adopted, removing the limit on how many terms in office the first president can serve and guaranteeing Nazarbaev's immunity and protection from any form of prosecution.

As for economic reforms, Kazakhstan undertook extensive privatization and liberalization measures between 1993 and 1996. In 1993, vouchers were distributed to citizens so that they could purchase state-owned assets through Privatization Investment Funds (PIFs). Once privatization of small- and medium-size enterprises was complete, the case by case privatization of major state-owned companies began. Kazhegeldin's government employed foreign experts extensively to manage state-owned enterprises using management contracts. Price liberalization was completed in 1994. The government established a liberal trade regime with all export quotas and many export and important licensing requirements lifted. Tariffs were drastically reduced towards 1997. Foreign direct investments started to flow significantly into the country, predominately into the oil and gas sectors.

The local currency became freely convertible in 1996, and the Kazakh government floated its first Eurobond. Government-directed credits in the banking sector were abolished in 1995 and limits placed on borrowing by the government from the National Bank of Kazakhstan (NBK). In the banking sector, the NBK started gradually to allow foreign bank entry, and worked on improving prudential regulation and supervision practices, as well as accounting standards.[38] The NBK continued to deal with the bulk of NPLs by closing small non-viable banks, and creating asset management companies to deal with the NPLs of the larger banks. Loans equaling 11 per cent of GDP were transferred from original banks to specialized institutions.[39]

Kazakhstan's GDP experienced a larger and longer decline than that of Uzbekistan in this period. Unlike Uzbekistan, Kazakhstan had to deal with the problem of a declining population as a result of considerable emigration. Both investment and savings rates declined but they were partly offset by the rapid growth in FDI. As a result of adopting a smaller social programme, Kazakhstan maintained a better budget position, and got inflation under control much earlier. Table 10.4 summarizes Kazakhstan's economic performance between 1991 and 1997.

Table 10.4: Kazakhstan's economic performance during 1991–7.

Indicator	1991	1992	1993	1994	1995	1996	1997
GDP growth, %	-11.0	-5.3	-9.3	-12.6	-8.2	0.5	1.7
GDP per capita*	2718	2576	2355	2088	1951	1990	2056
GDP per capita[†]	6270	5942	5431	4816	4499	4591	4743
Domestic savings/GDP	N/A	30.2	11.2	18.7	18.7	15.4	13.1
Investments /GDP	N/A	30.4	27.9	26.1	23.1	17.2	16.3
FDI/GDP (%)	N/A	0.4	5.4	3.1	4.7	5.4	6.0
Inflation (GDP deflator, %)	96	1472	1243	1547	161	39	16
Budget deficit (% of GDP)	-7.9	-7.3	-4.1	-7.5	-2.7	-4.7	-6.8

* Constant, year 2005 USD
[†] PPP method; in USD
Source: EBRD (1995, 2003); World Bank (2014)

Challenges to Political Stability and Economic Revival, 1998–2007

The next challenge to the president's rule came from much a closer source; the president's inner circle. The president's son-in-law, who played an important role in thwarting Kazhegeldin's challenge, gradually accumulated considerable wealth and influence. His aggressive tactics to gain control over various sectors of the economy attracted strong opposition from various stakeholders, including influential members of the president's inner circle. As a result, Aliev was relocated from his job as a deputy chairman of the Committee of State Security to the post of a deputy head of Nazarbaev's bodyguard. Aliev was then sent as an Ambassador to Austria, where he later asked for 'political asylum'. Dariga Nazarbaeva subsequently divorced Aliev, officially ending his political career in Kazakhstan.

In 2003, Nazarbaev's economic advisor was arrested in the US as part of a corruption investigation into alleged bribery payments by US companies to Nazarbaev and Prime Minister Nurlan Balgimbaev in return for oil development contracts. This undermined Nazarbaev's reputation both domestically and internationally. The scope of the problems led some commentators to predict Nazarbaev's imminent resignation in a complex succession plan.[40] Nazarbaev's political career survived, proving yet again his ability to manage political problems.

The 2004 parliamentary elections were again dominated by the pro-presidential *Otan* party which took over 60 per cent of the votes cast. The elections failed to meet democratic standards yet again. Some of Nazarbaev's allies left the party and their ministerial posts in protest at the electoral irregularities and joined the opposition.[41] In the 2005 presidential elections, Nazarbaev received over 91 per cent of votes. Soon after the elections, a number of high profile killings of prominent politicians and critics of Nazarbaev's regime, including the former minister for information, Altynbek Sarsenbaev, further damaged Nazarbaev's reputation.

In 2006, Dariga Nazarbaeva's *Asar* (Together) party, as well as the Agrarian and Civic parties merged with *Otan* under the new name of *Nur-Otan* (Light of Fatherland). A range of constitutional changes took place in 2007 including increasing the size of the parliament. The new parliamentary elections took place in 2007 with none of the opposition parties able to reach required threshold of 7 per cent.

As for economic progress, after widespread reforms in the mid-1990s, where the basis for future growth was laid, Kazakhstan enjoyed a period of economic revival. The GDP growth rate of around 10 per cent experienced in the early 2000s was largely driven by the growing output of the hydrocarbon sector, high market prices and continuing foreign investment. Moreover, the financial sector also developed rapidly with the gradual reduction of the state's involvement in the banking sector. Improved access to credit by both business and consumers contributed to the rapid growth in the construction, retailing and services sectors. Rediscovered confidence in the banking sector helped to improve savings and investment rates.

Foreign direct investment remained high throughout the period. Budget deficit turned into surplus from 2001 and remained positive and strong until the GFC.

Rapid growth in capital inflows led to high inflation rates of over 10 per cent and the real appreciation the currency. This, coupled with easy access to relatively cheap foreign currency denominated credit started to create challenges for the regulators. Overall though, Kazakhstan received high praise for its success in economic reforms and growth. Table 10.5 summarizes the major economic indicators for 1998–2007 period.

Table 10.5: Kazakhstan's economic performance during 1998–2007.

Indicator	1998	1999	2000	2001	2002	2003	2004	2005	2006	2007
GDP growth, %	-1.9	2.7	9.8	13.5	9.8	9.3	9.6	9.7	10.7	8.9
GDP per capita[*]	2052	2127	2344	2664	2925	3187	3469	3771	4131	4447
GDP per capita[†]	4734	4909	5406	6146	6748	7351	8001	8699	9529	10259
Domestic savings/GDP	15.9	16.0	25.6	25.8	27.2	31.1	34.9	39.8	44.6	42.2
Investments/GDP	15.7	16.2	17.3	23.7	24.0	23.0	25.1	28.0	30.2	30.0
FDI/GDP (%)	5.2	9.4	7.0	12.8	10.5	6.8	9.6	4.5	9.4	11.4
Inflation (GDP deflator, %)	5.7	13.3	17.4	10.2	5.8	11.7	16.1	17.9	21.6	15.5
Budget deficit (% of GDP)	-8.0	-5.2	-1.0	1.8	1.0	3.0	2.5	5.8	7.2	4.7

[*] Constant, year 2005 USD
[†] PPP method; in USD
Source: EBRD (2002, 2005, 2007, 2010); World Bank (2014)

Political and Economic Developments in the Post-GFC Era

In the lead-up to Kazakhstan's Presidency of the Organization for Security and Co-operation (OSCE) in Europe, Kazakhstan undertook reforms in electoral law which guaranteed a runner-up party to gain some parliamentary seats even if it failed to reach the 7 per cent threshold. In the latest presidential elections in 2011, Nazarbaev received over 95 per cent of votes against only three little known contestants who were allowed to run for the presidency. In the 2012 parliamentary elections, *Nur-Otan*'s domination continued gaining over 80 per cent of the votes cast.

The most notable political event in Kazakhstan's recent political history occurred in Zhana-Ozen in 2011. Oil field workers, whose protest for better job and pay conditions remained ignored by the state-run oil companies, staged a strike to voice dissatisfaction with the level of civil liberties in Kazakhstan. The protest was crushed by the police with at least sixteen killed and scores injured. The president responded by sacking a number of regional and government officials, including his son-in-law Timur Kulibaev, head of the government fund *Samryk Kazyna*, which controlled strategic government oil assets. Protest organizers were put on trial.

In April 2014, Dariga Nazarbaeva was appointed a deputy speaker of the lower house of parliament and head of the *Nur-Otan* parliamentary group. This is likely to bring new speculations about Nazarbaev's succession plan. Even if these speculations have some credibility, it is highly unlikely that Nazarbaev will step down in the near future. Health permitting, Nazarbaev will run for office in 2016 and win with the decisive majority as has happened in the past.

In terms of economic performance, due to a greater degree of integration of the Kazakh economy into the global economy, Kazakhstan felt the impact of the GFC much more than Uzbekistan. Firstly, as a major exporter of energy resources, it faced a sharp decline in demand for energy towards the end of 2008. As a result Kazakhstan's GDP declined by 1.9 per cent in 2008. However, with a healthy macroeconomic position and large international currency reserves, it did not shake investors' confidence, and they continued to participate in energy related projects. GDP growth turned positive in 2009, and the pre-crisis trend returned in 2010. The main post-GFC economic indicators are summarized in Table 10.6.

Table 10.6: Kazakhstan's economic performance during 2008–2012.

Indicator	2008	2009	2010	2011	2012	change 1990–2012
GDP growth, %	-1.9	2.7	9.8	13.5	9.8	74.5%
GDP per capita[*]	4538	4473	4732	5015	5191	68.9%
GDP per capita[†]	10469	10318	10916	11568	11973	68.9%
Domestic savings/GDP	47.6	37.6	40.1	43.9	40.5	–
Investments /GDP	26.8	27.8	24.3	20.7	20.8	–
FDI/ GDP (%)	12.6	12.4	5.0	7.6	7.4	–
Inflation (GDP deflator, %)	20.9	4.7	19.5	17.6	4.8	–
Budget deficit (% of GDP)	1.2	-1.2	1.5	5.9	3.6	–

[*] Constant, year 2005 USD
[†] PPP method; in USD
Source: EBRD (2010, 2012); World Bank (2014).

With the rapid growth of foreign borrowing to finance a hungry construction sector in the pre-GFC period, Kazakhstan's banking system became increasingly vulnerable to external shocks. Lending practices in banks became lax, corporate governance remained poor and bank regulation and supervision did not keep up with the rapid developments. Although, there was no direct exposure to the US subprime mortgages by Kazakh banks, their dependence on foreign finance cost them dearly when the flow of cheap credit suddenly dried up during the credit crunch. In turn, Kazakh banks stopped extending new credit facilities to the local market, which froze new property development and property prices plummeted. As a result, Kazakh banks discovered that many of their borrowers were unable to service their debts and non-performing loan ratios grew rapidly. Two of the largest four banks, Bank Turan Alem (BTA) and Aliance Bank, were particularly hit hard.[42]

In response the government through the National Fund *Samruk Kazyna,* acquired a 75 per cent stake in BTA, as well as a 28 per cent and 18 per cent stake in the second and third largest banks of Kazakhstan (Halyk bank and Kazkommertsbank). Moreover, to prevent bank runs, it increased its deposit guarantee to 5 million tenge ($33,500). The government extended a $3 billion support package to the struggling real estate sector and $1 billion each to small and medium businesses, agriculture and infrastructure projects.[43]

To solve the bank debt problem, the Kazakh government successfully negotiated a partial debt write-off with the bondholders of the Alliance Bank in 2010 and BTA in 2010 and 2012. This brought the capital adequacy of the Kazakh banking system back to acceptable levels. However, the process of cleaning the portfolio of NPLs remains slow and incomplete, with major banks reluctant to transfer their assets to the Problem Loan Relief Fund run by the NBK, which took back the prudential regulation and supervision functions from the Financial Supervisory Agency to better coordinate banking sector relief efforts.[44]

Looking at the Kazakhstan's post-independence performance and development, Nazarbaev was able to lead the country towards significant economic openness and freedoms, without compromising his tight grip on political power. The economic success of the 2000s gave legitimacy to the political regime and allowed Nazarbaev to gain political capital in regional affairs.

A Comparative Case Study of Uzbekistan and Kazakhstan Using the Political Economy of Dictatorship Framework

Evaluation of the Political Reforms

As can be seen from the discussions above, the reform effort towards the goals of democratization and the shift towards a market economy was uneven in both countries. The processes of democratization and electoral reform started by Gorbachev, in the final years of the USSR, was extended to both republics. This relative freedom achieved before the USSR's dissolution continued in the early 1990s. Political leaders in both countries announced plans for further democratization. However, the reality proved to be different. The Uzbek leadership swiftly tightened up on political freedoms.[45] The referendum in 1995 to extend Karimov's powers to 2000 was symbolic proof of the dominance of the president's powers. Since then, little has changed in the political landscape and the Uzbek president enjoys a complete monopoly of power. Civil liberties have diminished from the level of 'Partly free' in 1991–2 to 'Not free' in 1993 and have remained unchanged since then.

Tightening powers in the hands of the president in Kazakhstan was a much more gradual process with various pockets of resistance and challenges coming from the parliament and then from the president's inner circle. Arguably, in his quest to consolidate power, Nazarbaev had to take into account a more complex political landscape, including the ethnic composition, as well as the large geographic size of the country. Nevertheless, Nazarbaev proved a shrewd politician; navigated through these constraints and achieved political domination. Kazakhstan has enjoyed and still enjoys much greater civil liberties. Although most of the official media is now under governmental control, unlike Uzbekistan, Kazakhstan does not censor/restrict the access of their citizens to the internet. Table 10.7 presents a comparison of the dynamics of political freedoms and civil liberties in Kazakhstan and Uzbekistan from 1991 to 2013. The ratings range from 1 which stands for 'most free' to 7 which means 'least free'. The ratings reflect the Freedom House's assessment of rights and freedoms enjoyed by individuals in each country.[46]

Table 10.7: Dynamics of political freedoms and civil liberties during 1991–2013.

	1991	1992	1993	1994	1995	1996–2000	2001–5	2006–10	2010–13
					Political rights				
Kazakhstan	5	5	6	6	6	6	6	6	6
Uzbekistan	6	6	7	7	7	7	7	7	7
					Civil liberties				
Kazakhstan	4	5	4	5	5	5	5	5	5
Uzbekistan	5	6	7	7	7	6	6	7	7

Source: Freedom House (2014)

Overall, and in stark contrast to the experiences of the Eastern European transition countries, the general public in Kazakhstan and Uzbekistan failed to influence the political agenda.[47] By the mid-1990s, presidents in both countries established a monopoly over power and voters lost any possible avenue for change through the election process. In this sense, the announced process of political transition has never really commenced. To the contrary, by the mid-1990s, highly autocratic regimes were established in both countries with no interest from the ruling elite in advancing democracy.

Evaluation of Economic and Financial Reforms

Kazakhstan advanced much further in its economic liberalization and shift towards a market economy. It introduced much deeper market reforms in the early years of transition, especially in terms of privatization, and the liberalization of prices, international trade and foreign exchange. In the 2000s, Kazakhstan undertook more extensive reforms in its financial system, which improved businesses' and individuals' access to formal financial services. However, both countries failed to undertake significant reforms in governance, enterprise restructuring and competition policy, although Kazakhstan is slightly ahead in terms of EBRD transition indicators (see Table 10.8).

Although the more radical reforms in Kazakhstan in the early years of transition proved costly in terms of lost output, they did help the economy rebound stronger in subsequent years. A higher level of economic freedom in Kazakhstan, as evidenced by the country's rank of a 'moderately free' country in the index of economic freedom,[48] provided incentives to entrepreneurs to exercise initiatives. The Kazakh economy's relative openness and stronger integration into the world economy exposed the country more to global economic cycles. An obvious example of this is the rapid rise and bust of the country's financial system pre- and post-the GFC.

In contrast, Uzbekistan has progressed slowly towards a market economy. The authorities continue to have strong involvement in the economic process, constraining private economic activity. Hence, it is not a surprise that the country was ranked as 'repressed' in the index of economic freedom.[49] However, through tight economic management, Uzbekistan was able to go through the early years of transition in a better shape. Moreover, it also enjoyed strong growth in the 2000s thanks to favourable terms for its exports. The closed nature of the Uzbek financial system largely insulated it from the global economic downturn and the country has continued to report strong economic growth in the post-GFC period. However, one may question the reliability of government statistics due to their opaqueness and lack of audit by international organizations.

Overall, it is evident that by 2000 the leadership in both Uzbekistan and Kazakhstan had largely established the political and economic structures that they desired and were reluctant to undertake any further economic and political liberalization. Therefore, the term 'transition economies', as it was originally proposed to describe the process of shifting command based communist systems of the Eastern bloc towards democratic governments of Western style with a market economy, seems to be no longer relevant to both countries. It is no surprise that some commentators, such as Boris Rumer quite rightly concluded that the period of transition has ended in these countries.[50] Table 10.8 provides the dynamics of the EBRD transition indicators in Uzbekistan and Kazakhstan. The scores reflect the EBRD's assessment of the reform in particular areas, with 1 indicating 'no or little progress' and 4.3 reflecting 'standards and performance typical of advanced industrial economies'.[51]

Classification of Dictatorships

Taking into account the regimes established in Uzbekistan and Kazakhstan, it is more appropriate to analyse their reforms from the point of view of the political economy of dictatorship.

Table 10.8: Selected transition indicators in Uzbekistan and Kazakhstan.

	1990	1993	1998	2003	2008	2013
Uzbekistan:						
Large- scale privatization	1.0	1.0	2.7	2.7	2.7	2.7
Small-scale privatization	1.0	2.0	3.0	3.0	3.3	3.3
Governance and enterprise restructuring	1.0	1.0	2.0	1.7	1.7	1.7
Price liberalization	1.0	2.7	2.7	2.7	2.7	2.7
Trade & Forex system	1.0	1.0	1.7	1.7	2.0	1.7
Competition Policy	1.0	2.0	2.0	1.7	1.7	1.7
Banking reforms	1.0	1.0	1.7	1.7	1.7	1.0
Non-bank financial institutions	1.0	1.0	2.0	2.0	2.0	2.0
Kazakhstan:						
Large scale privatization	1.0	2.0	3.0	3.0	3.0	3.0
Small scale privatization	1.0	2.0	4.0	4.0	4.0	4.0
Governance and enterprise restructuring	1.0	1.0	2.0	2.0	2.0	2.0
Price liberalization	1.0	2.7	4.0	4.0	4.0	3.7
Trade & Forex system	1.0	2.0	4.0	3.3	3.7	3.7
Competition Policy	1.0	1.0	2.0	2.0	2.0	2.0
Banking reforms	1.0	1.0	2.3	3.0	3.0	2.7
Non-bank financial institutions	1.0	1.0	2.0	2.3	2.7	2.3

Source: EBRD (1998, 2003, 2008, 2013)

The literature that describes dictators, their types and models of their behaviour is somewhat limited. Ronald Wintrobe has offered the most comprehensive classification of regimes to-date using economic criteria.[52] The framework offered by Wintrobe tries to describe what the various types of authoritarian regimes are trying to maximize. He identifies four types of authoritarian regime: totalitarian, tinpot, tyranny and timocracy. Differentiation comes from the level of repression used to maintain the regime and level of loyalty the dictators enjoy from the general public. This is shown in Table 10.9. The dictator's power is considered to be a function of loyalty and repression. His surplus comes from the difference between generated taxes and spending on public goods and repressions.

Table 10.9: Classification of authoritarian regimes

Repression Loyalty	High	Low
High	Totalitarianism	Timocracy
Low	Tyranny	Tinpot

Source: Wintrobe (1998)

A totalitarian regime is assumed to maximize a dictator's power subject to a positive surplus. Tyranny is similar to totalitarianism except with much lower levels of loyalty. Tinpot dictatorships are assumed to maximize the surplus provided the level of power is sufficient to stay in the office. Finally, timocracy is an example of benevolent dictatorships, which try to maximize citizen's utility subject to positive surplus and sufficient power to remain in the office.

To be able to understand the functioning and longevity of authoritarian regimes in Uzbekistan and Kazakhstan, it is important to choose an appropriate category into which the regimes fit. President Karimov's style of leadership is well-documented in his earlier publications where he advocates a strong leadership role for the state in undertaking reforms in all spheres.[53] His actions to establish complete dominance in the political sphere, including oppressing even the mildest forms of opposition, suppressing civil liberties and freedom of speech, continuing the state's involvement in economic affairs, and maintaining an extensive law enforcement machine represented by the police and security services, clearly indicate a high level of repression. It is hard to determine the exact level of loyalty Karimov enjoys amongst the ruling elite or the general public and how it changed over time. This is a common problem for dictatorships: repression of democratic institutions and freedom of speech reduce the regime's capacity to accurately estimate the level of loyalty it enjoys.[54] Better economic performance in comparison with other post-Soviet countries, as well as maintenance of the majority of social programmes in early years, suggest that in the 1990s, Karimov enjoyed genuine public popularity and support. His vision for Uzbekistan, backed by successes in the early period of transition, and the continued effectiveness of Uzbekistan's administrative institutions attracted popular support from both the general public and some commentators.[55] With the rise of extreme opposition however, after the 1999 terrorist attacks and subsequent attempt by small radical Islamist groups to invade the country, the source of popular support has changed its form. Many residents would still support Karimov as a guarantor of peace and tranquility despite his lack of economic success.[56] However, with the rising cost of living, levels of corruption and continued lack of civil liberties; support for the president appears to be gradually fading. This is evident from the pockets of resistance that appeared in the mid–2000s, most notably the Andijan events.

However, even now, anecdotal evidence suggests that, despite their dissatisfaction with the current state of affairs, the general public does not believe that regieme change would bring any improvements. This indicates that citizen loyalty is more a case of 'status quo' bias rather than true belief in the positive contribution and benevolence of the current regime. In this sense, based on the high level of repression and loyalty, the Uzbek regime should be classified as totalitarian. Karimov has satisfied all the requirements to ensure longevity and the relative stability of the regime: periodical re-shuffling of the ruling elite, managing inter-elite rivalries to ensure overall balance, and substantial incentives created for those who secure his regime, such as the police, security services and judicial powers as well as bureaucrats. These incentives encompass relative job security and better pay packages, as well as access to rent-seeking opportunities. As a trained *apparatchik*, he also recognized the importance of national ideology. Therefore, the ideology of national independence was developed to assist in maintaining the regime. Although penetration of this ideology is somewhat limited, and its effectiveness is well below the levels achieved in the former USSR, it still plays a significant part in maintaining the regime. As a result, he was able to achieve an adequate level of legitimacy to stay in power.[57]

Classifying the authoritarian regime in Kazakhstan is more difficult. Nazarbaev adopted a different style of power and 'governamentality'.[58] Instead of positioning himself as a strict 'father', who controls all aspects of life of young children, Nazarbaev chose an 'owner of a large private corporation' style of rule. This regime allowed more political and especially economic freedom on the ground. The approach allowed some talented managers, provided they maintained the loyalty to the president, to grow within the system. Reform-minded individuals were appointed to high posts at various time periods. Skilful management of the balance of various interest groups, economic successes of the late 1990s and the 2000s, and higher levels of civil liberties ensured the popularity of the president both in the 1990s and the 2000s. In addition, the Nazarbaev regime was able to credibly commit to sustaining various institutions (democratic or otherwise) that were necessary to support investment in physical and human capital. Gilson and Milhaupt label such regimes as 'economically benevolent autocracies'.[59]

However, not dissimilar to Uzbekistan's case, over time, perhaps from the second half of the 2000s with the repression of the democratic opposition and various other corruption-related scandals, loyalty driven by Nazarbaev's personal charisma has declined as evidenced by the Zhana-Uzen protests. To compensate for diminishing loyalty, Nazarbaev's regime has been tightening political freedoms and civil rights. All in all, it appears that Nazarbaev's regime might be included in the illusive category of benevolent dictators (timocracy in Wintrobe's classification) with a high level of loyalty and moderate levels of repressions. This, however, may change if Nazarbaev continues tightening up on civil liberties opts for economic reform reversals.

Conclusion

The above discussion of the Uzbek transition experience since the 1990s explains why there has been very little effort to reform both the economy and the political landscape in Uzbekistan. A similar conclusion can be reached on Kazakhstan with its lack of progress on democratization and its slower progress towards economic reforms since the 2000s. One of the key conclusions that can be drawn from this analysis is that given the political environment, both countries have reached their respective steady states in their reform paths. Since the maintenance of this status quo is in the interests of the respective leaders and the ruling elites, no further significant reform changes, albeit for tactical purposes and/or in response to external shocks, should be expected. This suggests that the period of transition, which is usually associated with a deliberate move towards Western-style civil and market institutions, might well be over in both countries.

A totalitarian regime maximizes its power by maintaining high levels of repression and loyalty, but also ensures a positive dictator's surplus to be distributed to the ruling elite. The Uzbek president kept his personal reputation intact with no corruption scandals similar to those in Kazakhstan. The same though cannot be said about his family as Karimov recently had his eldest daughter reprimanded for her dubious business dealings.[60] This indicates that Karimov may not see his office as a means for accumulating personal wealth; he may see himself more as a 'father' of the nation. Nevertheless, his failure to establish institutions that facilitate investments in human and physical capital does not allow him to be classified as an 'economically benevolent' dictator; an idea on which he attempted to model his leadership.

Timocracy assumes that a dictator strives to improve his citizens prosperity without compromising his grip on power and endangering the benefits he enjoys. The level of economic freedom that the population in Kazakhstan has enjoyed shows that this may well have been Nazarbaev's goal. However, the challenges to his regime may have created a sense of insecurity for his regime too. This, in turn, may have encouraged him to consolidate his power through increased levels of political repressions and limitations on civil liberties.

Kazakhstan's reform implementation and economic performance in the years preceding the GFC were clearly superior to those of Uzbekistan. However, much higher exposure to the GFC through its more integrated financial system and trade links made Kazakhstan more vulnerable to its negative effects. Uzbekistan's performance during the GFC was proudly portrayed by the local media as visionary achievement of a leader who deliberately avoided significant integration with global capital markets. If anything, the GFC re-enforced the belief that further liberalization was unnecessary and might be harmful to both the stability of the economy and the country in general.

11 AN OVERVIEW OF THE SECURITIES MARKET REFORM IN POST-LIBERALIZATION CHINA AND INDIA

Malay K. Dey and Chaoyan Wang

The policy of being too cautious is the greatest risk of all.

> J. L. Nehru, first Prime Minster of India and a Socialist

To get rich is glorious.

> Deng Xiaoping, Chinese Communist Party Leader

The wave of economic liberalization that has swept across much of the developing economies of the world since the mid-1980s has many facets to it; yet, perhaps the most compelling aspect of it has been financial liberalization, which broadly encompasses financial sector deregulation and opening up of the capital accounts.[1] The financial sector deregulation entails securities market reform; and for the most part, this involves 'opening up' of securities markets (primarily stock markets), which aims to achieve free movement of capital both inside and outside of a country. The finance and growth literature postulates that active securities markets foster economic growth.[2] Although numerous cross sectional studies find positive correlation between stock market activity and economic growth, the evidence is mixed with respect to the direction of causality.[3]

Securities markets perform two essential functions in an economy: they offer alternative source of financing for the real sector; and they allow information aggregation for price discovery that is critical for securities trading. Hence financial economists evaluate the performance of security markets by how efficiently firms can raise capital (primary market function), and how efficiently securities are priced and traded in the market (secondary market function). However, the experiences of well-functioning, and wealth building, financial markets of the prosperous nations in Western Europe and North America, indicate that, to be a successful a securities market must provide:

a) protection of property and contractual rights including those of minority shareholders; b) full and fair disclosure laws; c) independent and external monitoring of corporate boards; d) transparent accounting practices; and last, but not least, f) timely and strict enforcement of rules and regulations.[4] Hence, the Western style securities market regulatory and corporate governance structures underlie the architecture for securities market reforms in all emerging economies, including in China and India. It must be noted though that for many emerging markets, this typical market reform agenda, containing a set of 'best practices', is only aspirational. In reality, effective reforms entail sustained, coordinated, and wilful actions by the government to promote 'fair and effective' securities market legislation with strong enforcement mechanisms (regulatory reform), and also by businesses to initiate changes in their respective corporate governance practices (governance reform).[5]

The literature on corporate governance argues that incentive alignment measures, combined with improvements in the legal environment, can help reduce excessive agency costs implicit in concentrated ownership that often leads to weak protection of minority shareholders' rights.[6] Incentive alignment measures, e.g. anti-tunnelling resolution, cross listing as a bonding device, etc., are largely voluntary inside boardroom decisions. By contrast, the extent to which managers can promote positive changes in the legal environment that promotes shareholders' welfare and trust in delegated authority depends on societal norms, e.g. the role of corporation in the society, corporate ownership structure, and the level of shareholder activism, which varies from one country to another.

In this chapter, we focus on a selection of broad country level rules and practices with respect to minority shareholder protection and disclosure laws in China and India that can serve as proxies for corporate governance. Our intent is to assess and compare the progress of China and India in terms of their security market reforms. In doing so, we consider the fact that the initial settings in China and India were very different when they embarked on their respective reform processes. In other words, China's primary challenge was designing an efficient and fully participative market based on free market principles from ground zero; whereas India's central problem was to win over the coalition of entrenched interests favouring *status quo* and to build an efficient system of laws backed by a robust enforcement mechanism. Taking these peculiarities into account, we evaluate each country's reforms independently.

By analysing the historical background and the up-to-date status of the securities market reform processes in both China and India, we argue that the reform process in China never got off the ground until very recently, mainly because it lacked a comprehensive and deliberate plan for implementation, a full commitment of the Chinese leadership to free markets, and a broad base public understanding and appreciation of a market economy. Despite such failings, however, certain domestic and international events, and the government's reactions to them, shaped China's stock market in the last 25 years. In contrast, the principal impediment to reform in India has been old-fashioned social norms and conventions including frail civil society rules and widespread transgressions of laws and regulations with impunity.[7] Successive post-colonial governments, immersed in unprecedented social, economic, and political problems, did very little to enforce the laws of the country and to educate the general public about the rewards of living under the rule of law and the perils of failing to do so. As a result, over time, the Indian polity developed indifference to, and perhaps even disregard for, laws and institutions of the country. Further, the democratic multi-party electoral politics in India created an environment characterized by chronic myopia, endless resistance to change, and self-indulging *quid pro quo* among corrupt and incompetent politicians and their network of highly politicized civil servants and businessmen, who thrive on the *status quo* of the absence of the rule of law. This institutional economics perspective, addressed in comprehensive annual survey reports from the World Justice Project, offers a convincing and nuanced explanation of the turbulent path of securities market reforms in China and India.[8]

The rest of the chapter progresses as follows. A historical perspective on the status of financial markets in China and India is first presented, followed by an overview of the reform agenda. We then catalogue the regulatory and governance reforms as part of the security market reforms in China and India respectively. Concluding remarks are then presented.

Securities Markets in China and India from 1980 to 2012: A Brief Overview and Historical Context

Before the 1980s, China and India had followed distinctly different paths to economic development. But, both were at the same historical crossroad roughly during a ten-year period, 1984–94, when each country had to put forth and pursue an aggressive financial liberalization package, including securities market reform to meet the demands and expectations of its own people. While China pursued a socialist planned economy with virtually all means of productions under the direct control of the state and complete suspension of property rights and stock markets, India, in spite of its heavy-handed control over many sectors of the economy and a large unwieldy public sector, mostly retained a private enterprise and market-based character of the economy.[9] Nowhere is this difference more obvious than in the capital markets, where despite state control and nationalization of certain vital sectors of the economy such as banking and insurance industries, stock markets continued to play a significant role in the economic process in India. Due to these evolving historic differences, China and India had markedly different initial conditions at the onset of their respective reform efforts. These early conditions were essential in each country's journey forward. Table 11.1 below contains a snapshot of the economic and financial landscape of China and India in 1980, 1990, 2000, and 2012.

Table 11.1 points to the fact that China and India enjoyed significant but asymmetric success in terms of economic and financial market growth over the past

Table 11.1: Selection of economic and financial indicators for China and India in 1980, 1990, 2000 and 2012.

	1980		1990		2000		2012	
	China	India	China	India	China	India	China	India
Population, thousand	981,235	698,965	1,135,185	868,890	1,262,645	1,042,261	1,350,695	1,236,686
Population growth rate, per cent	1.2	2.3	1.5	2.0	0.8	1.7	0.5	1.3
GDP, millions of US$	189,399	189,594	356,936	326,608	1,198,474	476,609	8,358,363	1,841,717
Rate of GDP growth, per cent	7.8	6.7	3.8	5.5	8.4	4.0	7.8	3.2
Per capita GDP, US$	193.02	271.25	314.43	375.89	949.18	455.44	6091.01	1489.24
FDI, per cent of GDP	0.0	0.0	1.0	0.1	3.2	0.8	3.0	1.7
Banking sector credit, per cent of GDP	53.3	37.0	89.4	51.4	119.7	51.4	152.7	76.6
Market capitalization, per cent of GDP	0.0	0.0	0.5 (1991)	11.8	48.5	31.1	44.2	68.6
Nos. of listed securities	0	NA	14 (1991)	2435	1086	5937	2494	5191

Source: World Bank (2012)

two decades. For our purpose, perhaps the most telling statistics is the link between per capita GDP and financial market activities denoted by market capitalization and securities listing. Between 1990 and 2012, per capita GDP grewfrom $314 to $6091 in China and from $375 to $1489 in India. During the same period, market capitalization as a percentage of GDP (number of exchange listed securities) increased from 0.5 per cent (14) to 44.2 per cent (2494) in China, and from 11.8 per cent (2435) to 68.6 per cent (5191) in India. Indeed, both China and India achieved measurable economic progress over the last two decades. Nevertheless, the lingering question remains as to how much of this growth is due to the Western style financial market reforms initiated by each country. Critics point to China's weak infrastructure with respect to securities market, lack of democratic institutions, and continued resistance to free and open markets, and yet, China's economic and financial progress on many counts dwarf those of India's and the rest of the developing economies of the world. In the World Justice Project's Rule of Law Index for 2014, China ranks 76 out of 99 countries in the world with a score of 0.45. By contrast, India ranks is 66 out of 99 countries with a score of 0.48.[10] Such evidence calls into question the logic of Western style financial market reforms as means to achieve sustainable economic growth. Some commentators have identified a largely decentralized Chinese economy during Mao years as a reason behind its success in quick transformation to a localized private sector-based economy, while others, comparing the business and entrepreneurial environments in China and India, predict that India's domestic entrepreneur-based growth model will in the long run win over China's Foreign Direct Investment (FDI) based growth.[11] It's also worth noting that despite China's poor corporate governance practice, market capitalization in China is relatively large and interest in Chinese equities by foreign investors remains strong. Some commentators call this phenomenon a 'China puzzle'.[12]

The Chinese Securities Market Reforms Since the 1990s

Phases of Stock Market Development in China: 1990–2012[13]

During the 1980s, China first experimented with issuing redeemable shares to the employees of a few large and medium-sized enterprises. The first such security, Shanghai Fei Le, was issued on November 18, 1984 and by 1990, 14 additional securities were issued. These securities were sold as bonds at par with guaranteed fixed dividends and redeemed at maturity and the local governments were responsible for the oversight and monitoring of their trading. On September 26 1986, China's earliest over-the-counter (OTC) market, Jing An Trust, was established and for the first time trading of shares began officially in a regulated secondary market. The People's

Bank of China (PBC), China's Central Bank, particularly its Shanghai and Shenzhen branches, were responsible for the regulation and surveillance of the market.

In 1990, the Chinese government approved the establishment of two stock exchanges in Shanghai and Shenzhen.[14] By the end of 1991, only eight and six stocks were listed on the Shanghai (SSE) and the Shenzhen (SZSE) Stock Exchanges respectively. From that humble beginning, over the past two decades, China's stock markets have experienced dramatic expansion. By the end of 2012, in terms of market capitalization, the SSE was the 7th largest stock exchange in the world, just behind the Hong Kong Stock Exchange (SEHK), and the SZSE ranked the 16th in the world.[15] Table 11.2 below enumerates three important indicators of equity market size and performance in China – number of listings, capital raised by the listed firms, and market capitalization.

Table 11.2: Number of listed firms and market capitalization in China in 2003–2012.

		2003	2004	2005	2006	2007	2008	2009	2010	2011	2012
Number of listed firms	A shares	1287	1377	1381	1434	1550	1625	1718	2063	2342	2494
	B shares	111	110	109	109	109	109	108	108	108	107
	H shares	93	111	122	143	148	153	159	165	171	179
Capital raised	Total*	6428	7149	7629	14897	22416	24522	26162	33184	36095	38395
Market capital	Total*	42457	37055	32430	89403	327140	121366	243939	265422	214758	230357

* in 10 Renminbi Yuans.
Source: China Securities Regulatory Commissions Statistics (2012)

Table 11.2 shows the growth in the number of listed firms in two share classes, A and B shares, and their respective market capitalization.[16] Note that the domestic securities market in China consists of A- and B-shares listed in the SSE and SZSE. However, the SSE is the principal market and hence, in order to chronicle the Chinese stock market, we plot in Figure 11.1 below the SSE Composite Index over the period 1990 to 2012.[17]

As Figure 1.1 indicates, the SSE index grew only by fits and starts and not without major hiccups on the way, Indeed, we identify three distinct phases: Phase 1 (1990–7), Phase 2 (1997–2005), and the most recent phase beginning in 2005 along the time path of the SSE index and the Chinese stock markets. During the first phase, 1990–7, the stock market grew modestly almost on its own while the Chinese government made very few strides to developing a consolidated securities regulation system. The second phase, 1997–2005, the early part of which coincided with the transfer of sovereignty of Hong Kong in July 1997 and the lead up to China's World Trade Organization (WTO) membership in 2001, brought much international attention to China and its fledgling stock market.[18] The US and European institutional investors looking for investment opportunities abroad flocked to China to invest, which might have contributed to the stock market boom and the subsequent bust that took place between 1999 and 2001, the latter coinciding with the dot.com bust and the US stock market crash in 2000–1. Perhaps, the turbulence in the equities market led the central government in Beijing to accelerate long pending fundamental market reforms, which were to be implemented only in the next stage.

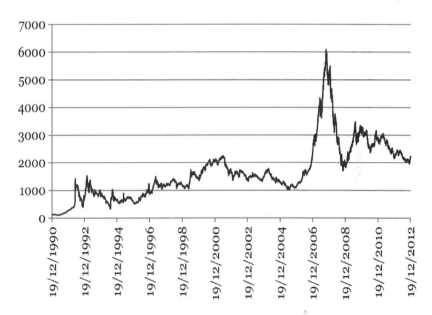

Figure 11.1: Shanghai Stock Exchange composite (SSEC) index for the period 1990 to 2012; Shanghai Stock Exchange (2012)

The last phase started in 2005 and continues at the time of this study. This period is characterized by a sharp upturn and a deep downturn in the SSE index, the latter coinciding with the global financial meltdown in 2008. In addition to further privatization and deregulation, a financial futures exchange and a second board market were opened in 2006 and 2009 respectively.

Events and Regulatory Reforms Related to China's Securities Markets Since 1990
We begin this section with a chronology of major relevant events and reforms in China, which helped shape China's securities markets. The summary of the main events are presented in Table 11.3. Further, we provide wherever possible, facts – and quotes-based assessments of the intended and/or actual outcomes of some of the reform measures undertaken by the government.

Table 11.3: A Chronology of events and regulatory reforms related to China's securities markets since 1990.

Month /Year	Events/Reform Measures	Results, Expected and/or Desired vs. Actual
1990–6	1990 – Shanghai and Shenzhen stock exchanges established. 1993 – Company law passed.	Limited privatization aimed at improving performances of state owned enterprises (SOEs); Recognition of individual's right to form 'for profit' corporation; sets the ground rules for forming joint stock companies. Until 1991, only 8 stocks in Shanghai and 6 stocks in Shenzhen were listed; The government retained large portion of SOEs shares as non-tradable shares.
1997–2004	1997 – The Hong Kong Accession Treaty 1998 – The Securities Law passed without adequate market discipline and control. Many features of incomplete and fragmented markets remained in place. 1999–2001 – the SSE index crossed 1000 and increased by over 100 per cent in 2 years (May 1999–June 2001). 2001 – China gains WTO membership.	In an effort to attract foreign institutional investors, guiding principles for primary and secondary market operations were laid out; increased pressure to reform transparency and disclosure laws as per international standards and allowing foreign institutional investors to participate directly in the domestic market. Increased investments by foreign institutional investors in A-shares traded in domestic Shanghai and Shenzhen exchanges. By the end of April 2011, 103 licensed QFII investors had been granted a combined quota of $20.7 billion to invest in China's capital markets under the QFII program. Lack of market discipline allowed speculative trading and bubble formation. A four year downturn in the stock market begins in June 2001.

Month /Year	Events/Reform Measures	Results, Expected and/or Desired vs. Actual
2005–12	Split ownership reform – Non tradable state shares become tradable. 'Quota' system for IPOs abolished. 2006 – Qualified Domestic Institutional Investor (QDII) announced.	Removing market frictions – artificial shortages, quotas in IPOs Allow Chinese institutions to invest in foreign money markets and fixed income securities abroad. Derivatives market opened. Since the reform was completed in 2008, the liquidity of the listed firms in China has been significantly increased. It has not significantly changed the market's ownership structure and the state's dominance. And the state's role in the governance structure has not changed.

As it is apparent from Table 11.3, the two main pillars of the regulatory structure for publicly listed corporations in China, the Company Law of 1993 and the Securities Law of 1998 have been jointly in force only since 1998. The Company Law passed by the legislature in 1993 laid out the fundamental features of all incorporated business entities in China, including state owned enterprises (SOE), corporations eligible to receive foreign investment, as well as listed and non-listed companies. It defined a listed company and specified the conditions and procedures for going public, information disclosure requirements for a listed company, and suspension and termination of the trading of shares. In addition, it also contained broad principles for securities regulation.

On the other hand, security market regulation in China moved through three distinct phases. First, between 1990 and 1992, there was no central regulatory authority. The PBC was the 'deemed' securities market regulator, but in fact, the actual regulation and supervision was carried on by the local governments and the regional branches of the PBC.

Second, during 1992–8, although there was no specific legislation, the China Securities Regulatory Commissions (CSRC) was entrusted with broad authority to regulate securities market and related activities in the country. The CSRC, formed in 1992, is China's equivalent of the Securities Exchange Commission (SEC) in the US. The CSRC oversees China's nationwide centralized securities supervisory system, with the power to regulate and supervise securities issuers, as well as to investigate, and impose penalties for illegal activities related to securities. However, compared to the mission of the conventional market regulators, which aim to protect investors, maintain fair, orderly, and efficient markets, and facilitate capital formation, the dominant mission of the CSRC was to provide preferential capital for state-owned enterprises, increase the value of state assets, and promote consumers' and producers' trust in overall economic performance through, for example, higher share prices.[19]

Finally, in 1998, China's first comprehensive securities legislation, the Securities Law of 1998, spelt out for the first time rules on the issuance and transactions of securities, rights and obligations of investors and market participants, as well as the powers and authorities of the securities regulator, the CSRC in a statute. It is also worth noting that while the securities law was initially drafted in 1992, it was perhaps the Asian Financial Crisis of 1997 that prompted the Chinese authorities, who were concerned about the fragility of the financial system, to finalize its passage in 1998. The law imposed strict restrictions on banks, insurance companies, and trusts with regard to forming holding companies and investing in risky securities.

Another conspicuous feature of the Securities Law of 1998 was a quota system that was used in selecting firms eligible for public listing. Under the quota system, the Planning Commission and various provincial leaders receive a listing quota for that particular region, which constitutes a certain amount of shares of government property that may be securitized and sold. These government officials then assign their shares to Initial Public Offering (IPO) candidates, which are usually state-owned enterprises (SOEs).

The main criticisms of the Securities Law of 1998 are over-regulation and under-protection. Since the law was enacted in the backdrop of the 1997 Asian Financial Crisis, the Act tilted towards being conservative and cautious vis-à-vis the securities market. It was criticized to be over-prudent in the way of regulation and enforcement while leaving little room for market development and financial innovation. For instance, derivative transactions and short selling were strictly forbidden. Further, critics viewed the 1998 Act inherently as a 'planned economy' effort to expand SOEs' capital raising opportunities and divest off troubled SOEs. The critics of the government's policy argued that the absence of regulation on civil litigations related to securities, in case investors are found to have been harmed, led to insufficient protection for investors. Further, due to the lack of civil liability imposed for the matters such as false information disclosure, insider trading, and other securities crimes, investors' confidence was seriously hampered, which critics point to as the reason for a stagnant market during the early 2000s.

From 1998 to 2004, the regulatory system went through a series of amendments, consolidations, and adjustments. In October 2005, the Chinese Congress adopted a comprehensive revision of the Securities Law that made sweeping changes in many aspects of securities market such as abandoning a CSRC approval of listing and lifting restrictions on derivative transaction and short selling. The 2005 revision of the law is a significant milestone (perhaps the beginning of the *de facto* reform!) in the development of China's stock market regulatory system and hence in the next section, we focus on the reform progress since 2005 and its intended effect on ownership, corporate governance, and market frictions.

Table 11.4: Detailed market structure of publicly listed securities in China, 2003–12.

		2003	2004	2005	2006	2007	2008	2009	2010	2011	2012
Number of listed firms	A shares	1287	1377	1381	1434	1550	1625	1718	2063	2342	2494
	B shares	111	110	109	109	109	109	108	108	108	107
	H shares	93	111	122	143	148	153	159	165	171	179
Capital raised	Total*	6428	7149	7629	14897	22416	24522	26162	33184	36095	38395
	Tradeable shares*	2267	5577	2914	5637	10331	12578	19759	25642	28850	31339
	Tradeable shares per cent	0.35	0.36	0.38	0.38	0.46	0.51	0.76	0.77	0.80	0.82
Market capital	Total*	42457	37055	32430	89403	327140	121366	243939	265422	214758	230357
	Tradeable shares*	13178	11688	10630	25003	93064	45213	151258	193110	164921	181658
	Tradeable shares per cent	0.31	0.32	0.33	0.28	0.28	0.37	0.62	0.73	0.77	0.79

Source: China Securities Regulatory Commissions Statistics (2012)

Securities Market Reform: 2005 and Beyond

While limited initiatives to curb frictions in the securities market were launched earlier during the reform process, the amended Securities Law 2005 focused solely on three key issues: segmentation, foreign investors' participation, and state control of ownership interest and governance of publicly listed companies in China. Segmentation has remained as one of the dogged features right from the early stage of China's stock market development. As reflected in Table 11.4 below, segmentation is reflected in many aspects of market design. First, the investors are segmented because Chinese listed firms have multiple classes of shares outstanding: shares listed domestically which can only be traded by domestic investors (A-shares) and shares listed domestically but denominated in foreign currencies (US and Hong Kong dollars) and reserved for foreign investors (B-shares). This form of segmentation has given rise to 'price discount puzzle', where B-shares consistently trade at a discount relative to A-shares, although both shares have similar voting and cash flow rights.[20]

Second, besides multiple classes of shares, Chinese listed companies also have a split ownership structure with tradable and non-tradable shares. Table 11.4 breaks up capital raised and market capitalization into tradable and non-tradable shares. Typically, the holders of non-tradable shares are financial institutions owned by central or local governments. The state shareholders had no interest in firm value maximization because their shares could not be transacted at market price. Further, since the majority of the shares are owned directly or indirectly by the state, there is a conflict of interest for the state to pass legislation for safeguarding investors, including minority shareholders.

Table 11.5 provides a snapshot of Chinese listed firms' ownership structures in 2005 and 2012. As can be seen from the table, in 2005 (2012), tradable shares accounted for approximately 33 per cent (76 per cent), leaving more than 67 per cent (24 per cent) of the shares in the Chinese stock market to non-tradable shares. In 2005, among the non-tradable shares, state-owned shares denoted approximately 45 per cent; by contrast, tradable A- and B-shares held by private individual and institutional investors summed up to slightly over 30 per cent. This split ownership structure, particularly the fact that tradable shares are outweighed by non-tradable shares created an artificial shortage, led to high turnover rates of 291 per cent and 351 per cent in 2005 for A-shares listed in Shanghai and Shenzhen Stock Exchanges respectively.[21] Finance theory postulates that high turnover rates contribute to developing speculative bubbles in asset markets and promote insider trading and price manipulation. Not surprisingly, such activities were quite common at the time, in the Chinese markets, especially among small – and medium-cap stocks, which are typically more vulnerable to manipulation than large cap stocks.

Table 11.5: Ownership structure of Chinese public firms in 2005 and 2012.

		Number of shares (bn.) (2005)	per cent of total (2005)	Number of shares (bn.) (2012)	per cent of total (2012)
Non-tradable	State-owned shares	343.3	44.82	13.92	0.00
	Sponsor's legal person shares	55.2	7.21	766.92	0.26
	Foreign legal person's shares	22.6	2.95	103.4	0.03
	Private placement of legal person's shares	24.3	3.17	0.00	0.00
	Employee shares	0.4	0.05	0.00	0.00
	Others	28.7	3.75	0.00	0.00
Tradable	A-shares	228.1	29.78	2,220.4	75.14
	B-Shares	21.8	2.84	29.53	0.99

Source: China Securities and Futures Statistical Yearbook (2006, 2013)

In April 2005, the CSRC launched a state share reform to make all non-tradable state shares tradable on the market, thus facilitating privatization and change of control rights of the publicly listed SOEs. Prior to the reform in 2005, non-tradable shares could be traded only via equity transfer between state shareholders. Further, these transactions were not market-based and resulted from agreements approved by the respective government authorities and regulators. By contrast, the state share reform was a market-based negotiation between private shareholders and state shareholders. It was a market-based negotiation in the sense that share merger gives 'consideration' to private shareholders and used 'consideration' to transfer trading rights. The consideration includes bonus shares, warrants, and cash as compensation to holders of tradable shares. For example, in order for non-tradable shares to be tradable, each public shareholder will receive a certain number of shares, or a number of warrants, or certain cash as consideration. The general public as shareholders will decide at the shareholder meetings whether they consider it a fair deal and hence accept it.

As is evident from Tables 4 and 5 above, after the implementation of the 2008 reform, the proportion of tradable shares in the market increased significantly. The non-tradable shares reform has enhanced the liquidity of the listed firms in China although it has not significantly changed the market's ownership structure and the state's dominance. Even though in principle, the state's directly and indirectly controlled shares are now eligible for market transfer, in practice, the state and its agencies still cannot do so. Consequently, the state's role in the governance structure has not changed.

Besides the issues associated with the state ownership of listed Chinese corporations, there is also a problem of concentrated ownership. At the end of 2005,

74 per cent of the domestic listed public firms had fewer than 50,000 share-holders and fewer than 2 per cent had more than 150,000 shareholders.[22] The combination of state and concentrated ownership of the Chinese listed firms brings up the problem of asset stripping where the institutional state sharehold-ers resort to asset-stripping via cash dividends which is a regular way to pay out company profits. For example, before April 2003, 657 out of 1,236 listed compa-nies declared either a cash or stock dividend. Among them, 622 listed firms paid a total cash dividends amounting to Renminbi Yuan (RMB) 45.8 billion (US$ 5.5 billion), which is around 53 per cent of these companies' total net profits. Of the RMB 45.8 billion (US$ 5.5 billion) worth of dividends announced by April 2003, the holders of traded shares received only RMB 16 billion (US$ 1.9 bil-lion), the rest going to institutional state shareholders.[23]

Finally, prior to 2005, China's stock market was relied on an administrative governance structure based on a quota system. The quota system that was inte-gral to the IPO process was completely abandoned after the enactment of the newly revised Securities Law, indicating China's affirmation of 'growing out' of a planned economy. Under the 2005 Act, it is no longer the CSRC but the stock exchanges are responsible for approval of applications for IPOs. And the quota system was replaced by a sponsor system on securities issuance and listing. Under the sponsor system, a prospective listing firm must be sponsored by a securities company and the sponsor must assign sponsor representatives to the listing firm. The sponsor is responsible for information disclosed by listing firms during the process of IPO as well as in its aftermath.

With regards to transparency and investor protection, the 2005 Act has cre-ated private right of action for misrepresentation, insider trading, and market manipulation. Listed companies, directors and officers thereof, as well as respon-sible intermediaries, are liable for the resulting losses.

In summary, we posit that China undertook a cautious and gradual approach to market reform. It initiated limited reform measures, e.g. opening stock exchanges and allowing partial privatization of state enterprises primarily due to its concern for the ailing state enterprises, rather than paving a no-return path to a free market economy. The lack of commitment on the part of the Chinese political leadership to free markets is evident from their piecemeal legislative ini-tiatives and low priority in building democratic institutions; on the other hand, the Chinese public, due to their lack of exposure to market economy and politi-cal freedom, accepted the reforms albeit only tacitly. Besides China's overall rank of 76 out of 99 countries in the world in The World Justice Project's 2014 Rule of Law Index table, more importantly and to our point, it ranks 92 out of 99 and 96 out of 99 countries in 'constraints on government power' and 'funda-mental rights' of its citizens respectively. Further, it ranks 74 out of 99, 78 out of 99, and 79 out of 99 countries in questions of 'open government', 'regulatory enforcement', and 'civil justice' respectively.[24] More recently, a few aggressive and fundamental reform initiatives have been put in place; however, the effects of those reforms are still pending.

Indian Financial Market Reform Experience since the 1990s

The Beginning of Reforms in the 1990s

The Indian financial liberalization began in the early 1990s under the steward-ship of Dr Manmohan Singh, then the Finance Minister and the erstwhile Prime Minister of India at the time of this study. It was triggered by India's staggering external debt leading to the balance of payments (BOP) crisis of 1990–1 that had been building for decades and ignored by the political leadership deeply entrenched in petty election politics. Hence the reform in India began with the opening of the capital accounts, specifically, relaxing foreign exchange, dividend, and investment repatriation rules to entice foreign investments. In addition, the liberalization program, specifically its deregulation component made new and/ or previously 'exclusively or preferred' public sector industries open to private investment; it relaxed administrative controls on the formation, operation, and financing of business enterprises; it set performance benchmarks for the public sector that included the largest commercial banks in the country; and it allowed public sector companies to invest disposable surplus in no-interest-rate ceil-ing bank deposits. All these bode well for the Indian stock market and led the Bombay Stock Exchange Sensitive Index (BSE SENSEX), India's principal stock market index to rise from approximately Indian Lira (INR) 1000 in February 1991 to INR 4500 in March 1992.

The Harshad Mehta Scandal as the Turning Point

By all accounts, India's focus on modernizing and reforming its securities mar-ket is the direct after-effect of a series of scandals culminating in the notorious Harshad Mehta scandal that broke out in 1992, when India had just emerged from a massive balance of payments crisis. The scandal not only jolted the Indian financial market and the economy but also created a lasting distrust in the Indian financial system among international investors. For the benefit of the readers not familiar with the scandal, below is a quick summary that also provides a contex-tual understanding of the securities market reform in the aftermath of the scandal.

The Harshad Mehta scandal, or the 'securities scam' as it is popularly known, began with an initial press report in April 1992 of a shortfall in government secu-rities held by the State Bank of India, the largest public sector commercial bank in India. Preliminary investigations showed that the extent of diversions of funds from the banking system, specifically through the inter-bank government securities market to brokers, who used the funds to finance their stock purchases amounted to approximately $1.2 billion. Within two months from the initial press report, the BSE SENSEX lost 40 per cent of its peak value of INR 4500 in March 1992.

Multiple investigations and court documents later revealed that a network of brokers and several public and private sector bank officials were involved in the scam to abuse two common but highly susceptible instruments used in the Indian financial market operations known as Ready Forward (RF) and Bank Receipt (BR) respectively.[25] In essence, the perpetrators used uncovered BRs (bank authorizations guaranteeing receipt of government securities as collateral, without actually receiving the collateral) to secure interbank borrowing privileges; they borrowed money under RFs (short term debt instruments used for inter-bank borrowing) as required to invest in a rapidly growing equity market. The scam caused huge losses to many investors, brought down a few small-town banks and brokerage firms directly involved in the scam. But, arguably, it dealt the gravest blow to the Indian financial system and completely stalled the parts of the reform process dealing with liberalization, including a plan to increase equity market participation by foreign mutual funds.[26]

Reforms in the India's Stock Market after 1992

Unlike China, India had a long tradition and infrastructure of capital markets activities with as many as twenty regional stock exchanges and a dominant Bombay Stock Exchange (BSE) established in 1876 as the leading stock exchange of the country and the oldest in the region. Nevertheless, the industry operated with outdated technology; its market structure glaringly anti-competitive; and the exchanges' regulatory and surveillance systems lagged significantly behind modern securities markets in terms of handling large quantities of complex securities trading. Dr. R. H. Patil, the first managing director of the National Stock Exchange (NSE), the premier stock exchange in India today laments, 'Indian capital markets around the early 1990s were akin to the Stone Age'.[27] Yet, prior to the Harshad Mehta scandal, no one truly paid attention to how badly the stock markets were run.

Many of the securities market reforms were introduced in response to the 'securities scam' that exposed many of the structural inadequacies, e.g. lack of integration among different segments of the securities markets and lax control over high volume structured instruments including RFs and BRs, which were used by brokers to secure loans from banks to finance purchase of stocks during an unprecedented bull market. These practices were overseen by the Reserve Bank of India (RBI), India's central bank. The RBI used an inefficient and technologically outdated control system, presumably, also manned by incompetent officials with little or no training in securities trading. In a system, where transgression with impunity is the norm and corruption among public officials is rampant, it is not surprising that a large number of individuals alleged to have been involved with the scam, including the chairman of a commission investigating the scam, were convicted.[28] We now turn our attention to a few post–1992 consequential regulatory and institutional reforms related to the Indian securities market.

Table 11.6: List of financial liberalization programmes initiated since 1992.

Month /Year	Events/Reform Measures	Results, Expected and/or Desired vs. Actual
1990–4	Capitalmarket reform – 1992 – Securities and Exchange Board of India (SEBI) passed a key provision was to create a securities market regulator, Securities and Exchange Board of India with broad and sweeping power to regulate securities market; curb insider trading; Ban 'Badla', a unique instrument used in the Indian securities trading to defer settlement in 1993. 1994 – National Stock Exchange with a fully electronic trading platform opened	The SEBI was set up with the fundamental objective, 'to protect the interest of investors in securities market...' and to gain foreign institutional investors' trust in the equity market. NSE was opened to curtail BSE's almost monopoly power over trade execution. The electronic trading system on the NSE and BSE enhanced transparency of listed firms. The 'badla' ban was lifted in 1995 and a weaker version of the instrument still prevails post 1997.
1990–4	Deregulation in Banking, Insurance, and Mutual Funds sectors Dismantling interest rate control, RBI approval requirements for jumbo loans, and mandatory investment in government securities; prudential regulation with respect to capital adequacy; allowing private sector competition; Recovery of debts due to banks and the Financial Institutions Act 1993 was passed; privatize public sector banks up to 67 per cent of equity but retain control. Introduce bankruptcy law 1994 – Malhotra committee recommended opening up the insurance industry to private companies.	Government pre-emption of banks' resources through statutory liquidity ratio (SLR) and cash reserve ratio (CRR) brought down in steps; Interest rates on the deposits and lending sides almost entirely were deregulated; special recovery tribunals set up to facilitate quicker recovery of loan arrears. The RBI has given licenses to new private sector banks as part of the liberalization process. The RBI has also been granting licenses to industrial houses. PSBs are still dominating the commercial banking system although shares of the leading PSBs are traded on the stock exchanges. Opening up of mutual funds to the private sector in 1992, which ended the monopoly of Unit Trust of India (UTI)

| 1998–2004 | Mutual fund sector – Withdraw government control on governance through board appointments and simultaneously special privileges to UTI, public sector mutual fund | Between 1993 and 2001, Foreign Institutional Investors (FII) had invested $21 billion in Indian equities. Beginning with VSNL divestment via public offer in 1999–2000, 50 Central Public Sector Enterprises (CPSE) have been partially divested, out of which 15 were divested recently, since 2009. |

1998–   Mutual fund sector – Withdraw govern-   Between 1993 and 2001, Foreign
2004   ment control on governance through   Institutional Investors (FII) had
board appointments and simultaneously   invested $21 billion in Indian equities.
special privileges to UTI, public sector   Beginning with VSNL divestment via
mutual fund   public offer in 1999–2000, 50

Insurance sector – After years of stale-   Central Public Sector Enterprises
mate due to political opposition, a   (CPSE) have been partially divested,
law was finally passed to allow private   out of which 15 were divested
insurance companies with up to 26 per   recently, since 2009.
cent foreign equity offer insurance and
annuity products

Corporate governance Clause 49 stipulates
i) composition of the board of directors
and audit committee members along
with their functional responsibilities;
ii) governance and disclosure of subsidiaries;
iii) disclosures by companies;
iv) certification by CEO/CFO of companies of all financial reports; and
v) corporate governance reporting as part
of periodic financial reports.

The highlights of the post-1992 market reform agenda contained in Table 11.6 above are as follows:

Broadening the power of the Securities and Exchange Board of India (SEBI) to include market regulation: SEBI was created in 1988; however, in 1992, under the provisions of the SEBI Act, it was given broad and sweeping power to regulate and reform the equity markets with explicit focus on regulatory effectiveness and improving market conditions. One of the most critical features of the pre-1992 India's stock market was the asymmetric regulatory standards between the primary and secondary markets. On the one hand, the IPO market was overregulated. For example, in order to sell shares in the market, new companies needed to obtain permission from the government, which would also approve the price at which new equity could be sold. On the other hand, the secondary market was poorly regulated. This is exemplified by the numerous financial market scandals, including the 1992 scam. After 1992, major policy changes and new guidelines concerning IPOs were put into effect eliminating the bureaucratic and regulatory control over new share issues. The new regulatory framework also sought to strengthen investor protection by ensuring disclosure and transparency, rather than through regulatory control.

Incorporating and opening the National Stock Exchange (NSE): The NSE, the first ever demutualized stock exchange in India and the Asia Pacific region was created in the aftermath of the 1992 trading scandal to curb the virtual monopoly power of the BSE in execution services. The NSE started trading on 4 November 1994.

In less than a year, traded volume of the NSE exceeded that of the BSE and that gap has only widened over time. Figure 11.2 depicts the growing trading volume gap in recent years between BSE and NSE in terms of cash market equity trading. The NSE introduced an automated screen-based trading system, known as the National Exchange for Automated Trading (NEAT) system. The electronic trading system at NSE ensured transparency in the trading environment while reducing transaction costs and enabling real time surveillance of the securities market. The NEAT also enhanced transparency by requiring its listed companies to increase the frequency of their earnings and other corporate announcements. The BSE adopted similar automated trading technology soon afterwards.

Reforming the mutual funds sector: Another important development under the reform process has been the opening up of the mutual funds sector to the private sector in 1992, which ended the monopoly of the Unit Trust of India (UTI), a public sector entity. Further, a so called 'Disinvestment Policy' was adopted, which would enable the government to divest its holding in non-strategic public sector units including public sector mutual funds and financial institutions, such as the UTI, the insurance companies, and the Development Finance Institutions (DFIs). This would imply a significant privatization of the state portfolio holdings in the stock market. Another policy initiative in the mutual funds sector is the follow up on the 1989 breakup of the UTI and the gradual passing of its management to a professional board. The Trust had to be bailed out once in 1998, when its net asset value fell below the declared redemption price of the units, and again in 2001, when the problem recurred. It has now been decided that in the future, investors in the Unit Trust of India will bear the full risk of any loss in capital value. Competition in this sector was also enhanced by increasing the number of participants including private sector mutual funds and foreign institutional investors (FIIs), who were permitted to participate in the equity market. This proved to be a hugely successful step. Since 1993, foreign institutional investors have invested a cumulative $21 billion in Indian stocks.

Streamlining transferability, settlement, and clearing for securities transactions: Finally, to ensure transferability of securities with speed, accuracy and security, the Depositories Act was passed in 1996, which enabled the establishment of securities depositories and allowed securities to be dematerialized. Following the legislation, the National Securities Depository Limited (NSDL), India's first depository was launched. At the same time, NSE created a wholly owned subsidiary, National Securities Clearing Corporation (NSCC) as its futures clearing house.

We contend that the post-1992 reforms failed to identify and address the basic problem of lack of enforcement. It is unlikely that setting higher and rigorous standards and putting more laws into the books will solve India's problem with rampant improprieties in the securities market. In fact, despite a long standing equity market and a fairly extensive banking system with well-developed lending norms and recovery procedures, the efficacy of these norms has always been a question due to lack of enforcement. For instance, by some estimate, one-fifth of the listed companies in India do not even comply with basic shareholding reporting norms set by the regulator.[29] Further, the fact that even after all the legislative initiatives and surveillance put in place, between 1995 and 2001, four additional crises hit the equity market adequately supports our contention.[30]

The Current Status of the Indian Equity Market

We begin this section with Table 11.7 below providing an overview of the activities in the Indian securities market since 1993.

Table 11.7: Snapshot of India's publicly listed securities (equities) markets.

Year	Number of listed firms	Market capitalization (million Indian rupee)	
		BSE	NSE
1994	4413	3999999	NA
1995	5398	4472970	3489374
1996	5999	4392310	3666134
1997	5843	5037160	4415034
1998	5724	4770100	3941785
1999	5789	8033530	8529847
2000	5853	6911620	7603908
2001	5795	5668970	5420053
2002	5620	NA	NA
2003	5644	12733610	11538260
2004	4725	16859890	15791608
2005	4763	24893849	23223921
2006	4796	36243566	34262356
2007	4887	71699847	65432719
2008	4921	31447680	29167684
2009	4955	60798920	56996368
2010	5034	72967258	71393098
2011	5112	53486448	52322733
2012	5191	69218152	67637814

Source: World Federation of Exchanges (2012)

As Table 11.7 shows, India experienced significant growth in the number of new listings and market capitalization, which partially reflects increased capital raising activities by new and seasoned firms; in addition, an upward trending price level has contributed to the steep increase in market capitalization over the past two decades. Figure 11.3 below plots the BSE SENSEX index over the period 1990–2012.

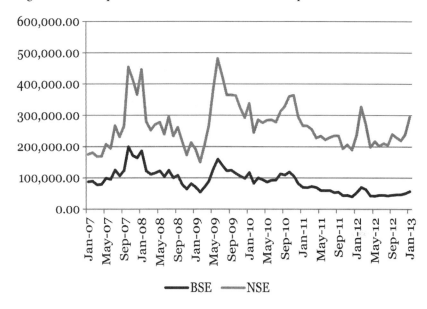

Figure 11.2: Monthly turnover of BSE and NSE in 2007–12; moneycontrol.com (2014)

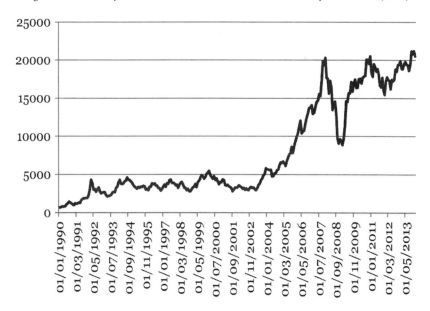

Figure 11.3: S&P BSE Index in 1990–2012; Centre for Monitoring Indian Economy (2013)

It's clear from Figure 11.3 that after a decade of reforms, in 2004, the Indian securities market, as measured by the BSE SENSEX index, crossed the March 1992 high watermark. While the market gained substantial momentum since then, the worldwide recession in 2008 once again brought the market to its knees and it lost more than half of its value. Since 2009, the market has been recovering but with a much higher volatility than before. Remarkably though, as evident from Figure 11.2, trading volumes at both NSE and BSE are still muted and have not gained much ground since early to mid–2009.

Brief Overview and Critique of the Regulatory Framework Relating to Corporate Governance

At the time of independence, in 1947, India inherited an elaborate English common laws-based corporate and securities law system. The core statute dealing with joint-stock companies in India is the 1956 Companies Act, which enumerates the functioning principles of corporations and protection of investors' rights including minority rights.[31]

The legal framework in terms of minority shareholders protection is clear and well-defined. For example, the Companies Act of 1956 provides legal protection for minority shareholders who may approach the appropriate court with original jurisdiction or the Company Court and ask for winding-up a company, and a company can be wound up on the ground that the court is of the opinion that it is just and equitable to do so. Although it is rare that shareholders indeed pursue such ownership rights, mainly because the value of a company as a wound-up is far less than its value as a going-concern. Also, the Courts have been exercising the power to force liquidate companies very cautiously. Nonetheless, they do provide the ultimate resort for minority shareholders.

Instead of referring to a court, the minority shareholders may also approach the Company Law Board. By law, the Company Law Board possesses enormous powers to resolve and dispose of any dispute brought under its authority and hence the Company Law Board is deemed to be more effective than the court system.

Yet, another safeguard in the company law is the requirement that certain major decisions have to be approved by a supermajority of 75 per cent – 90 per cent of the shareholders by value. However, in practice, many rules and regulations are violated, especially in closely held companies where the issue of corporate governance is complicated by the fact that 'majority rule' and protection of minority shareholders often runs contrary to each other.

Arguably, the central problem of corporate governance in India is the conflict between the dominant and the minority shareholders, which is deeply rooted in its historically concentrated corporate ownership structure. Unlike China's listed companies, in which shareholdings have remained largely state-owned until the recent split share structure reform, in India, dominant shareholders belong to one of following three categories: first, the government is the majority and/or dominant shareholder in public or joint sector units; second, foreign companies are the dominant shareholders in the multinational corporations; and finally, Indian business groups, where the promoters' families are the dominant share-holders of a majority of India's listed companies. As of 2006, family business groups (public sector units (PSUs), PSUs with state and federal governments holding substantial or majority shares) accounted for 60 per cent (11 per cent) of India's 500 largest companies' market capitalization and approximately 65 per cent (22 per cent) of the total market capitalization of the BSE. Also, in 2006, five out of six Indian companies on the Fortune 500 list belonged to PSUs.[32] Further, almost all (a majority) of the top twenty (50) most actively traded stocks at the NSE belong to either PSUs, e.g. State Bank of India (SBI), Oil and Natural Gas Corporation, or significant holding by the government or family and Business groups, e.g. Ambanis (Reliance), Birlas, and Tatas.

There are several legitimate concerns about the disproportionately large number of highly concentrated publicly listed corporations in India. First, the PSU firms are too large (50 Central Public Sector Enterprises accounts for more than 16 per cent of the BSE/NSE market capitalization), poorly managed, and inefficient. The foreign firms, as parent corporations of Indian subsidiaries for the most part, may not have a long term commitment to the economic growth of the country. And finally, although family and business group firms are generally associated with higher agency costs, lower profit margins and firm valuation, they are found to outperform their control groups, mainly due to the protection they traditionally receive from the Indian government. This concentrated ownership exerts a direct influence on corporate governance, particularly of business group firms. Over 40 per cent of the Indian companies had a promoter, who is either a founding controlling shareholder, an influential member of a business family, or representing a public sector financial institution, on the board of directors and in over 30 per cent of the companies, the promoter also served as the Chair of the Board.[33]

Finally, a distinctive corporate governance issue in India is the "tunnelling effect", which refers to the efforts by firms' controlling owners to indulge in personal financial gains at the expense of minority shareholders. In practice, tunnelling may take the form of a large salary, subsidized personal loans, non-arms-length asset transactions, and, in some cases, outright theft. Tunnelling may also take the form of executive compensation as it was exempted from strict regulation by the Companies Act of 1994. For instance, between 1998 and 2004, the average Indian CEO executive compensation as a fraction of profits has almost doubled, from 0.55 per cent to 1.06 per cent.[34]

A significant milestone in tightening corporate governance has been the SEBI's adoption of Clause 49 in the listing agreement initiated in 2001 and further amended in 2004. Clause 49 deals with the following issues relating to corporate governance: i) composition of the board of directors and audit committee members along with their functional responsibilities; ii) governance and disclosure of subsidiaries; iii) disclosures by companies; iv) certification by CEO/CFO of companies of all financial reports; and v) corporate governance reporting as part of periodic financial reports.

Clause 49 has been received well both by the market and the independent observers from both inside and outside the country. However, for India, it is rarely the absence of laws that is the main problem; rather, their enforcement has always been an overarching concern. In fact, the 2014 'Rule of Law' report nails down the issues of lack of enforcement and civil society orders as two principal factors for India's low overall rating. Subsequently, India ranks 95, 81, and 90 out of 99 countries in terms of 'order and security', 'regulatory enforcement' and 'civil justice' respectively.[35]

Conclusion

During the mid-1980s, China and India woke up to the unprecedented challenge of reforming their respective economies in the spirit of economic freedom, private enterprises, and open markets in a just and civil society. The two economies had very different settings, as they embarked on the process of reform, particularly the securities market reform to establish their credentials as credible alternatives to the developed economies in the West for business and investment. Yet, after more than three decades, the reform processes in both countries are still ongoing and the results are only mixed. This is confirmed by the 2014 'Rule of Law' report by the World Justice Project, which finds China and India score 0.45 and 0.48 respectively on the overall index. The low scores of China and India on the overall index, which measures socio-political stability essential for economic growth, places them among the lowest one-third among 99 countries in the World Justice Project's list.[36] A further breakdown of the overall scores indicate only minor shifts in some of the factors but the structural rigidities and obstacles to a transformative society remain firmly grounded in both China and India.

In China, at the onset, capital markets didn't exist and hence it had to start building everything anew. The government did not start with either a comprehensive plan or a disciplined approach to implement it. Yet, it laid the foundation for capital market activities, e.g. opening stock exchanges, passing laws recognizing property rights, and allowing firms to raise capital in the primary market and investors to benefit from trading in the secondary market. Evidently, the primary interest of the government was not a 'free market' reform but a limited and controlled privatization of the behemoth state enterprises (SOE), a process that is still ongoing. Besides, the building of democratic institutions necessary for ensuring a wider participation in a truly 'free and open' market is still a work-in-progress.

Like China, India is also riddled with the problems associated with the large and inefficient public sector, albeit the magnitude is much smaller. Setting that apart, in terms of market reform for India, the primary concern seems to be the rampant transgression of laws with impunity due to weak enforcement of laws and orders. Disregard of laws and institutions is evident in many walks of life in India. Nonetheless, with respect to the securities markets, where there are many sound laws and yet, the large number of scandals linked to securities markets and the corruption charges against a wide range of public officials indicate the depth of the enforcement problem in the country. In the end, rules written in the book serve no purpose unless they are wilfully adopted and enforced by the state. Hence, the ongoing challenge for India is to have fewer 'smart' laws backed by rigorous enforcements. Serious policy research from leading Indian think tanks echoes a similar sentiment.[37]

All in all, despite some progress in the legislative agenda, the vital and difficult process of building appropriate institutions, which would implement and oversee the reform, is yet to materialize in both China and India albeit for different reasons. In case of China, the resistance comes from the 'old guard' communists who fear change and 'losing control' to democratic ideals and the general public who have not completely bought into the idea of the free market. For India, reforms threaten economic interests and the way of life of the coalition of entrenched interests comprised of the elites, the bureaucratic establishment, and the power brokers, who all then stand in the way of effective enforcement. Ironically, the solutions for China and India are in complete contrast to one another. China needs an open and democratic legislative process to succeed; India requires an assertive executive branch to will its way into the future.

Acknowledgement

We are grateful to P. Srikant for our extensive discussions on Indian corporate governance practices and to Arnab Bhattacharya for Indian stock exchange data.

12 FINANCIAL SECTOR DEVELOPMENT IN SUB-SAHARAN AFRICA: A SURVEY OF EMPIRICAL LITERATURE

Radha Upadhyaya

A major irony of African development history is that the theories and models employed have largely come from outside the continent. No other region of the world has been so dominated by external ideas and models.

Thandika Mkandawire and Charles Soludo (1999)[1]

It is widely recognized that financial systems in Africa are both shallow and fragile and therefore cannot sustainably facilitate economic growth and poverty eradication.[2] This fragility and shallowness is reflected in low lending levels, high interest rate spreads, high levels of non-performing loans (NPLs) and frequent episodes of bank failures throughout Sub-Saharan Africa (SSA).[3] The financial systems in SSA were particularly fragile and bank failures were common between the mid-1980s and the mid-1990s, which also coincided with the introduction of financial liberalization reforms in the region.[4] More recent institutional changes, such as advancements in prudential regulation, improved stability in the various banking sectors, but poor access to credit, high interest rate spreads and low savings levels continue to be prevalent in the region.[5] This chapter aims to provide a critical survey of the empirical literature on financial sector development in SSA over the last twenty years.[6]

While financial systems in SSA have deepened since 2000, they remain underdeveloped and inefficient by international standards.[7] This is evident from the information provided in Table 12.1, which shows that:

- Between 2000 and 2010, private sector credit as a share of GDP increased from 15 per cent to 25 per cent. This, however, remains low when compared to similar figures for upper-middle income countries (53 per cent) and high-income countries (130 per cent).[8]

- Between 2000 and 2010, the ratio of liquid liabilities to GDP grew from 55 per cent to 37 per cent. Again, this is low when compared to similar figures for upper-middle income countries (66 per cent) and high-income countries (120 per cent).
- Finally, banking systems still remain inefficient. Interest rate spreads in SSA averaged 5 per cent in 2010 compared to 3 per cent in upper-middle income countries and 2 per cent in high-income countries.

Table 12.1: Comparative financial depth indicators for SSA in 2000 and 2010.

	SSA	SSA	SSA	Upper Middle Income	Upper Middle Income	Upper Middle Income	High Income	High Income	High Income
	2000	2005	2010	2000	2005	2010	2000	2005	2010
Liquid Liabilities /GDP	25%	28%	37%	47%	52%	66%	86%	91%	120%
Private Credit /GDP	15%	17%	25%	38%	40%	53%	82%	98%	130%
Interest Rate Spread/Margin	6%	3%	5%	4%	3%	3%	2%	2%	2%

Source: Authors calculation of means of each indicator from Financial Indicators Database (Beck et al. 2000 – revised 2009 and 2012)

In order to describe and explain the persistence of financial system underdevelopment in the region, we have grouped the surveyed empirical studies under the following four streams:

- The link between financial development and economic growth in Africa;
- The impact of financial liberalization on financial deepening in Africa;
- Bank competition in Africa; and
- Bank efficiency in Africa.

In each section, we start with an examination of cross-country studies followed by country case studies. A summary of the key findings is then presented which suggests alternative approaches to undertaking research on financial sector development in SSA.

Link between Financial Development and Economic Growth in Africa

Economic theory suggests that financial development facilitates economic growth in market economies. The proponents of this conjecture claim that the theory enjoys strong empirical evidence. The view is held so strongly among mainstream economists that some authors have referred to it as 'the Finance and Growth Consensus.'[9] Thorsten Beck and Ross Levine, applying the generalized method of moments (GMM) technique for panel data from forty countries for the period 1976–98, find a positive relationship between financial development and economic growth. They explain the transmission channel of the link as follows: financial development leads to a reduction in information and transaction costs, which, by helping to ease enterprise liquidity constrains, subsequently fosters aggregate economic activity.[10]

Using a similar approach, several scholars have also tried to investigate the empirical relationship between financial development and economic growth in SSA. In one of the early cross-country studies, John Ndebbio investigates the empirical link between financial development and economic growth using two proxy variables for financial deepening: the ratio of broad money (M2) to GDP, and the growth rate of per capita money balances.[11] The author uses the ordinary least squares (OLS) method in his estimation which covers the period 1980–9 and 32 SSA countries. He concludes that financial deepening positively affects per capita output growth. A closer investigation of his results, however, indicates that the coefficient associated with the ratio of M2 to GDP is actually statistically insignificant. But, inexplicably, the fact that both variables' estimated coefficients have expected signs is sufficient for him to conclude that his findings have important policy implications.

In another cross-country panel data study of African countries, Teame Ghirmay uses cointegration analysis and error-correction models for the period 1970–2000.[12] The study measures economic growth in terms of real GDP, and financial development in terms of the size of private sector credit. He finds that there is a positive relationship between financial development and economic growth, and concludes that the causation runs from finance to growth. Again, a closer investigation of the results show that while the theoretically expected causality is confirmed in 8 countries in the study sample, there is an apparent reverse causality in 9 countries in the sample. This, combined with the fact that there is also evidence of bi-directional causality in 6 countries in the sample, makes the generalization of the conclusion highly questionable.

Let us now discuss a selection of single-country case studies that investigate the relationship between finance and growth empirically. Oludele Akinboade investigated the relationship between financial deepening and growth in Tanzania using total bank deposits as a measure of financial deepening for the period 1966–96.[13] Using the static ordinary least squares (SOLS) method and the dynamic ordinary least squares (DOLS) method, the author found that the removal of interest rate restrictions since 1982 led to positive real interest rates, which subsequently resulted in an increase in bank deposits.[14] However, contrary to expectations, the regression results indicate that the relationship between financial deepening and economic growth is negative and statistically significant during the period of financial liberalization (1982–96), hence failing to support the finance and growth argument. In another study, Nicholas Odhiambo employs a tri-variate causality model to explore the link between and growth in Kenya for the period 1991–2005 using savings as an intermitting variable.[15] This study can be seen as

a genuine improvement on the studies that simply measure the impact of financial development on growth. The paper uses a Granger causality error-correction
model where financial deepening is measured in terms of the ratio of M2 to GDP.
The paper finds that there is a uni-directional causal flow from economic growth
to financial development. It also shows that economic growth Granger causes savings, while savings drive the development of the financial sector in Kenya. Based
on these findings, Odhiambo notes that any argument that financial development
unambiguously leads to economic growth should be treated with extreme caution.

In another study, the same author, Odhiambo uses a bi-variate causality model
to investigate the link between financial development and economic growth in
Kenya.[16] The period under consideration is longer in this study, from 1968 to
2004. The methodology of estimation is the same in both papers although the
second paper does not employ savings as an intermitting variable. Surprisingly,
however, the second paper provides a completely opposite conclusion:

> The results from the causality test show that by and large the finance-led growth cau-
> sality predominates in Kenya. Although there is evidence of a weak bi-directional
> relationship between financial depth and economic growth in Kenya, the causal link
> from finance to growth seems to override the causal link from growth to finance.[17]

As our brief overview of the empirical studies shows, it is difficult to establish a
strong empirical link between finance and growth and the results are often sensitive to changes in model specifications, sampling periods, countries in the sample,
and variables used as proxies for financial deepening. Charles Kenny and David
Williams convincingly argue that empirical results based on econometric estimations will inevitably have disappointing results as they assume that the process of
development is homogenous across countries, whereas history has shown that it
is highly heterogeneous.[18] Similar criticism can also be levied against the finance
and growth studies mentioned above. Unfortunately, however, the limitations of
estimation methodologies are often ignored and the robustness of the empirical
link between finance and growth is taken for granted without due scrutiny. For
example, while recognizing empirical inconsistencies in the literature, a recent survey study by Victor Murinde argues that the weight of evidence is still in favour of
finance facilitating growth.[19] According to this study, these inconsistencies can be
resolved by the use of more sophisticated technical methods of data analysis.

All in all, the economics profession's obsession with formal modelling and
associated econometric testing has masked the real question in this subject area:
under what circumstances does finance actually lead to economic growth, and
more specifically pro-poor, growth? According to Laurence Harris, formal models should be used sparingly as a basis for policy making for African countries as
they provide very little information on the transmission channels from finance to
growth.[20]

Impact of Financial Liberalization on Financial Deepening in Africa

The 'financial repression' literature, pioneered by Ronald McKinnon and Edward Shaw in the 1970s, advocated that financial liberalization would end credit rationing by the state, thereby ensuring more efficient allocation of scarce formal credit resources on the basis of market risk and return.[21] This argument formed the rationale for financial liberalization reforms undertaken in most African countries in the 1980s and the early 1990s as part of the structural adjustment policies advocated by the World Bank and the International Monetary Fund (IMF). It was expected that, by fostering financial deepening and improving mobilization of private savings to their most productive use, financial liberalization would ultimately facilitate economic growth. In particular, the main mechanism through which liberalization would influence resource mobilization was through savings. A study of a cross section of African countries found that the effect of real interest rates on savings is weak or non-existent.[22] Further, a general consensus in the literature is that financial sector reforms did not lead to an increase in savings and investments, improvements in financial sector intermediation, and reductions in interest rate spreads.[23] There is also recognition that financial liberalization was accompanied by increased instability and higher incidence of bank insolvencies.[24] Experience from African countries suggests that credit to the private sector did not grow after liberalization and in fact banks shifted their portfolios towards government stocks.[25] It was observed that post-liberalization, banks moved in two dramatically opposite directions: they either avoided all but the lowest risk lending, or exhibited a reckless expansion of lending even to insolvent clients.[26] Therefore, instead of granting long-term loans, banks maintained highly liquid portfolios and there was a high incidence of non-performing loans.[27]

As a result, the failure of liberalization reforms created a vigorous debate in the literature. At a theoretical level, working within a new institutional framework, Joseph Stiglitz has emphasized that credit rationing in financial markets is not merely the result of 'financial repression', but is rather inherent to any financial market due to pervasive information asymmetries and incomplete markets.[28] Furthermore, the increase in interest rates following liberalization tends to worsen the risk composition of banks' loan portfolios, aggravating the problems of adverse selection and moral hazard.[29]

In general, mainstream authors have argued that liberalization failed mainly due to the incompleteness of reforms, poor sequencing and lack of government will.[30] Furthermore, it has been argued that certain 'initial conditions' must be met before financial sector reform is embarked upon. These include: reasonably stable macroeconomic conditions, sound financial conditions of banks and their borrowers, attainment by bank personnel of basic minimum financial skills, and checks and balances to minimize collusion amongst banks.[31] In other words, there is a firm acknowledgement of the need to build 'institutional capacity' before undertaking reforms.[32] According to the World Bank:

> In designing reform programs, African governments and external donors have some-
> times placed too much faith in quick fixes. Reform programs overestimated the benefits
> of restructuring balance sheets and recapitalising banks – and underestimated the time it
> takes to improve financial infrastructure in an environment where the main borrowers (the
> government and public enterprises) are financially distressed and institutionally weak.[33]

The recognition of the importance of institutional factors is useful. However, there is a methodological issue with this sort of analysis as it reduces historical development to a small set of 'initial conditions'. Further, given the international financial institutions' involvement in the process of liberalization in most SSA countries, it is hypocritical of the World Bank to talk about 'poor sequencing' of reforms. Liberalization was based on the explicit principle that once prices (in this case interest rates) were set free, market forces would ensure the efficient mobilization of savings.

A survey article reviewing studies that attempt to explain why financial liberalization did not achieve the desired results in SSA notes that the peculiarity of African economies and the low quality of their institutions might have been a primary culprit.[34] But, in methodological terms, the idea of institutions 'peculiar' to Africa implies a bias towards a monolithic idea of what constitutes a good institution. A review of institutional developments in Europe and Asia reveals great institutional diversity, yet this is not reflected in work on African institutions. The underlying reasons behind the failure of financial liberalization policies in SSA are extremely complicated. For example, in countries such as Ghana and Malawi reform was more gradual. However, they experienced only a few positive changes in financial indicators, and on balance the results were no different compared to those in faster reforming countries.[35] A more credible explanation points to fragmentation and segmentation of markets in SSA and the fact that liberalization was carried out as a response to severe economic crises and acute macroeconomic instability.[36]

Bank Competition in Africa

Neoclassical economics begins with the assumption that increased competition will lead to lower costs and enhanced efficiency in financial markets. However, there is a growing recognition, even in the mainstream literature, that this is a rather naïve assumption and that the information-intensive nature of the banking industry implies that banking is bound to be naturally less competitive than other sectors.[37] Theoretically, therefore, an oligopolistic (highly concentrated) banking sector can either lead to more efficient market outcomes due to economies of scale, or to higher interest rate spreads and inefficiency due to the collusive practices of the few large banks.[38] In this sense, the links between competition and efficiency are not clear as far as the banking industry is concerned.

The banking systems in SSA are highly concentrated as shown in Table 12.2, where the bank is defined as the asset shares of the three largest banks to total banking sector assets. While bank concentration ratios in SSA have fallen from 84 per cent in 2000 to 72 per cent in 2010, they are still high by international standards. For comparison, the bank concentration ratio in 2010 for upper-middle income countries was 61 per cent and for high-income countries 64 per cent.

Table 12.2: Bank concentration ratios for SSA, upper-middle, and high income countries in 2000, 2005, and 2010.

	Year	Bank Concentration Ratio
SSA	2000	84.04
	2005	77.17
	2010	72.80
Upper-middle	2000	64.43
	2005	64.10
	2010	61.06
High income	2000	64.85
	2005	64.00
	2010	63.63

Source: Authors calculation of means of each indicator from Financial Indicators Database (T. Beck, A. Demirgüç-Kunt and R. Levine, 'A New Database on Financial Development and Structure', *World Bank Economic Review*, 14:3 (2000; revised 2009 and 2012), pp. 597–605).

Despite the general recognition in the literature that countries differ in their optimal level of competition intensity, empirical work on Africa continues to follow a Structure-Conduct-Performance (S-C-P) paradigm where it is assumed that the low levels of competition is the main contributor of poor bank performance in the region.[39] More crucially, studies assume that a high level of concentration automatically results in lower competition. For example, using data from 13 African countries, Mthuli Ncube argues that the oligopolistic nature of the banking market is the key reason for the observed high interest rate spreads in his study.[40] Ephraim Chirwa, in an extensive study of the Malawian banking industry, also carries out a test of the S-C-P hypothesis by analysing the determinants of bank profitability.[41] He finds that market concentration has a positive and significant impact on profitability in the Malawian banking industry, lending support to the collusion hypothesis. He also argues that competition exists only on the fringes, e.g. nine private banks account for 25 per cent of the market share and two state-owned banks control 75 per cent of the market. This leads to a policy conclusion that there is a need to privatize state-owned banks to encourage competition. But, without going into the extensive debate on the merits of privatization, experience shows that privatization of state-owned banks did not reduce the concentration problem in other African countries.[42]

By contrast, the industrial organization literature shows that competition is determined by not only concentration and market structure, but also by contestability.[43] Numerous empirical studies were conducted to measure competition defined in terms of contestability, following the seminal work by John Panzar and James Rosse.[44] The Panzar and Rosse model investigates the extent to which a change in factor input prices is reflected in (equilibrium) revenues earned by a specific bank. The model provides a statistic (H statistic) as a measure of the degree of competition. Table 12.3 below explains the interpretative value of the H statistic. Stijn Claessens and Luc Laeven use this model to estimate the degree of competitiveness in a cross section of 50 developed and developing countries for the period 1994–2001.[45] Thierry Buchs and Johan Mathisen also apply the Panzar and Rosse model to estimate the H statistic for Ghana for the same period.[46] A selection of the results from these studies is summarized in Table 12.4. As can be seen from Table 12.4, an H statistic of between zero and one seem to be the 'default' result of applying this methodology, which makes the usefulness of this model to establish the level of competitiveness highly questionable.[47] Furthermore, the model is based on several restrictive assumptions, including the (long run) equilibrium operating capacity of banks. Buchs and Mathisen recognize this problem, but they justify their use of the model by stating that they are abiding by the existing literature.

Table 12.3: Interpretation of H statistic.

Value of H	Implied Market Structure
$H \leq 0$	Monopoly, colluding oligopoly
0	Monopolistic competition
$H = 1$	Perfect competition, natural monopoly in perfectly contestable market

Source: Claessens and Laeven (2003)

Table 12.4: Estimates of the H Statistic for different countries/regions.

Country	Period	H – Statistic
Kenya	1994–2001	0.58
Ghana	1998–2003	0.56
Nigeria	1994–2001	0.67
South Africa	1994–2001	0.85
North America (median)	1994–2001	0.67

South America (median)	1994–2001	0.73
East Asia (median)	1994–2001	0.67
South Asia (median)	1994–2001	0.53
Western Europe (median)	1994–2001	0.67
Eastern Europe (median)	1994–2001	0.68

Source: T. Buchs and J. Mathisen, 'Competition and Efficiency in Banking: Behavioural Evidence from Ghana', *IMF Working Paper, 05*:17 (Washington, DC: IMF, 2005) and Claessens and Laeven (2003)

In another study, Adam Mugume uses the Panzar and Rosse methodology to analyse the competitiveness of the Ugandan banking sector from 1995 to 2005 and finds the following results: the H statistic is 0.28 for the entire period, 0.40 for the 2000–05 period and 0.31 for the 1995–99.[48] He argues that this suggests that the Ugandan banking sector is characterized by monopolistic competition with improved competition in the later period. However, a closer investigation of the results indicate that concentration did not change dramatically in the period under consideration and there is little specific analysis to explain why this might have been the case.

In another related study, Musonda uses the Panzar and Rosse methodology to analyse competitiveness of the Zambian banking sector from 1998 to 2006.[49] Table 12.5 below summarizes his results. Since the five largest banks in Zambia control over 80 per cent of the industry, the concentration ratios would imply that the industry is oligopolistic. However, using the Panzar-Rosse model, Musonda argues that key findings of the study are that Zambian banks earned their income under conditions of monopolistic competition. Also, despite the fact that the results show a rather mixed picture, e.g. competition is higher amongst foreign banks for total income but it is lower when looking at interest income, he concludes that foreign banks compete more intensely than domestic banks. It can be argued that while this study is sophisticated in its application of econometric techniques, it fails to explain the true nature of competition in the Zambian banking market. In particular, the social and historical factors that shape the reputation of banks and the impact of this on competition between banks are completely ignored.

In this sense, it is more useful to assess the nature of competition in its full complexity and to discuss whether an increase in competition is associated with improvements in performance or not. Samuel Maimbo carries out a similar analysis in an interesting study that links competition issues to bank failures in Zambia.[50] The study highlights that in addition to monitoring CAMELs financial ratios, in depth analysis of other factors such as the business strategies of local banks, e.g. reliance on cost-based competition, can reveal more fundamental weaknesses in the banks that are likely to fail.[51]

Table 12.5: Summary of H statistic for Zambia.

	H – **Statistic**
Total Revenue (all banks)	0.711
Interest Revenue (all banks)	0.721
Foreign Banks (total income)	0.678
Local Banks (total income)	0.594
Foreign Banks (interest income)	0.64
Local Banks (interest income)	0.654
Large Banks (total income)	0.592
Small Banks (total income)	0.656
Large Banks (interest income)	0.656
Small Banks (interest income)	0.667

Source: A. Musonda, 'Deregulation, Market Power and Competition: An Empirical Investigation of the Zambian Banking Industry', *CSAE Conference 2008– Economic Development
in Africa* (Oxford: CSAE, 2008).

Bank Efficiency in Africa

Another recent stream in the literature is the estimation of bank efficiency in
SSA. This follows a similar trend in the mainstream literature where there are
many studies that attempt to move beyond a simple comparison of financial
ratios to econometric modelling, measuring the efficiency of financial institutions using frontier analysis. In this section, we will discuss briefly the theory of
frontier analysis followed by its application to measuring bank efficiency in SSA.
The main aim of this section is to show that despite its popularity, the method
is based on a false sense of rigour and subsequently does not contribute to a
deeper understanding of the fundamental problems inherent in the SSA banking systems.

In general, this method involves establishing an efficient benchmark; a frontier.
The distance of a firm from this frontier measures the extent of the firm's inefficiency.
The frontier is usually established in terms of either cost efficiency (maximum output for given input) or allocative efficiency (given output for minimum input).
Hasan provides a good critical summary of the theoretical underpinnings of these
studies and highlights that although allocative and technical efficiency measures
are used interchangeably in the empirical literature, theoretically they are different
concepts.[52]

The majority of empirical studies in this area follow two stages. In the first stage
(in)efficiency from the frontier is measured. The two most common methods of
measuring efficiency are: a parametric stochastic frontier analysis (SFA) and a non-
parametric data envelopment analysis (DEA). The models of output and input
functions have become highly sophisticated deploying translog and other flexible

functional forms in preference to the more traditional Cobb-Douglass production function. Frontier analysis can be applied across a variety of industries.

In studies of banking, there are no consistent measures of input or output used to define the frontier. Popular input measures include labour costs, physical capital costs, the cost of deposits and the total value of deposits. Popular measures of output include total value of loans, total assets, income from loans and off balance sheet items. The efficiency results are sometimes decomposed using a Malmquist decomposition into technical efficiency and technological change, with the former further decomposed into a pure efficiency change and scale efficiency change. This helps to explain changes over time, changes between companies, changes between regions.[53]

In the second stage of the analysis, the calculated measures of (in)efficiency are used as a dependent variable in a model with a selection of determinants of (in)efficiency as independent variables. Allen Berger and David Humphrey provide a summary of 121 studies in 21 countries that used these efficiency models and highlight some of limitations of the approach.[54] Here we discuss two such studies that focus on the SSA region: Kenneth Egesa who attempts to understand the efficiency of banks in Uganda and Jehovaness Aikaeli whose analysis looks at banks in Tanzania.[55]

Egesa measures the changes in bank efficiency from 1993–2005 for 11 banks in Uganda where reforms of the financial sector started in 1992. He measures bank efficiency using a non-parametric Malmquist Index. At an aggregate level, the author finds an overall decline in efficiency between 1993–2005. However, the steep decline in efficiency after 1993 is slightly reversed by the increase in productivity from 2002. Results for efficiency change at an individual bank level are shown in Table 12.6. According Egesa, improvements among four foreign banks and one local bank over the entire period can be explained entirely by technological improvements. But, besides giving an explanation of the results, this analysis does not provide any meaningful explanations of the changes in bank efficiency in Uganda from 1993–2005, including the nature of technological improvements that took place. In the second stage, the author then assesses the determinants of efficiency using a two way error components model. The results are summarized in Table 12.7.[56] Unfortunately, very little thought appears to have been given in deciding the independent variables in the model. For example, it is tautological to use the return on assets as an independent variable. This variable is an output that is used to calculate the efficiency frontier in the first stage. Therefore, it is not surprising that the most significant variable in the model is the return on assets.[57] Furthermore, while the econometric model is sophisticated, there is little analysis as to why the results of the analysis are in most cases opposite to what is expected.

Table 12.6: Bank and ownership efficiency change measures in Uganda, 1993–2005.

	Bank Ownership	Technical Efficiency change index	Technological change index	Pure efficiency change index	Scale efficiency change index	Total factor productivity change index
1	Foreign	0.997	1.009	0.996	1.001	1.006
2	Foreign	1.000	1.013	1.000	1.000	1.013
3	Foreign	1.000	0.982	1.000	1.000	0.982
4	Local	0.985	1.021	0.992	0.993	1.006
5	Local	1.000	0.974	1.000	1.000	0.974
6	Foreign	1.000	0.999	1.000	1.000	0.999
7	Foreign	0.994	1.011	0.996	0.999	1.005
8	Local	1.000	0.984	1.000	1.000	0.984
9	Foreign	1.000	0.975	1.000	1.000	0.975
10	Foreign	1.000	1.025	1.000	1.000	1.025
11	Foreign	0.994	0.980	0.998	0.996	0.974
Mean		0.997	0.997	0.998	0.999	0.995

Source: K. Egesa, 'Financial Sector Liberalisation and Productivity Change in Uganda's Commercial Banking Sector', *AERC Biannual Research Workshop* (Nairobi: AERC, 2006).

Table 12.7: Regression results of the determinants of productivity in Uganda, 1993–2005.

Variable	Measured by	Expected sign	Hypothesis	Empirical results
Size	Assets of bank / Total assets of banks in industry	+ve	Economies of scale, large size → high productivity	-ve but not significant
Capital adequacy	Core capital / Risk weighted assets	+ve	High capital → high productivity	-ve
Asset quality	Non-performing loans / Total loans	-ve	High non performing loans → low productivity	+ve but not significant
Shareholder stake in Bank	Equity / total assets	+ve	High shareholder stake, reduced agency problems → high productivity	+ve
Liquidity	Total Assets / Total Deposits	-ve	High (excess) liquidity → low productivity	+ve
Return on Assets	Return on Assets	+ve	Higher profits → increased productivity	+ve

positive = +ve; negative = -ve

Source: Egesa, 'Financial Sector Liberalisation and Productivity Change in Uganda's Commercial Banking Sector', p. 26

Aikaeli's study on the other hand is based on the banking system in Tanzania using data from 1998–2004. The author uses three different methods in his analysis: a non-parametric DEA, anon-parametric Malmquist index of efficiency change, and a parametric SFA. The paper is useful as it tries to explain the segmentation in the market by calculating efficiency indexes for different segments.[58] Results for efficiency change using the non-parametric Malmquist index at the segment level are shown in Table 12.8. The results indicate that the largest change in efficiency occurred amongst the largest privately-owned banks, and that the overall efficiency of smaller privately-owned banks decreased. This finding contradicts the estimation results obtained using the other two models: the efficiency of small banks increased under both the DEA and SFA approaches. Again, the author makes no attempt to explain why the models gave differing results.

In the second part of the analysis, the indexes of inefficiency, calculated using the SFA model, are regressed against possible determinants of inefficiency using a Tobit model. The estimation results, which are presented in Table 12.9, have serious flaws. The model specifies that the second variable is capital adequacy. In banking, capital adequacy refers to shareholder funds that are viewed as a cushion in case of a bank run.[59] But, in the empirical operationalization of the regression, Aikaeli uses expenditure on capital goods and spending on fixed assets as the measure of capital adequacy. This shows a clear lack of understanding of bank balance sheet as assets are confused with equity measures.[60] Again, there is no clear attempt to explain why the coefficient of the bank size variable has an opposite sign, and why asset quality, which according to theory should be a significant determinant of efficiency, is not statistically significant.

Table 12.8: Bank and ownership efficiency change measures in Tanzania, 1998–2005.

Group	Technical efficiency change index	Technological change index	Pure efficiency change index	Scale efficiency change index	Total factor productivity change index
Large private-owned	1.000	1.131	1.000	1.000	1.131
Large foreign-owned	1.000	1.056	1.000	1.000	1.056
Small private-owned	1.002	0.992	1.000	1.002	0.994
Mean	1.001	1.058	1.000	1.001	1.059

Source: J. Aikaeli, 'Commercial Banks Efficiency in Tanzania', *CSAE Conference - Economic Development in Africa* (Oxford: CSAE, 2008).

Table 12.9: Regression results of the determinants of bank efficiency in Tanzania.

Variable	Measured by	Expected sign	Hypothesis	Empirical results
Size	Assets of bank / Total assets of banks in industry	-ve	Economies of scale, small size → high inefficiency	+ve and significant
Capital adequacy	Spending on capital goods (fixed assets, office fittings)/ Non-tax expenses	- ve	Low capital → high inefficiency	-ve and significant
Assets quality	Non-performing Loans / Total Loans	+ve	Low asset quality → high inefficiency	Not significant
Labour compensation	Salaries and remuneration / Other non-tax expenses	-ve	Low compensation → high inefficiency	-ve and significant
Excess liquidity	Liquidity – statutory liquidity	+ve	High (excess) liquidity → high inefficiency	+ve and significant
Pseudo R squared				-0.1634

positive = +ve; negative = -ve

Source: J. Aikaeli, 'Efficiency and the Problem of Excess Liquidity in Commercial Banks in Tanzania' (PhD dissertation, University of Dar es Salaam, 2006)

In short, although both of these papers employ the mainstream methodology, they do not meet the standards of rigour set by mainstream researchers. They do not acknowledge the limitations of efficiency models, which are noted even by the strongest proponents of the frontier analysis approach. For instance, the key difference between the parametric SFA method and the non-parametric DEA method is that they maintain different assumptions about the probability distribution of banking data.[61] The caveat is that there is no simple rule for determining the true distribution of banking data, yet the choice of measurement method strongly affects the measurement of inefficiency and therefore extreme care needs to be taken when deciding which method should ultimately be used. Neither of the papers makes an attempt to explain how this limitation would impact their results.

Egesa uses a non-parametric model on the grounds that a parametric model requires large data sets which are not available for African countries.[62] However, if the banking process in the sampled countries is characterized largely by stochastic elements, then the non-parametric approach may not be appropriate.

Further, the cross-country comparisons of, even simple banking ratios is fraught with difficulties due to differences in product mix, capital structures, accounting conventions and macroeconomic environments.[63] Hence, it should not come as a surprise that when Aikaeli employs all three methods – a non-parametric DEA, a non-parametric Malmquist decomposition and a parametric SFA – for the Tanzanian banking sector, he gets conflicting results.[64]

Hence, the studies can be criticized as lacking sufficient rigour because they draw strong conclusions on thin evidence. For example, in the Aikaeli study, using the DEA model, the average efficiency of all banks during the study period in Tanzania is 97 per cent, which is higher than the comparator figures for the UK banking sector (83 per cent) and the Italian banking sector (80 per cent). The study makes no attempt to explain this anomaly. Rather, it simply interprets the result as an indication of the high efficiency of commercial banks in Tanzania. Aikaeli's conclusion is also startling in light of all the problems of the Tanzanian banking system, including high interest rate margins and regionally low levels of credit to the private sector which the author highlights in the study.

In summary, at least six methodological criticisms can be raised against the approach. First, innumerable factors can influence efficiency including: agency problems, regulatory issues, legal issues, organizational issues, scale and scope issues and the CAMELs rating issues. But, the tendency in practice is to use a 'pick-and-mix' approach in choosing independent variables as the determinants of efficiency in the second stage of the analysis. Second, the link between bank efficiency and intermediation is not necessarily direct. It is argued that more efficient banks mean improved profitability, greater intermediation, lower prices and better service quality for consumers; provided some of the efficiency savings are applied towards improving capital buffers, even safety and soundness of banks can be improved.[65] But, while efficiency may lead to more profitable institutions, it is a leap of faith to assume that allocative efficiency will automatically lead to lower prices for clients, higher lending levels, and increased safety of institutions.

Third, due to the specialization of banks, it is problematic to assume that all banks produce homogenous outputs and operate on the same efficiency frontier.[66] Therefore the comparability of efficiency of institutions even within a single banking sector can be problematic. Fourth, it is the nature of bank lending to reject applications that do not meet banks' criteria of creditworthiness. These decisions usually improve bank efficiency by reducing future non-performing loans. Yet, under frontier analysis, this process would correspond to a use of inputs without any corresponding increase in output, and therefore it would be measured as a reduction in efficiency. Fifth, frontier analysis does not capture non-price and social factors such as interpersonal networks which are extremely important in lending processes in developing countries. Finally, and most crucially, the analysis cannot account for the impact of market segmentation, implying it is unrealistic to assume that banks operate on a single efficiency frontier, particularly in markets that are segmented. In this sense, the frontier models cannot truly measure intermediation efficiency, which is the key function of banking institutions.

Concluding Remarks

This chapter critically reviewed the extant empirical literature on financial sector developments in SSA. There is a general recognition in the literature that financial sector liberalization in SSA did not generate the expected results. Studies written from the perspectives of orthodox as well as heterodox schools attempt to explain the reasons for the failure of reforms. However, most of the studies we surveyed here fail to shed lights on why financial systems in SSA remain shallow and inefficient. In particular we observe the following weaknesses in the literature.

- Cross-country and single-country studies that attempt to find an empirical link between finance and growth are methodologically weak as they do not take into account specificity of country mechanisms.
- Single-country case studies often employ the S-C-P paradigm where it is assumed that the poor performance of African banking in terms of high interest rate spreads can be attributed to high levels of concentration and low levels of competition. These studies do not recognize that in banking economies of scale do not always lead to efficiency, but can lead to improved reputation and stability of banks with complex effects on competition.
- Some of the single-country case studies that measure efficiency of banks, place mathematical and econometric complexity above theoretical clarity and practical relevance.

There is a consensus in the literature that finance plays an important role the economic process in market economies. However, country specific fundamental institutional factors, such as social factors and interpersonal networks, that are precursors to financial deepening, need further research in SSA. The current methodologies used by African economists are insufficiently rigorous to explain fundamental issues and problems. On the whole, it seems that the studies we surveyed here have followed the trend in mainstream economics by appearing to become more scientifically rigorous, with an increased focus on econometrics. In reality, they lack theoretical insights to explain real world phenomena.[67]

It has been argued that future research on financial sector development should focus on relevance. In this we argue the William Reddaway dictum, which states that it is better to be technically crude and relevant than to be technically sophisticated and irrelevant, should be a guiding principle for researchers.[68] This applies especially to African researchers because there can be no 'African Renaissance' without an African-focused intelligentsia driving it.[69] This approach involves a shift from a traditional research paradigm to the one that asks not only 'what' questions but also scrutinizes 'how' these questions are answered. Some suggestions for more fruitful research questions, for example, may include the following:

- Under what circumstances and institutional conditions does financial development lead to economic growth?
- What are the most likely transmission channels from finance to growth?
- How do banks make lending decisions in specific African countries and what are the constraints that they face in terms of increasing the supply of credit to the private sector?
- How do banks raise deposits in specific African countries and what are the constraints that they face to increase their deposit bases?
- What is the country specific role of social factors in turn influencing competition and resource allocation?[70]

Finally, this chapter is a plea by the author for African economists to follow a pluralist methodology in conducting research that is critical and relevant.

13 MICROCREDIT, MICRO-ENTERPRISES, AND SELF-EMPLOYMENT OF WOMEN: EXPERIENCE FROM THE GRAMEEN BANK IN BANGLADESH

M. Jahangir Alam Chowdhury

By breaking the vicious cycle of poverty through self-empowerment, respect and social dignity, micro-enterprises contribute to poverty reduction. They allow poor people to increase their income, accumulate assets, and enter into mainstream society. Benefits of starting a micro-enterprise go beyond an individual and a household. Others in society also benefit from microenterprise development as it fosters social relations and networks, civic engagement, community solidarity, and social capital.[1] Micro-enterprises' contribution to aggregate economic activity is also important; they engage in innovative activities, create jobs, and facilitate economic growth. According to the Bangladesh Economic Census of 2001 and 2003, there were 3.6 million microenterprises[2] in the country.[3] Of these, 56 per cent were located in rural areas and 40 per cent operated in household premises. Microenterprises created more than 3 million jobs in 2011 in Bangladesh, contributing to just over 5 per cent of the country's GDP.[4]

Microenterprises not only create self-employment, but also generate jobs for others. More specifically, risk-oriented entrepreneurship has a positive and large impact on regional labour productivity and growth.[5] Entrepreneurial activities that promote innovation play an important role in facilitating economic growth.[6] Similarly, it is found that newly established firms with high potential to grow in future have significant impact on the economic growth of a country.[7] Fast growing new small and medium enterprises (SMEs) usually account for most of the newly-created jobs in developing countries.

A recent study found a negative relationship between economic development and the level of self-employment in the labour force.[8] More specifically, it has been argued that the relationship between economic development and entrepreneurship is U-shaped.[9] At the initial stage of economic development, when per capita income is low but growing fast, a shift occurs in economies from agriculture to manufacturing, implying economies of scale in production. During this period, larger enterprises become more cost efficient, while small and medium enterprises become comparatively cost inefficient,[10] resulting in the closure of many SMEs.[11] In addition, rising real wages increase the opportunity cost of self-employment; as a result, many individuals leave self-employment and join large enterprises as wage earners. But, as the prospect of economic development improves, so does household income and wealth, which increases consumers' demand for goods and services, and subsequently creates opportunities for people to start new micro-enterprises.

However, the relationship between entrepreneurship and economic development is likely to be more complex than the above-described U-shaped relationship. Some scholars argued that the relationship may in fact be S-shaped.[12] According to this view, at the initial stage of economic development, entrepreneurship is *factor* driven, enabling entrepreneurs to take advantage of cheap labour and natural resource endowments. In the next stage, entrepreneurship becomes *efficiency* driven. At this stage, entrepreneurs take advantage of efficient infrastructure, the business–friendly environment, the improved skills of workers etc. In the final stage, entrepreneurship becomes *innovation* driven: entrepreneurs use the most advanced technologies which give them a competitive advantage over those who find themselves in the earlier two stages. The relationship between economic development and entrepreneurship in the factor driven stage is positive and has a relatively flat slope. A similar relationship also exists in the innovation driven stage. But, the slope of the positive relationship becomes increasingly steep in the efficiency driven stage, hence giving an overall S-shape to the relationship.

Lack of access to external finance is one of the main factors constraining microenterprise operations and growth.[13] Poor people are excluded from the formal credit markets for a number of reasons: (i) poor people do not possess adequate collateral, (ii) formal financial institutions such as banks ration credit and prefer working with high income clients, and (iii) bureaucratic and lengthy procedures of loan sanctioning are too complex and time consuming for the poor. On the other hand, informal financial sources are exploitative in nature.[14]

Microcredit programmes were developed to deal with the limitations of formal and informal financial institutions in providing, especially women, with the required funds for starting micro-enterprises. Microcredit can broadly be defined as small loans that are given to poor people without collateral for income generating purposes. While formal financial institutions such as commercial banks tend to lend predominantly to men, as a rule microcredit programmes target women. Currently, 96 per cent of all members of the Grameen Bank, which pioneered microcredit programmes in Bangladesh, are women. The reason why women have been targeted for giving microcredit in Bangladesh is that women's access to credit has been recognized as an important factor that significantly contributes to the household welfare.[15] It has been found that the access of women to microcredit increases consumption,[16] improves the nutritional levels of household consumption, enhances aspirations for children's education in households,[17] and contributes to the reduction of household poverty.[18] Another reason for targeting women is to empower women in their households by helping them establish micro-enterprises and hence to create a stable source of income. One may confuse these women-run micro-enterprises with the family-run micro-enterprises that are managed and controlled by male members in the household. Usually women do not have any control in family-run micro-enterprises.

Considering the main objective of microfinance institutions is to empower women through self-employment, this chapter intends to evaluate whether access to microcredit from the Grameen Bank has enabled females to become self-employed by owning micro-enterprises which are fully managed and owned by them. For this purpose, we analyse a household level data set of 521 households ($N=521$). The data set contains detailed information on the self-employment status of all household members, and loans from various sources as well as information on other socio-economic aspects of households. The decision to participate in a microcredit programme depends upon some observable as well as unobservable characteristics. Participants in microcredit programmes are self-selecting and they differ from those who do not participate. Arguably, the participants are more entrepreneurial than the non-participants. For these reasons, microcredit programme participants are going to be different from non-participants. Therefore, a comparison between microcredit programme participants and non-microcredit programme participants may overestimate or underestimate the impact of microcredit programme participation on the self-employment status of women. Keeping this in mind, a comparison has been made between more established programme participants and new programme-participants that have just received their first loans or have not received any loans yet. Considering the nature of the dependent variables, a Probit model has been used for estimation purposes.

The remainder of this chapter is organized as follows. First, the microcredit sector and the Grameen Bank in Bangladesh are described. Then, a theoretical framework on credit constraint and other determinants of womens' self-employment is outlined. The estimation strategy is then discussed. The penultimate section discusses the nature of the data used in the study. Finally, results, summary and conclusions are presented.

The Microcredit Sector and the Grameen Bank in Bangladesh

Muhammad Yunus, the founder of the Grameen Bank, undertook a research project in 1976 to identify the causes and the extent of poverty in the villages surrounding the University of Chittagong in Bangladesh. He found that some poor women were forced to sell their handicraft products to middlemen at prices that were much lower than the market price, partly because they obtained their raw materials from the middlemen on credit. Then Professor Yunus tried to estimate the amount of capital required to buy the necessary raw materials to produce the handicraft products. Professor Yunus, to his surprise, found that a mere Taka (Tk.) 856 ($21) would be sufficient to buy the necessary raw materials for forty-two women. Out of these forty-two women, some required as little capital as Tk. 10, and the highest required amount was Tk 65.[19] Professor Yunus thus realized that the lack of capital was the root cause of poverty as it was the main obstacle preventing the continuation or the starting-up of income generating activities in rural areas. He then decided to provide these forty-two poor women with the required capital amount of Tk. 856 from his own pocket. After that, he started contacting and pursuing formal sector commercial banks to provide poor but economically active women the necessary external finance to start production of handicraft products and/or to expand the capacity of already existing production. Initially, formal financial institutions refused to provide credit as poor women lacked the appropriate collateral to secure bank loans. Formal financial institutions also argued that the proposed loans to poor women were so tiny that the interest income from these loans would not cover administrative costs. In response, Professor Yunus offered himself as a guarantor. The process in the establishment of the Grameen Bank began from this humble arrangement.

Professor Yunus and his colleagues devised a unique technology to provide small credit to poor people without collateral, which is now known as the Grameen Bank model; and the small loans provided to poor people are known as microcredit. In 1983, the result of Professor Yunus' research project became a specialized formal bank through a government statute and it was named as the Grameen Bank. It is now regulated by the Central Bank of Bangladesh, like any other formal financial institution. As can be seen from Table 13.1, the Grameen Bank achieved a growth rate of 23 per cent per annum in cumulative disbursement of all loans during the period 1986 to 2012. In 1986, the cumulative disbursement of all loans was $57 million. It went up to $13,043 million in 2012. The annual disbursement of loans was $18 million in 1986 and it increased to $1,447 million in 2012 which translates into an annual growth rate of 18 per cent. The Grameen Bank also provides its members with loans for constructing houses; between 1986 to 2012, 69 thousand houses were constructed with these loans. In 1986, member deposits accounted for $4 million but had increased to $1,628 million in 2012; an annual growth rate of 26 per cent. Membership of the Grameen Bank grew from 0.23 million in 1986 to 8.3 million in 2012 which translates into a annual growth rate of 15 per cent over this period. Currently, the Grameen Bank's microcredit programme covers more than 90 per cent of the total area of the country or 81 thousand villages out of 86 thousand villages in the country.[20]

Table 13.1: Performance of the Grameen Bank.

Performance indicators	1986	2012
Cumulative disbursement (all loans, in million USD)	57	13,043
Disbursement during the year (all loans, in million USD)	18	1,447
Number of houses built cum (in thousand)	2.04	69.3

Total deposits (balance) (in million USD)	4	1,628
Number of members (in million)	0.2	8.3
Female members (per cent)	74	96
Number of villages covered	5,170	81,386
Number of branches	295	2567

Source: Annual reports of Grameen Bank 1987 and 2013

Credit Constraint and Other Determinants of Women's Self-Employment

Anna Paulson and Robert Townsend assert that financial constraints serve an important role in determining the shape of the patterns of entrepreneurship in Thailand.[21] The availability of the required funds determines the probability of survival of small and new businesses.[22] Wealthier households are more likely to start a business.[23] Robert Cressy has an opposite view in this regard; he argues that human capital is the main factor in determining the probability of survival of businesses and the correlation that exists between financial capital and survival is spurious.[24]

The constraints, particularly financial, that entrepreneurs face in establishing businesses, especially micro-enterprises, have a gender dimension. Women are more likely to be constrained than men and they have on average a smaller amount of capital for startups.[25] Leann Tiggers and Gary Green[26] have identified three reasons that contribute towards women's disadvantageous position in capital markets: i) women are likely to have less equity and less business experience; ii) resource lenders may discriminate against women due to their outmoded gender beliefs; and iii) the low number of applications for loans by women may also be due to women's beliefs that they will be discriminated against.[27] Diana Fletschner[28] argues that women are more likely to be non-price rationed and women's demand for capital and the supply of funds to them are determined by the legal, social, cultural and economic constraints they face. From the available literature, Fletschner also finds the collateral requirement, finding a male guarantor for the loan, the authorization of a loan application by a husband or a male family member, preference of lenders for financing of those activities that are usually run by men, lack of knowledge about the availability of funding, transaction costs, the risk averse behavior of women, and literacy requirement as factors lying behind gender discrimination in the financial sector.

Intra-household dynamics are more important in determining the financial constraints placed on women rather than men. Women have approximately a 42 per cent higher probability to be constrained in finding adequate funds when their husbands are also constrained. On the other hand, men are only 12 per cent likely to be financially constrained when their wives are also financially constrained. Women who have more control of the family budget have a higher probability of meeting their capital needs.[29]

The credit constraint is not the only factor that determines the self-employment status of women.[30] Among other factors, age has also been found as an important determinant.[31] A negative non-linear relationship has been found between age and the decision to start a business.[32] On the other hand, Xiangyu Yang, Yuan Cheng, and Jian Gao[33] do not find a significant impact of age for nascent entrepreneurship. Education is considered as an important factor in terms of making self-employment decisions by individuals. Education enhances the likelihood of becoming self-employed as it increases an individual's managerial ability.[34] In contrast, it is argued that education is also likely to affect the self-employment decisions of individuals negatively as it increases the opportunity cost of forgoing wage employment for self-employment.[35] The self-employment decision has a gender dimension as women are less likely to become self-employed, and similarly, they are more likely to leave self-employment than men.[36] However, Yang, Cheng, and Gao[37] have not found any likely impact of gender on entrepreneurship. Religion is likely to influence the self-employment status of microcredit programme members. David Audretsch, Werner Bonte, and Jagannadha Tamvada[38] conclude that religious minorities, such as Muslims and Christians, are more likely to become entrepreneurs compared to religious majority Hindus in India.

Household dynamics play an important role in the self-employment decisions of individuals.[39] The results regarding the impact of the number of children and other members in the household on the entrepreneurial decision are mixed.[40] The number of household members has a positive impact on the likelihood of becoming an entrepreneur for a household member, especially a woman member of the household, as it increases the availability of free labour from other non-owner household members. In contrast, the likelihood of becoming an entrepreneur for a household member declines when the number of household members goes up as more household members absorb more resources of the household which reduces the availability of capital for starting a new business. The marital status of women contributes significantly to their self-employment decision. Women are more likely to be self-employed if they are married.[41] For women the likelihood of becoming self-employed nearly doubles if the husband has some exposure to self-employment.[42]

Paulson and Townsend assert that the ownership of household assets and their size are likely to positively influence the entrepreneurial decision of household members as they increase the ability of household members to raise the necessary external finance to start a business from commercial banks.[43] The likelihood of business failure declines with the availability of the required amount of capital in the household.[44] Chowdhury finds the total area of cultivable land as a negative determinant of the entrepreneurial decision of household members in Bangladesh as it increases the opportunity cost of leaving agricultural activities and starting a business.[45] He also finds that the size of the ownership of non-land assets of households increases the likelihood of starting a businesses by household members. Evans and Jovanovic find that an adequate amount of assets is required for starting one's own business.[46]

The availability of local infrastructural facilities is also likely to influence individuals' entrepreneurial decisions. For example, it was found that the availability of paved roads in a locality would increase the likelihood of starting businesses by local people in rural areas of Bangladesh.[47] According to Junbo Yu and Roger Stough, entrepreneurial development activities are enhanced with proximity to markets and improvements in business infrastructure.[48]

Hence, on the basis of the above mentioned literature, we hypothesize that:

H: There is a positive relationship between access to microcredit and female entrepreneurship in Bangladesh.

In the process of testing this hypothesis, and following the relevant literature, we control for other important variables including: household ownership of assets including land, the human capital of household members, the age of the individual, religious status of the household, the number of household members in different age categories, marital status, husband's employment status and the availability of different infrastructural facilities.

Estimation Strategy

Given the extensive geographic coverage of microcredit in Bangladesh, it is difficult to find a perfect 'control' group that could be used to estimate the impact of microcredit on women's ownership of micro-enterprises and self-employment. In this study, we assume that the choice of a household to engage with a microcredit programme is related to the outcome of interest, i.e. the self-employment status of women through the ownership of micro-enterprises. Given the outcome for household j, we estimate the following simple model:

$$SEMPLOY_{ij} = \beta' \chi_i + \gamma MC + u_i \ (1)$$

where SEMPLOY is the self-employment status of women and it is assigned 1 if women members of the household j in village i own businesses and 0 otherwise. In equation (1), x is a vector of control variables that we assume to be exogenous (for example, education of the household members, distance of the household from the nearest market, etc.), and MC represents the microcredit programme participation, and u_i is the error term.

Participation in microcredit programmes in turn is defined by the following model.

$$MC_i = \delta' z_i + v_i \ (2)$$

Where z_i represent some control variables and v_i represent the error term of the model.

While the impact of *MC* is estimated using the equation (1), it is assumed that the error terms of equations (1) and (2), i.e. u_i and v_i, are not correlated. But, if the characteristics of the household that influence the microcredit programme participation decision also determine the outcome variable, i.e. SEMPLOY$_i$ in equation (1), these two error terms may become correlated. This problem is known as the selection bias problem. In such a situation, the straightforward estimation of equation (1) using data from participants and non-participants yields a biased estimate of the parameter of interest γ. Typically, two types of selection biases make u_i and v_i correlated: (1) non-random selection of households to participate in the microcredit programme, and (2) non-random selection of places to establish the branches of microcredit institutions like the Grameen Bank.

The Grameen Bank in Bangladesh accepts people as members who have less than 50 decimals of land.[49] This selection criteria generates the first of the two types of biases mentioned above. Besides the selection criteria of the Grameen Bank, the self-selection of programme participants is also another source of the first bias. It could be the case that participants have more entrepreneurial capabilities than non-participants. This may also bias the econometric estimation of programme benefits. The non-random programme placement also creates biases in estimating the potential benefits of the programme. For example, if the Grameen Bank establishes branches in areas which have more business opportunities or have a better communication infrastructure or have more dynamic leaders or are poorer, then such criteria for selecting places for programme implementation create biases in estimating programme benefits.

On the basis of the above arguments, we can say that a comparison between a group of microcredit programme participants, who are self selected, and a group of non-participants, who are not self-selected, would generate a bias in estimating the impact of microcredit on outcome variables. In the same way, the estimates will be biased if programme group members are selected from a place that has been non-randomly selected by the Grameen Bank on the basis of some characteristics for the establishment of a branch and comparison group members from a place without those characteristics. Based on the above, this study uses a survey method that is different from that commonly employed.[50] We selected new members from a newly established branch as well as those from old branches of the Grameen Bank, who were yet to receive or just received their first loans, and included them as members of the comparison group. Since, the comparison group members are also self-selected like the programme members, the bias arising from self-selection in estimating programme benefits disappears. The Grameen Bank selects all areas for the establishment of branches for microcredit operations non-randomly according to their own criteria. Thus, in our investigation, both the programme branch and the comparison branch have been selected under similar criteria. Therefore, the bias, which arises from non-random programme placement, is also avoided from our sample so that the programme impacts can be estimated now using a single equation described below.

$$\text{SEMPLOY}_{ij} = H_{ij}\alpha_y + L_j\Theta_y + MC_{ij}\beta_y + \nu_{ij} \quad (3)$$

where, $SEMPLOY_{ij}$, H_{ij}, L_j and MC_j are micro-enterprise ownership of women, vector of household characteristics, and vector of local characteristics and micro-credit respectively; and ν_i represents the error of the model that arises from the household and village level variables that are not included in the model.

The Data

A four-stage random sampling technique has been applied in selecting program households and comparison households. In the first stage, one district was randomly selected out of 64 districts in Bangladesh in 1998. In the second stage of random sampling, three branches of the Grameen Bank, two branches for selecting program households and the other one for selecting comparison households, were selected randomly for data collection purposes. Program households were selected from two branches of the Grameen Bank which were more than eight years old (program branch) and comparison households were selected from a newly established Grameen Bank branch (comparison branch). In the third stage, thirty centres from the comparison branch and sixty centres from two program branches were selected. In the fourth and final stage, the study randomly selected six members from each of the program branch centres and seven members from each of the comparison branch centres. Each Grameen Bank branch consists of fifty to sixty centres, each centre consists of eight groups and each group consists of five members.

In total, the study collected information on about 210-member households of the comparison branch and about 360-member households of program branches. However, during the examination of the completed questionnaires, it was found that some contained incomplete answers and other inaccuracies, and were subsequently dropped. This left the study with 205 useable questionnaires from the comparison branch and 316 useable questionnaires from two program branches. So, in total, the sample size for the study is 521 ($N=521$).

In addition to information on microcredit and self-employment, the survey also collected detailed information on a variety of other relevant factors. For example, demographic information (age, sex, marital status, etc.) and socio-economic information (education, employment, food consumption, expenditure on health, etc.) were collected for all household members. Detailed village-level information was also collected, such as distance to the nearest primary school, secondary school, the market and the district headquarters, along with variables describing village infrastructure, such as the presence of schools, markets, roads, electricity supply, etc.

Information relating to the size of loan received, date of joining and other membership characteristics was provided by branch officials and matched to the data.

Dependent Variables

Our outcome variables are the self-employment status of women members of the Grameen Bank and their husbands through the ownership of micro-enterprises. These are binary variables. The dependent variable SEMPLOYPM represents the self-employment status of women members of the Grameen Bank's microcredit program and it is assigned '1' if a woman member of the household j is self-employed through owning at least one business and '0' otherwise. The variable SEMPLOYHUS represents the self-employment status of husbands of women members of the Grameen Bank's microcredit program and it has been defined similar to SEMPLOYPM. Due to the binary characteristic of these two variables, SEMPLOYPM and SEMPLOYHUS, the probit regression technique has been applied to estimate the parameters of interest.

Independent Variables

The target variable on the right hand side of the equation is microcredit program participation (MC). In equation (3), MC is represented by the membership duration (in months) of the household j in the village i in the *Grameen* Bank's microcredit program (DURATIONMC). Five variables (AGEPM, AGE2PM, EDUPM, MARITALPM, and RELIGION) related to the characteristics of women members of the microcredit program of the Grameen Bank have been included in the model to control for their impact on self employment status. The age (AGEPM) of the microcredit program member of the household has been included to test the statistical significance of the relationship between the age and the self-employment status. The non-linearity in the relationship between age and self-employment has been examined by incorporating the square term of AGEPM (AGE2PM). The impact of education on self-employment is assessed by incorporating a variable on the level of education of female members of the microcredit program (EDUPM) in terms of the number of years of schooling. The marital status of female members of microcredit programs (MARITALPM) is included to check whether or not this factor has any impact on women's self-employment status. The variable on the women members' religious status (RELIGION) is also included to investigate the likely impact of religion on the self-employment status of women.

On the right hand side of the model, three variables on age (AGEHUS), age square (AGE2HUS), and education (EDUHUS) of husbands of female microcredit members are added to examine the influence of these three variables on the self-employment status of female microcredit members of households. There are twelve variables in total in the model (MALE00T05, MALE06T15,

MALE16T25, MALE26T40, MALE41T60, MALE61A, FEMALE00T05, FEMALE06T15, FEMALE16T25, FEMALE16T40, FEMALE41T60, and FEMALE61A) which relate to the household composition of members by age (in years) and sex. For example, MALE00T05 represents the number of male household members in the age category of more than zero to five years; the household male members who are aged less than five years belong to this age category. These variables are used to control for impact of the size of households in different age categories on the entrepreneurial status of individuals.

It is anticipated that the level of asset positively influences the entrepreneurial status of an individual, as it increases the ability of that individual to generate capital for investing in businesses. Keeping this in mind, two more variables on the total area of agricultural land (LAND) and the total value of non-land assets (OASSETS) are included in the model as independent variables. The variable LAND is measured in decimals and OASSETS are measured in Taka. In equation (3), six variables relating to the infrastructural facilities at the village level are included as it is considered that local infrastructural facilities affect the self-employments of individuals living in the village. These include: the availability of primary (PSCHOOL) and secondary schools (SSCHOOL) in the village, the availability of electricity supply in the village (ELECTRICITY), the distance of the nearest market from the household (MARKET), the distance of the nearest paved road from the household (ROAD), and the distance of the nearest commercial bank branch from the household (BANK). The variables PSCHOOL, SSCHOOL and ELECTRICITY are dummy variables and these variables are assigned 1 if a primary school, a secondary school and the electricity respectively are available in the village and 0 otherwise. On the other hand, distance related variables, MARKET, ROAD and BANK, are measured in kilometers. The descriptive statistics of the dependent and independent variables are given in Table 13.2.

Table 13.2: Basic descriptive statistics of the variables used in the analysis.

Variables	Labels	Mean	Std. Dev.
SEMPLOYPM	Micro-enterprise ownership of the Grameen Bank (GB) Member (dummy)	0.06	–
SEMPLOYHUS	Micro-enterprise ownership of the Husband of the GB member (dummy)	0.32	–
DURATIONMC	Microcredit programme membership duration (in months)	43.2	37.2
RELIGION	Religion of the household	0.91	–
AGEPM	Microcredit programme member's age	29.50	11.37
AGE2PM	Square of AGE2PM	999.56	776.48
EDUCATIONPM	Total years of schooling of microcredit programme member	2.26	3.22

Variables	Labels	Mean	Std. Dev.
MARITALPM	Microcredit programme member's marital status (dummy)	0.91	–
AGEHUS	Age of microcredit programme member's husband	39.71	10.00
AGE2HUS	Square of AGEHUS	1676.95	905.99
EDUCATION-HUS	Education of microcredit programme member's husband	3.21	3.99
MALE00T05	Total number of household male members between 0 to 5 years	0.24	0.48
MALE06T15	Total number of household male members between 6 to 15 years	0.99	0.97
MALE16T25	Total number of household male members between 16 to 25	0.46	0.73
MALE26T40	Total number of household male members between 26 to 40	0.62	0.58
MALE41T59	Total number of household male members between 41 to 59	0.46	0.50
MALE60A	Total number of household male members between 60 and above	0.08	0.27
FEMALE00T05	Total number of household female members between 0 to 5 years	0.25	0.48
FEMALE06T15	Total number of household female members between 6 to 15 years	0.93	0.99
FEMALE16T25	Total number of household female members between 16 to 25	0.36	0.59
FEMALE26T40	Total number of household female members between 26 to 40	0.65	0.49
FEMALE41T59	Total number of household female members between 41 to 59	0.22	0.42
FEMALE60A	Total number of household female members between 60 and above	0.05	0.23
LAND	Total area of agricultural land (in decimal)	7.52	7.63
OASSETS	Total value of non-land assets (in Taka)	9386	17956
PSCHOOL	Existence of a primary school in the village (dummy)	0.79	–
SSCHOOL	Existence of a higher secondary school in the village (dummy)	0.26	–
ELECTRICITY	Existence of electricity in the village (dummy)	0.79	–
MARKET	Distance to the nearest market from the household (in kilometers)	0.81	0.74
ROAD	Distance of the nearest paved road from the household (in kilometres)	0.67	0.67
BANK	Distance to the nearest commercial ban branch from the household (in kilometres)	1.32	0.94

Source: Author's calculations

The Results

The self-employment status of women in the programme as well as in the comparison group is illustrated in Table 13.3. As can be seen from Table 13.3 relatively more women in the comparison group are self-employed through micro-enterprise ownership than women in the programme group; only six per-cent of women in the programme group are self-employed. On the other hand, approximately seven percent of women are self-employed in the comparison group. This comparative scenario indicates that one's participation in the micro-credit programme of the Grameen Bank does not improve the self-employment status through micro-enterprise ownership. The Chi square test also confirms that the self-employment status of women in the programme group is not statis-tically different from that of women in the comparison group.

Table 13.3: Employment status of women members of the Grameen Bank.

Employment status	Programme group		Comparison group	
Self-employed	19	6.0%	14	6.8%
Housewife	273	86.4%	177	86.3%
Others	24	7.6p%	14	6.8%
Total	316	100%	205	100%
Pearson Chi2		0.2309		

Source: Author's calculations.

Table 13.4 presents the results of the Probit model following equation (3) which was estimated to examine determinants of female self-employment through micro-enterprise ownership. The microcredit variable represented by the dura-tion of membership in the microcredit programme of the Grameen Bank, is not statistically significant, but it shows the expected positive sign. This result indicates that microcredit programme membership does not significantly help participating women members in becoming self-employed by starting their own micro-enterprises. The results in Table 13.4 also indicate that household dynam-ics are more important than access to microcredit in determining women's self-employment status. The age of the household head, the total number of male members in the age category of 6 to 15, and the total number of female members in the age category of 26 to 40 are all statistically significant determinants affect-ing women's self-employment status. The age of the household head and total number of female members in the age category of 26 to 40 positively influence the self-employment status of women. On the other hand, the total number of male members in the age category of 6 to 15 significantly negatively determines women's self-employment status. The reason might be that household members at this age category are attending school and the more members in this category indicates that a household needs to allocate money to meet educational expenditure. This, therefore, reduces the availability of funds that women members can access to start their business enterprises.

Table 13.4: Determinants of self-employment of women members of the Grameen Bank.

Variables	Estimated Coefficients
DURATIONMC	0.00147
RELIGION	-0.213
AGEPM	0.0148
AGE2PM	-0.000485
EDUCATIONPM	-0.0705
MARITALPM	-0.320
AGEHUS	0.0493***
EDUCATIONHUS	0.0414
SEMPLOYHUS	0.446**
MALE00T05	0.0259
MALE06T15	-0.286**
MALE16T25	-0.00997
MALE26T40	-0.103
MALE41T59	-0.550
MALE60A	-0.428
FEMALE00T05	-0.248
FEMALE06T15	-0.0677
FEMALE16T25	0.160
FEMALE26T40	0.569*
FEMALE41T59	0.295
LAND	-1.11e-05
OASSETS	0.00653
PSCHOOL	0.144
SSCHOOL	0.0959
ELECTRICITY	0.306
MARKET	-0.138
ROAD	-0.228
BANK	-0.0754
Constant	-3.119***
Observations	514

*** statistically significant at 1 per cent level
**statistically significant at 5 per cent level
 * statistically significant at 1 per cent level
Source: Author's calculations

All in all, the results from Tables 13.3 and 13.4 indicate that engagement in micro-credit programmes does not significantly improve women's self-employment status.

Now the question is what the participants do with their microcredit loans. In order to answer this question, we also need to assess the impact of participation by female members in the microcredit programme on the self-employment status of their husbands. For example, it is possible that instead of using microcredit loans for their own self-employment, women pass on their loans to their husbands.

The employment status of husbands of participating female microcredit programme members is presented in Table 13.5. The results from our sample data clearly indicate that the self-employment status through micro-enterprise ownership is higher among husbands in the programme group than husbands in the comparison group. In the programme group, 34 per cent husbands are self employed compared to 21 per cent husbands in the comparison group. The Chi-square test also indicates that the self-employment status of husbands in the programme group is statistically significantly different from that of husbands in the comparison group. The interpretation of this result is that women members of the Grameen Bank pass their microcredit loans over to their husbands who become self-employed by starting micro-enterprises that are run and managed by husbands. This finding is also evident from the additional results presented in Table 13.6 of the probit model following equation (3) on the determinants of self-employment of husbands of participating women members.

Table 13.5: Employment status of husbands of the Grameen Bank women borrowers.

Employment status	Programme group		Comparison group	
Self-employed	108	34.2%	43	21.0%
Agriculture	61	19.3%	49	23.9%
Daily labourer	26	8.23%	31	15.1%
Others	92	29.1%	65	31.7%
Total	316	100%	205	100%
Pearson Chi2		14.4		
Pr		0.002		

Source: Author's calculations

Table 13.6: Determinants of self-employment of husbands of women borrowers of the Grameen Bank.

Variables	Estimated Coefficients
DURATIONMC	0.00575***
RELIGION	-0.299
AGEHUS	-0.0342
AGE2HUS	0.000301
EDUCATIONHUS	7.33e-05
AGEPM	0.0162
EDUCATIONPM	0.0118
MALE00T05	-0.0678
MALE06T15	0.0513
MALE16T25	-0.0986
MALE26T40	0.0416

Variables	Estimated Coefficients
MALE41T59	0.160
MALE60A	-0.234
FEMALE00T05	0.242
FEMALE06T15	0.0696
FEMALE16T25	-0.0622
FEMALE26T40	-0.00502
FEMALE41T59	-0.0938
FEMALE60A	-0.455
LAND	1.07e-05***
OASSETS	0.00172
PSCHOOL	0.317*
SSCHOOL	-0.0488
ELECTRICITY	0.172
MARKET	0.0540
ROAD	0.0625
BANK	-0.262***
Constant	-0.521
Observations	472

*** statistically significant at 1 per cent level
**statistically significant at 5 per cent level
 * statistically significant at 1 per cent level
Source: Author's calculations

The results in Table 13.6 indicate that the microcredit variable in the model represented by the membership duration in the microcredit programme has a positive sign and it is statistically significant. These results imply that the participation of women in the microcredit programme of the Grameen Bank positively affects the self-employment status of husbands of participating women. It is evident from the results in Table 13.6 that intra-household dynamics are less important for male members than female members in the household in terms of self-employment. Only one household variable is significantly important for determining the self-employment status of husbands of participating female members. It is the total area of household agricultural land ownership and it positively determines the self-employment status of husbands as it reflects the ability of households to acquire loans from commercial banks through providing with land as collateral. Other two significant variables are: the distance to the nearest commercial bank branch from the household andthe existence of a primary school in the village. The existence of a primary school in the village is a significant determinant of the self-employment status of husbands as it is likely to increase the education level of husbands which consequently contributes to their self-employment status. On the other hand, the distance to the nearest commercial bank branch significantly reduces the probability of becoming self-employed by husbands. It means that when distance to the commercial bank branch goes up, the likelihood of becoming self-employed by owning a micro-enterprise goes down. The result is logical and it indicates that the longer distance to a commercial bank branch reduces access to bank loans. It is clear from these results that access to credit is not important for microcredit programme participating women members of the Grameen Bank. However, it is important for husbands of participating women members. Hence, it can be concluded from the estimated results that participation in the microcredit programme of the Grameen Bank does not enhance the ability of participating women to become self-employed. However, the same participation significantly enhances the ability of husbands of women members to become self-employed by starting micro-enterprises, which means the overall impact of the programme on the household income is still positive.

Discussion and Conclusion

Entrepreneurship and micro-enterprises have been recognized as factors that contribute to the economic development of a country. The ownership of a micro-enterprise helps an individual to become self-employed. Lack of external finance is one of the main constraints that individuals face in establishing a micro-enterprise and hence becoming self-employed. This financial constraint has a gender dimension as women are more likely to be constrained than men. In developing countries, formal sector financial institutions do not provide poor people with the necessary funds that are required for starting micro-enterprises. On the other hand, the terms of loan agreements in the informal credit sector are exploitative in nature. The Grameen Bank came into existence in the 1970s with its microcredit programme with the objective of removing the credit constraints on poor people. Women are specifically targeted for the giving of microcredit loans. Currently, 96 per cent of the members are women. It is assumed that access to microcredit helps women members of the Grameen Bank to become self-employed by starting micro-enterprises that are owned and managed by them.

In this regard, this chapter attempted to evaluate whether or not participation in the microcredit programme of the Grameen Bank would help women members in becoming self-employed. Both, the results from descriptive statistics of our sample and also the results from the multivariate techniques, indicate that participation in microcredit programmes does not help women members to become self-employed. We find that women are not using their microcredit loans from the Grameen Bank to establish micro-enterprises managed and run by them. Since over 96 per cent of the participating members in the Grameen Bank's microcredit programme are women, this seems a surprising finding. However, in the context of the socio-cultural environment in a predominantly Muslim country such as Bangladesh, it is not conducive for women to start micro-enterprises of their own. In spite of some positive changes in the socio-cultural attitudes of the society towards women's participation in the economic activities in the last three decades, in the rural areas, it is still regarded as unacceptable to see women running their businesses outside the home and in market places. The results of this study indicate that the participation of women in the microcredit programme of the Grameen Bank actually helps husbands of women members to become self-employed. It also means that the actual control of microcredit loans lies with husbands of participating women. Anna Goetz and Rina Gupta have also found similar results in their study.[51] They have found that the control of microcredit loans does not remain with women members in most of the cases. Although the microcredit programme of the Grameen Bank has been initiated with the objective of promoting micro-enterprise development among poor women, it is evident from the results of this chapter that a mere access to microcredit does not enhance female self-employment. To achieve the broader objectives of microcredit programmes, especially in view of the arguments regarding empowering the role of women in households, more needs to be done. For example, improvements and changes in the intra-household dynamics and the socio-cultural environment are also required along with providing microcredit to women to enable them to start up micro-enterprises owned and managed by them.

NOTES

1 Dow and Dow, 'Economic Development in the Scottish Enlightenment: Ideas as Cause and Effect'

1. R. L. Meek, *Social Science and the Ignoble Savage* (Cambridge: Cambridge University Press, 1976), p. 1 (original emphasis).
2. See for example J. Shields, 'Highlandisms: The Expanding Scope of Eighteenth-Century Scottish Studies', *Eighteenth-Century Life*, 33:1 (2009), pp. 54–60.
3. The character of the Enlightenment was complex, with differences within national traditions, and as these traditions evolved, and with interactions between thought in different traditions; the Scottish Enlightenment in particular was influenced by various strands of continental European thought as well as English thought. Here we draw out the main distinctive features of Scottish Enlightenment, see F. von Hayek, *Studies in Philosophy, Politics and Economics* (London: Routledge & Kegan Paul, 1967).
4. See S. Dow, 'Hume: A Re-assessment', in P. L. Porta, R. Scazzieri and A. S. Skinner (eds), *Knowledge, Division of Labour and Social Institutions* (Cheltenham: Edward Elgar, 2001), pp. 75–92.
5. B. J. Loasby, 'Closed Models and Open Systems', *Journal of Economic Methodology*, 10:3 (2003), pp. 285–306, on p. 287.
6. See S. Dow, 'Hume and Critical Realism', *Cambridge Journal of Economics*, 26:6 (2002), pp. 683–97.
7. See L. Montes, 'Adam Smith: Real Newtonian', in A. Dow and S. Dow (eds), *A History of Scottish Economic Thought* (London: Routledge, 2006), pp. 102–22, and F. Comim, 'Adam Smith: Common Sense and Aesthetics in the Age of Experiments', in A. Dow and S. Dow (eds), *A History of Scottish Economic Thought*, pp. 123–45. We thus emphasize the origins of ideas about system in experience, rather than the deductive reasoning then applied for further reference to experience as emphasized by Kwangsu Kim, 'Adam Smith's Theory of Economic History and Economic Development', *European Journal of the History of Economic Thought*, 16:1 (2009), pp. 41–64.
8. A. Smith, 'The History of Astronomy'(1795), in W. P. D. Wightman (ed.), *Essays on Philosophical Subjects* (Oxford: Oxford University Press, 1980), pp. 33–105.
9. A. Smith, *Lectures on Rethoric and Belles Lettres* (1762–3,b), ed. J. C. Bryce (Oxford: Oxford University Press, 1983).
10. G. Davie, *The Democratic Intellect* (Edinburgh: Edinburgh University Press, 1961).
11. A. Smith, *Lectures on Jurisprudence* (1762–3), ed. R. L. Meek, D. D. Raphael and G. P. Stein (Oxford: Oxford University Press, 1978), p. 493.

12. L. Montes, *Adam Smith in Context* (London: Palgrave, 2004).
13. See M. Schabas, *The Natural Origins of Economics* (Chicago, IL: University of Chicago Press, 2005).
14. Meek, *Social Science and the Ignoble Savage.*
15. A. Brewer, 'Adam Ferguson, Adam Smith, and the Concept of Economic Growth', *History of Political Economy*, 31:2 (1999), pp. 237–54.
16. Meek, *Social Science and the Ignoble Savage*; Schabas, *The Natural Origins of Economics*, ch. 3.
17. C. Wennerlind, 'David Hume as a *Political* Economist', in A. Dow and S. Dow (eds), *A History of Scottish Economic Thought* (London: Routledge, 2006), pp. 46–70; and Montes, *Adam Smith in Context.*
18. M. Brown, *Adam Smith's Economics* (London: Croom Helm, 1988), ch. 5.
19. Montes, *Adam Smith in Context*, ch. 2.
20. In the meantime, the *Wealth of Nations* had been interpreted as an advocacy of capitalism, drawing a range of critiques from, for example, Sismondi and Marx.
21. Notably his teacher, Hutcheson; see A. S. Skinner, 'Frances Hutcheson, 1694–1746', in A. Dow and S. Dow (eds), *A History of Scottish Economic Thought* (London: Routledge, 2006).
22. See, respectively, R. H. Campbell and A. S. Skinner, 'Introduction' to *An Inquiry into the Nature and Causes of the Wealth of Nations* (1776), ed. R. H. Campbell and A. S. Skinner (Oxford: Oxford University Press, 1976), pp. 1–60, and Brewer, 'Adam Ferguson, Adam Smith, and the Concept of Economic Growth'.
23. J. T. Young, *Economics as a Moral Science* (Cheltenham: Edward Elgar, 1997).
24. See A. Young, 'Increasing Returns and Economic Progress', *Economic Journal*, 28 (1928), pp. 523–42.
25. J. Rae, *Statement of Some New Principles on the Subject of Political Economy* (Boston, MA: Hilliard Gray, 1834).
26. D. Mair, 'John Rae', in A. Dow and S. Dow (eds), *A History of Scottish Economic Thought* (London: Routledge, 2006), pp. 198–212.
27. D. D. Raphael, *Adam Smith* (Oxford: Oxford University Press, 1985).
28. Skinner, 'Frances Hutcheson, 1694–1746'.
29. A. Smith, *The Theory of Moral Sentiments* (1759), ed. D. D. Raphael and A. Macfie (Oxford: Oxford University Press, 1976).
30. See further Schabas, *The Natural Origins of Economics*, p. 95.
31. See R. V. Eagly, 'Sir James Steuart and the "Aspiration Effect"', *Economica*, 28:1 (1961), pp. 53–61, and A. Brewer, 'Luxury and Economic Development: David Hume and Adam Smith', *Scottish Journal of Political Economy*, 45:1 (1998), pp. 78–98.
32. A. Smith, *An Inquiry into the Nature and Causes of the Wealth of Nations* (1776), ed. R. H. Campbell and A. S. Skinner (Oxford: Oxford University Press, 1976), p. I.ii.1).
33. C. Wennerlind, 'David Hume as a *Political* Economist', in A. Dow and S. Dow (eds), *A History of Scottish Economic Thought* (London: Routledge, 2006), pp. 46–70.
34. D. Hume, 'Of Money' (1742), in *David Hume: Essays Moral, Political and Literary*, ed. E. Rotwein (Indianapolis: Liberty, 1985), pp. 281–94. This interpretation differs from the conventional monetarist interpretations of Hume, where it is money itself, rather than the process of increasing productivity, which is causal; see further Skinner, 'David Hume'.
35. I. Hont, 'The "Rich Country–Poor Country" Debate in Scottish Classical Political Economy', in I. Hont and M. Ignatieff (eds), *Wealth and Virtue: The Shaping of Political Economy in the Scottish Enlightenment* (Cambridge: Cambridge University Press, 1983), pp. 271–316.
36. J. Steuart, *Principles of Political Oeconomy* (1767), ed. A. S. Skinner (Edinburgh:

Oliver & Boyd, 1966).

37. J. Anderson, *An Enquiry into the Nature of the Corn Laws, with a View to the New Corn Bill Proposed for Scotland* (Edinburgh, 1777); and J. Anderson, *An Account of the Present State of the Hebrides and Western Coasts of Scotland: In which an Attempt is made to Explain the Circumstances that have hitherto Repressed the Industry of the Natives; and some Hints are Suggested for Encouraging the Fisheries, and Promoting other Improvements in those Countries* (Edinburgh: C. Elliot, 1785). Also see Dow, A (2010) 'Anderson, James (1739–1808)', in D. Rutherford (ed), *The Biographical Dictionary of British Economists* (New York: Continuum), at http://www.oxfordreference.com/view/10.1093/acref/9780199754717 [accessed 11 July 2014].

38. A. Ferguson, *Essay on the History of Civil Society* (1767), ed. D. Forbes (Edinburgh: Edinburgh University Press, 1967). Also see M. G. H. Pittock, 'Historiography', in A. Broadie (ed.), *The Cambridge Companion to the Scottish Enlightenment* (Cambridge: Cambridge University Press, 2003), pp. 258–79.

39. Ferguson, *Essay on the History of Civil Society*, p. 19.

40. R. B. Sher, 'Adam Ferguson, Adam Smith, and the Problem of National Defense', *Journal of Modern History*, 61 (1989), pp. 240–68. Ferguson argued from personal experience, first from his upbringing in the Highlands characterized by militias, and then as a chaplain to the Black Watch regiment.

41. Montes, *Adam Smith in Context*, ch. 3.

42. A. Fitzgibbons, *Adam Smith's System of Liberty, Wealth and Virtue* (Oxford: Clarendon Press, 1995), ch. 11.

43. Smith, *The Theory of Moral Sentiments*.

44. Meek, *Social Science and the Ignoble Savage*, p. 150.

45. See for example D. Allan, *Virtue, Learning and the Scottish Enlightenment* (Edinburgh: Edinburgh University Press, 1993), A. Broadie, *The Tradition of Scottish Philosophy: A New Persceptive on the Enlightenment* (Edinburgh: Polygon, 1990), and A. Broadie (ed.), *The Cambridge Companion to the Scottish Enlightenment* (Cambridge: Cambridge University Press, 2003).

46. A. I. Macinnes, *Clanship, Commerce and the House of Stuart, 1603–1788* (East Linton: Tuckwell Press, 1996), p. x.

47. R. H. Campbell, 'The Enlightenment and the Economy', in R. H. Campbell and A. S. Skinner (eds), *The Origins and Nature of the Scottish Enlightenment* (Edinburgh: John Donald, 1982), pp. 8–25; R. Emerson, 'The Contexts of the Scottish Enlightenment', in A. Broadie (ed.), *The Cambridge Companion to the Scottish Enlightenment* (Cambridge: Cambridge University Press, 2003); and T. M. Devine, 'The Scottish Merchant Community, 1680–1740', in R. H. Campbell and A. S. Skinner (eds), *The Origins and Nature of the Scottish Enlightenment* (Edinburgh: John Donald, 1982), pp. 26–41.

48. S. G. Checkland, *Scottish Banking: A History, 1695–1973* (Glasgow & London: Collins, 1975).

49. See for example E. Cregeen, 'The Changing Role of the House of Argyll in the Scottish Highlands', in N. T. Philipson and R. Mitchison (eds), *Scotland in the Age of Improvement* (Edinburgh: Edinburgh University Press, 1970), pp. 5–23.

50. M. Newton, *A Handbook of the Scottish Gaelic World* (Dublin: Four Courts Press, 2000), p. 14.

51. T. M. Devine, 'A Conservative People? Scottish Gaeldom in the Age of Improvement', in T. M. Devine and J. R. Young (eds), *Eighteenth Century Scotland: New Perspectives* (Edinburgh: Tuckwell Press, 1999), pp. 225–36.

52. Newton, *A Handbook of the Scottish Gaelic World*, ch. 9.
53. R. Saville, 'Scottish Modernisation Prior to the Industrial Revolution, 1688–1763', in T. M. Devine and J. R. Young (eds), *Eighteenth Century Scotland: New Perspectives* (Edinburgh: Tuckwell Press, 1999), pp. 6–23.
54. Devine, 'The Scottish Merchant Community, 1680–1740'.
55. Campbell, 'The Enlightenment and the Economy'.
56. Devine, 'The Scottish Merchant Community, 1680–1740'.
57. R. H. Campbell, *Scotland since 1707*, 2nd edn (Edinburgh: John Donald, 1985), p.11.
58. Meek, *Social Science and the Ignoble Savage*.
59. Meek, *Social Science and the Ignoble Savage*, p. 127.
60. Hont, The "Rich Country–Poor Country" Debate in Scottish Classical Political Economy', n. 7; C. George Caffentzis, 'Hume, Money, and Civilization; or, Why was Hume a Metallist?', *Hume Studies*, 27:2 (2001), pp. 301–35; and R. Emerson, 'The Scottish Contexts for Hume's Political-Economic Thinking', in M. Schabas and C. Wennerlind (eds), *Hume's Political Economy* (London: Routledge, 2007).
61. Caffentzis, 'Hume, Money, and Civilization; or, Why was Hume a Metallist?'
62. Quoted from Hume's unpublished *Of the Authenticity of Ossian's Poems* by E. C.Mossner, *The Forgotten Hume* (New York: Columbia University Press, 1943, p. 96.
63. Meek, *Social Science and the Ignoble Savage*, p. 43 n. 46; pp. 154–5.
64. Meek, *Social Science and the Ignoble Savage*, p. 172.
65. R. L. Meek, *Smith Marx and After* (London: Chapman and Hall, 1977).
66. N. Philipson, 'The Scottish Enlightenment', in R. Porter and M. Teich (eds), *The Enlightenment in National Context* (Cambridge: Cambridge University Press, 1981), pp. 19–40, on pp. 21–2.
67. M. Gray, *The Highland Economy 1750–1850* (Westport, CT: Greenwood Press, 1957).
68. Philipson, 'The Scottish Enlightenment', pp. 30–1.
69. J. B. Davis, *The Theory of the Individual in Economics: Identity and Value* (London: Routledge, 2003), ch. 2.
70. M. Foucault, *The Archeology of Knowledge*, trans. A. M. Sheridan (London: Routledge, 1972).
71. I. V. de Lima, *Foucault's Archeology of Political Economy* (London: Palgrave, 2010).
72. Newton, *A Handbook of the Scottish Gaelic World*.

2 Grieve, 'Nearer to Sraffa than Marx: Adam Smith on Productive and Unproductive Labour'

1. M. Blaug comments that 'Smith's distinction between productive and unproductive labour is probably the most maligned concept in the history of economic doctrines' (M. Blaug, *Economic Theory in Retrospect* (Cambridge: Cambridge University Press, 1962), p. 53).
2. As by Petty, Cantillon and the Physiocrats; see respectively C. H. Hull (ed.), *The Economic Writings of Sir William Petty* (London: Routledge/Thoemmes, 1899); H. Higgs (ed.), *Cantillon's 'Essay sur la Nature du Commerce en Général'* (London: Macmillan, 1931); and R. L. Meek, *The Economics of Physiocracy* (London: Allen and Unwin, 1962).
3. A. Smith, *An Inquiry into the Nature and Causes of the Wealth of Nations* (1776; Oxford: Oxford University Press/Indianapolis: Liberty Fund, 1976), II.iii.
4. See T. Aspromourgos, 'Adam Smith on Labour and Capital', ch. 13 in C. J. Berry, M. P. Paganelli, and C. Smith (eds) *The Oxford Handbook of Adam Smith* (Oxford: Oxford

University Press, 2013), pp. 275–8.

5. Smith, *An Inquiry into the Nature and Causes of the Wealth of Nations*, II.iii: 330.
6. Smith, *An Inquiry into the Nature and Causes of the Wealth of Nations*, II.iii: 330.
7. Smith, *An Inquiry into the Nature and Causes of the Wealth of Nations*, II.iii: 330–1.
8. Smith, *An Inquiry into the Nature and Causes of the Wealth of Nations*, I.viii: 83–5.
9. Compare K. Marx, *Theories of Surplus Value* (London: Lawrence & Wishart, 1969). Marx gives examples of 'so-called' (by Smith) 'unproductive labour' which *he* counts as productive: 'An entrepreneur of theatres, concerts, brothels, etc., buys the temporary disposal over the labour-power of the actors, musicians, prostitutes, etc. . . . The sale of [the services of] this labour provides him with wages and profit'. By Smith's surplus value criterion, such labour *ought* to qualify as productive, as it does with Marx. Smith was apparently muddled on this.
10. See K. Marx, *Capital, Volume I* (1867; London: Penguin Classics, 1990), p. 644: 'Capitalist production is not merely the production of commodities, it is, by its very essence, the production of surplus-value. . . . The only worker who is productive is one who produces surplus-value for the capitalist, or in other words, contributes towards the self-valorization of capital'.
11. Note here an allegation by M. Dobb, *Theories of Value and Distribution since Adam Smith* (Cambridge: Cambridge University Press, 1973), pp. 62–4, to the effect that Smith did not have a clear understanding of the economy's investible surplus. In *Adam Smith's Theory of Value and Distribution: A Reappraisal* (Basingstoke and London, 1990) Rory O'Donnell has, however, convincingly refuted this charge, demonstrating that Dobb had misinterpreted the meaning of Smith's term 'nett' revenue.
12. Smith, *An Inquiry into the Nature and Causes of the Wealth of Nations*, II.iii: 339.
13. Smith, *An Inquiry into the Nature and Causes of the Wealth of Nations*, II.iii: 342.
14. Smith, *An Inquiry into the Nature and Causes of the Wealth of Nations*, II.iii: 331.
15. Smith, *An Inquiry into the Nature and Causes of the Wealth of Nations*, II.ii: 345.
16. See P. Sraffa, *Production of Commodities by Means of Commodities* (Cambridge: Cambridge University Press, 1960).
17. Smith, *An Inquiry into the Nature and Causes of the Wealth of Nations*, I.i: 22–3.
18. In 'Adam Smith's Theory of Economic Growth', in A. S. Skinner and T. Wilson (eds), *Essays on Adam Smith* (Oxford: Clarendon Press, 1975), Walter Eltis observes that, in modern economic theory, the 'sole echo of Smith's distinction [between productive and unproductive labour] is Piero Sraffa's classically based *Production of Commodities by Means of Commodities*' (p. 434).
19. Smith, *An Inquiry into the Nature and Causes of the Wealth of Nations*, II.v: 360–2.
20. See A. Gray, *The Development of Economic Doctrine: An Introductory Survey* (London: Longmans, Green, 1931), pp. 138–9.
21. Later authorities, for example J. Schumpeter, *History of Economic Analysis* (London: Allen & Unwin, 1954) and S. Hollander, *The Economics of Adam Smith* (London: Heinemann, 1973), are no less hostile to the Smithian distinction. Schumpeter dismisses the whole issue as a 'dusty museum piece' (pp. 628–30); Hollander refers to Smith's 'unfortunate choice of terminology' (p. 147) and seems to believe that Smith was mistakenly neglecting the importance of the service sector. Neither commentator appears to appreciate that Smith was warning that the consequence of employing labour 'unproductively' is that the growth potential of the economy is lessened.
22. Smith's critics have failed to distinguish 'productive labour' (the subject of Smith's discussion) from what Marx, *Capital*, I.iii:132–3, described as 'useful labour', i.e., labour

supplying goods and services which directly provide utility to users.

23. J. S. Mill, *Principles of Political Economy*, 8th (People's) edn (London: Longman, Green, Reader and Dyer, 1866), I.iii.

24. I. Gough, 'Marx's Theory of Productive and Unproductive Labour', *New Left Review* (November–December 1972), pp. 47–72.

25. J. M. Gillman, *Prosperity in Crisis* (New York: Marzani and Munsell, 1965).

26. J. Morris, 'Unemployment and Productive Employment', *Science and Society*, 22 (1958), pp. 194–5.

27. J. Blake, 'Jacob Morris on Unproductive Employment: A Criticism', *Science and Society*, 24 (1960), pp. 169–75.

28. I. I. Rubin, *A History of Economic Thought* (London: Pluto Press, 1989), p. 215.

29. M. Dobb, *Theories of Value and Distribution since Adam Smith*, p. 60.

30. E. Roll, *A History of Economic Thought* (London: Faber and Faber, 1973), p. 168.

31. H. Myint, *Theories of Welfare Economics* (London: London School of Economics and Political Science, 1948), p. 73.

32. Smith, *An Inquiry into the Nature and Causes of the Wealth of Nations*, II.iii: 346–9.

33. Covering too the status of 'some of the most frivolous professions'; see note 9 above.

34. Smith, *An Inquiry into the Nature and Causes of the Wealth of Nations*, II.iii: 332.

35. Smith, *An Inquiry into the Nature and Causes of the Wealth of Nations*, II.iii: 343.

3 Vazquez-Guzman, 'Ethical Issues in Key Aspects of Economic Development: Rationality and Justice'

1. Acts 17:18, *Holy Bible: New International Version* (Grand Rapids, MI: Zondervan, 1984).

2. P. Pattanaik and X. Yongsheng, 'The Ethical Bases of Public Policies: A Conceptual Framework', *Andrew Young School of Policy Studies Research Paper Series*, Working Paper 13-14 (2013), n. 1.

3. See for example A. K. Sen, *Development as Freedom* (Oxford: Oxford University Press, 1999), M. Schabas, *The Natural Origins of Economics* (Chicago, IL and London: University of Chicago Press, 2005), S. C. Dow, 'Hume: a Re-assessment', in P. L. Porta, R. Scazzieri and A. S. Skinner (eds), *Knowledge, Social Institutions and the Division of Labour* (Aldershot: Edward Elgar, 2001), pp. 75–92, and L. Montes, *Adam Smith in Context: A Critical Reassessment of Some Central Components of His Thought* (New York: Palgrave Macmillan, 2004).

4. R. S. Woolhouse, *A History of Western Philosophy. Book 5: The Empiricists* (Oxford University Press, 1988).

5. T. Lawson, 'The Current Economic Crisis: Its Nature and the Course of Academic Economics', *Cambridge Journal of Economics*, 33:4 (2009), pp. 759–77, and J. E. Stiglitz, *Freefall: America, Free Markets, and the Sinking of the World Economy* (New York and London: W. W. Norton & Company, 2010).

6. That cultural aspects can have an impact in present economic development might be an issue that deserves analysis (in J. A. Forson, J. Janrattanagul and E. Carsamer, 'Culture Matters: A Test of Rationality on Economic Growth', *Asian Social Science*, 9:9 (2013) because there are ancient records that might highlight regional negative habits in Greece, like those in the writings attributed to poet Epimenides (J. R. Harris, 'The Cretans Always Liars', in *The Expositor* (London: Hodder and Stoughton, 1906), vol. 2, pp. 305–17. and cited by Paul in the Letter to Titus 1:12, *Holy Bible: New International Version* (NIV).

7. S. Heargraves-Heap, *Rationality in Economics* (Oxford: Basil Blackwell, 1989), G. Gigerentzer, P. M. Todd, and The ABC Research Group, *Simple Heuristics that Make Us Smart* (New York: Oxford University Press, 1999), A. K. Sen, *Rationality and Freedom* (Cambridge, MA: Harvard University Press, England, 2002) and I. Gilboa, *Rational Choice* (Cambridge, MA: MIT Press, 2010).

8. As for example in A. K. Sen, 'The Possibility of Social Choice', in *Rationality and Freedom* (Cambridge, MA: Harvard University Press, 1998), pp. 65–118.

9. I have studied these notions elsewhere in D. Vazquez-Guzman, 'Why are You So Irrational? Decision-making Process and Notions of Rationality' (Mimeo, University of California Riverside, Spring 2004), D. Vazquez-Guzman, 'Notions of Rationality and Critiques: Beyond the as if Assumption' (Mimeo, University of Stirling, 2006) and D. Vazquez-Guzman, 'Historical Background of Rationality: Decision-making Insights Before and During the Enlightenment' (Mimeo, University of Stirling, 2006).

10. Vazquez-Guzman, 'Historical Background of Rationality: Decision-making Insights Before and During the Enlightenment'.

11. Woolhouse, *A History of Western Philosophy. Book 5: The Empiricists.*

12. E. M. Curley, *Descartes against the Skeptics* (Oxford: Basil Blackwell, 1978), p. 10.

13. Curley, *Descartes against the Skeptics*, p. 12.

14. D. Hume, *Treatise of Human Nature* (1739; The Project EBook 4705, 2010), at http://www.gutenberg.org/files/4705/4705-h/4705-h.htm [accessed 6 July 2014].

15. Explained as 'Stratonician' atheism in A. Flew, *David Hume: Writings on Religion* (La Salle, IL: Open Court, 1994).

16. Vazquez-Guzman, 'Historical Background of Rationality: Decision-making Insights Before and During the Enlightenment'.

17. Montes, *Adam Smith in Context: A Critical Reassessment of Some Central Components of His Thought.*

18. A. Smith, *The Theory of Moral Sentiments* (1759; Oxford: Clarendon Press, 1974), on p. 482.

19. A. Smith, *An Inquiry into the Nature and Causes of the Wealth of Nations* (1776; Oxford: Clarendon Press, 1976), p. i.ii.2.

20. Hume, *Treatise of Human Nature*, p. 3.II.1.

21. Hume, *Treatise of Human Nature*, p. 3.II.6.

22. Vazquez-Guzman, 'Historical Background of Rationality: Decision-making Insights Before and During the Enlightenment'.

23. A. Kenny, *Descartes, a Study of his Philosophy* (Bristol: Thoemmes Press, 1997), p. 4.

24. Kenny, *Descartes, a Study of his Philosophy*, on pp. 5–6.

25. R. Descartes,*Œuvres de Descartes* (Paris: L. Cerf, 1897), p. 18; or also see R. Descartes, *The Philosophical Works of Descartes*, trans. E. S. Haldane and G. R. T. Ross (Cambridge: Cambridge University Press, 1911), p. 145.

26. Descartes, *Œuvres de Descartes*, p. 20; and Descartes, *The Philosophical Works of Descartes*, p. 146.

27. Descartes, *Œuvres de Descartes*, p. 32; and Descartes, *The Philosophical Works of Descartes*, p. 101.

28. R. Descartes, *Discours de la Méthode* (1637; The Project EBook 13846, 2010) at http://www.gutenberg.org/ebooks/13846, part. IV [accessed 6 July 2014].

29. Descartes had a particular pleasure in mathematics as seen in J. F. Scott, *The Scientific Work of Rene Descartes* (London: Taylor and Francis, Ltd, 1952), on p. 15.

30. Descartes, *Œuvres de Descartes*, p. 420; and Descartes, *The Philosophical Works of Descartes*, p. 147.

31. R. Scruton. *A Short History of Modern Philosophy* (London and New York: Routledge, 1981), p. 29.

32. Descartes, *Œuvres de Descartes*, p. 315; and Descartes, *The Philosophical Works of Descartes*, p. 289.

33. Kenny, *Descartes, a Study of his Philosophy*, p. 216.

34. When it is said 'Church' or 'Catholic Church', it is usually referred to the Roman Catholic Church. I use the term 'Christian' as a generalization of people that believe in Jesus as the waited Messiah.

35. Unless stated otherwise, the Jewish tradition refers to the Pharisaic branch, because the other one, from the Sadducees, denied immortality and spiritual existence.

36. M. Maher and J. Boland, 'Soul', in *The Catholic Encyclopedia* (New York: Robert Appleton Company, 1912), vol. 14.

37. Mathew 22:37, *Holy Bible: New International Version*.

38. 5:23, *Holy Bible: New International Version*.

39. Paul's conception has been seen close to the Platonic dualism, yet for the latter there is no way to know the truth of any essence fully.

40. Genesis 1:26, *Holy Bible: New International Version*.

41. He was staunchingly critical of any Jewish-Christian religion as it can be clearly seen in his (in)famous quote 'So that, upon the whole, we may conclude, that the Christian Religion not only was at first attended with miracles, but even at this day cannot be believed by any reasonable person without one. Mere reason is insufficient to convince us of its veracity: And whoever is moved by Faith to assent to it, is conscious of a continued miracle in his own person, which subverts all the principles of his under-standing, and gives him a determination to believe what is most contrary to custom and experience'. in D. Hume, 'An Enquiry Concerning Human Understanding', in *Enquiries Concerning Human Understanding and Concerning the Principles of Morals*(1748; Oxford: Clarendon, 1975), sec. 10.

42. Hume, *Treatise of Human Nature,* p.1.I.3.

43. Hume, *Treatise of Human Nature,* p. 1.III.14.

44. ''Tis certain there is no question in philosophy more abstruse than that concerning identity, and the nature of the uniting principle, which constitutes a person. So far from being able by our senses merely to determine this question, answer to it; and in com-mon life 'tis evident these ideas of self and person are never very fix'd nor determinate. 'Tis absurd, therefore, to imagine the senses can ever distinguish betwixt ourselves and external objects'. In Hume, *Treatise of Human Nature*, p. 1.III.2.

45. For instance, see T. Lawson, 'Situated Rationality', *Journal of Economic Methodology*, 4:1 (1997), pp. 101–25.

46. J. Kemp, 'New Methods and Understanding in Economic Dynamics: An Introductory Guide to Chaos and Economics', *Economic Issues*, 2:1 (1997), pp. 1–26.

47. D. Vazquez-Guzman, 'Measurement of Income Inequality in Mexico: Methodology, Assessment and Empirical Relationship with Poverty and Human Development' (PhD Dissertation, University of Stirling, 2008), ch. 1.

48. J. Rawls, *A Theory of Justice* (Cambridge, MA: Harvard University Press, 1971), p. 11.

49. Rawls, *A Theory of Justice*, p. 3.

50. Plato (360 BC, trans. by B. Jowett), 'The Republic', in *The Dialogues of Plato*, 5 vols, 3rd rev. edn (Oxford: Oxford University Press: 1892).

51. M. C. Nussbaum, *The Fragility of Goodness, Luck and Ethics in Greek Tragedy and Philosophy* (Cambridge, MA: Cambridge University Press, 1986).

52. A. K. Sen, *Inequality Reexamined* (Oxford: Clarendon Press and Oxford University Press, 1992), p. 1980.

53. Vazquez-Guzman, *Measurement of Income Inequality in Mexico: Methodology, Assessment and Empirical Relationship with Poverty and Human Development*, ch. 1.

54. A. K. Sen, 'Social Justice and the Distribution of Income', in A. B. Atkinson and E. Bourguignon (eds), *Handbook of Income Distribution* (Amsterdam: North Holland, 2000), pp. 60–81, on p. 61, n. 2.

55. M. Slote, 'Justice as a Virtue', in *The Stanford Encyclopedia of Philosophy*, at http://plato.stanford.edu/entries/justice-virtue/ [accessed 6 Juy 2014].

56. Aristotle, *Politics*, trans. B. Jowett (Ontario: Batoche Books, 1999).

57. Slote, 'Justice as a Virtue'.

58. Nussbaum, *The Fragility of Goodness, Luck and Ethics in Greek Tragedy and Philosophy*, pp. 246, 304, 102, n. 33.

59. Nussbaum, *The Fragility of Goodness, Luck and Ethics in Greek Tragedy and Philosophy*, p. 349.

60. Nussbaum, *The Fragility of Goodness, Luck and Ethics in Greek Tragedy and Philosophy*, on p. 353.

61. Sen, 'Social Justice and the Distribution of Income', p. 73.

62. I. Abrahams, 'Judaism', in *Religions: Ancient and Modern* (London: Constable and Company, Ltd, 1921), on p. 14. See also 'Judaism' in *The New Encyclopaedia Brittanica* (Chicago, IL: Encyclopaedia Brittanica In., 1997), p. 419.

63. Exodus 16:17–18, *Holy Bible: New International Version*. More desert-based examples in 2 Samuel 12:7–8 and 1 Kings 3:3–15; general cases in 2 Chronicles 7:14, and healing as a result of people's loyalty to God, also in Deuteronomy 28:1–3.

64. Isaiah 56:1–2, *Holy Bible: New International Version*.

65. Genesis 15:6; Proverbs 2:1–9, *Holy Bible: New International Version*.

66. 'The LORD commanded us to obey all these decrees and to fear the LORD our God, so that we might always prosper and be kept alive, as is the case today. And if we are careful to obey all this law before the LORD our God, as he has commanded us, that will be our righteousness'. Deuteronomy 6:24–5, *Holy Bible: New International Version*.

67. Deuteronomy 6:25 and 9:4–6, *Holy Bible: New International Version*.

68. Matthew 22:36–40, *Holy Bible: New International Version*.

69. Slote, 'Justice as a Virtue' (emphasis added).

70. 2 Corinthian 8:14, *Holy Bible: New International Version* (emphasis added).

71. 1 Timothy 5:8, *Holy Bible: New International Version*. 'If anyone does not provide for his relatives, and especially for his immediate family, he has denied the faith and is worse than an unbeliever'.

72. Mark 7:9–13, *Holy Bible: New International Version*.

73. 1 Timothy 6:17–18, *Holy Bible: New International Version*.

4 Ghosh and Chick, 'Commodity Control: A Missing Element in Keynes's *General Theory*'

1. Dipak Ghosh presented a paper to the Association for Heterodox Economics at Kingston University in London in 2009. He left a revised draft of just under 3,000 words, dated October 2009, which has been fleshed out by Victoria Chick. She wishes to emphasize that references to her own work were in Dipak's original draft. Although

the draft bore the words 'Please do not use without consulting the author', we hope this use is appropriate and one which Dipak would have wished. While this paper was being expanded, Chick came across L. Fantacci, 'Keynes's Commodity and Currency Plans for the Post-War World', in M. C. Marcuzzo (ed.), *Speculation and Regulation in Commodity Markets: The Keynesian Approach in Theory and Practice* (Rome: Department of Statistical Sciences, Sapienza University of Rome, 2012), pp. 177–206. However, Fantacci's work does not make some of the connections this chapter brings out.

2.   G. L. S. Shackle, *The Years of High Theory* (Cambridge: Cambridge University Press, 1967), p. 182; V. Chick, 'On Open Systems', *Brazilian Journal of Political Economy*, 24:1 (2004), pp. 3–16, on p. 9; J. M. Keynes, *The General Theory of Employment, Interest and Money* (London: Macmillan, 1936). Reprinted in D. E. Moggridge (ed.), *The Collected Writings of John Maynard Keynes* (hereafter abbreviated as *CW*, with volume number in roman numerals), 30 vols (London: Macmillan, 1971–80), VII.

3.   Prices move just enough to cover changes in costs: Keynesassumed diminishing returns in the short period, so prices rise with increased output.

4.   N. Kaldor 'What is Wrong with Economic Theory', *Quarterly Journal of Economics*, 89:3 (1975), pp. 347–57, on p. 350.

5.   J. M. Keynes, 'The Policy of Government Storage of Food-Stuffs and Raw Materials', *Economic Journal*, 48:191 (1938), pp. 449–60, reprinted in *CW* XXI, pp. 456–70; 'Some Aspects of Commodity Markets', *Manchester Guardian Commercial, European Reconstruction Series*, section 13 (29 March 1923), in *CW* XII, pp. 255–66; 'The Control of Raw Materials by Governments', *Nation and Athenaeum* (June 1926), in *CW* XIX, pp. 546–52.

6.   Chapter 3 of *CW* XXVII contains materials on Keynes's war-time plan for commodity price stabilization. These papers only came to be known when they were released under the thirty-year rule. War-time government papers could not be published at the time.

7.   R. Skidelsky, 'Keynes, Globalisation and the Bretton Woods Institutions in the Light of Changing Ideas about Markets', *World Economics*, 6 (2005), pp. 15–29, on p. 16.

8.   Chick, 'On Open Systems', p. 9.

9.   Keynes, 'The Policy of Government Storage of Food-Stuffs and Raw Materials'.

10.   Keynes, 'The Policy of Government Storage of Food-Stuffs and Raw Materials', p. 454.

11.   Keynes, 'The Policy of Government Storage of Food-Stuffs and Raw Materials', p. 458.

12.   Keynes, 'The Policy of Government Storage of Food-Stuffs and Raw Materials', p. 451.

13.   Keynes, 'The Policy of Government Storage of Food-Stuffs and Raw Materials', p. 451.

14.   Keynes, 'The Policy of Government Storage of Food-Stuffs and Raw Materials', p. 450.

15.   Keynes, 'The Policy of Government Storage of Food-Stuffs and Raw Materials', p. 450.

16.   Keynes, 'The Policy of Government Storage of Food-Stuffs and Raw Materials', p. 453.

17.   Keynes, 'The Policy of Government Storage of Food-Stuffs and Raw Materials', p. 453.

18.   Keynes, 'The Policy of Government Storage of Food-Stuffs and Raw Materials', p. 453.

19.   The English version of this paper was published only in 1954. The references in the text are to its reprint: M. Kalecki, '"Cost-determined" and "Demand Determined" Prices', in Kalecki, *Selected Essays on the Dynamics of the Capitalist Economy, 1933–1970* (Cambridge: Cambridge University Press, 1971), pp. 43–61.

20.   Kalecki, '"Cost-determined" and "Demand Determined" Prices', p. 43.

21.   J. R. Hicks, *Capital and Growth* (Oxford: Clarendon Press, 1965).

22.   Kalecki, '"Cost-determined" and "Demand Determined" Prices'.

23.   Hicks, *Capital and Growth*, ch. 7.

24.   Hicks, *Capital and Growth*, p. 79.

25. Hicks, *Capital and Growth*, pp. 43–4.
26. Kaldor, 'What is Wrong with Economic Theory'.
27. Kaldor, 'What is Wrong with Economic Theory', p. 352.
28. Kaldor, 'What is Wrong with Economic Theory', p. 354.
29. Keynes, 'The Policy of Government Storage'.
30. J. M. Keynes, 'Some Aspects of Commodity Markets', *Manchester Guardian Commercial, European Reconstruction Series*, section 13 (29 March 1923), reprinted in *CW* XII, pp. 255–66.
31. J. M. Keynes, *Special Memorandum on Stocks of Staple Commodities*, London and Cambridge Economic Service special memorandum 1 (1923), in *CW* XII, pp. 267–314. Keynes, *Special Memorandum on Stocks of Staple Commodities*, London and Cambridge Economic Service special memorandum 6 (1924), in *CW* XII, pp. 314–57. Keynes, *Special Memorandum on Stocks of Staple Commodities*, London and Cambridge Economic Service special memorandum 32 (1930), in *CW* XII, pp. 574–647.
32. J. M. Keynes, 'The Control of Raw Materials by Governments', *The Nation and Athenaeum* (June 1926), in *CW* XIX, pp. 546–52.
33. Keynes, *CW* XIX, p. 550.
34. Keynes, 'The Policy of Government Storage', p. 458.
35. Keynes, 'The Policy of Government Storage', p. 455.
36. R. Skidelsky, *John Maynard Keynes,* vol. 3: *Fighting for Britain 1937–1946* (Basingstoke: Macmillan, 2000), p. 234.
37. Keynes, *CW* XXVII, p. 105.
38. J. M. Keynes, 'Some Aspects of Commodity Markets', *Manchester Guardian Commercial, European Reconstruction Series*, section 13 (29 March 1923), in *CW* XII, pp. 255–66.
39. Keynes, *CW* XXVII, p. 172.
40. Skidelsky, *John Maynard Keynes*, p. 236. For details of the response to Keynes's proposals see Chapter 7, as well as J. F. A. Pullinger, 'The Bank and the Commodity Markets', Appendix A in J. S. Fforde, *The Bank of England and Public Policy, 1941–58* (Cambridge: Cambridge University Press, 1992), pp. 785–95.
41. Pullinger, 'The Bank and the Commodity Markets', p. 795.
42. Pullinger, 'The Bank and the Commodity Markets', p. 787.
43. Keynes, *CW* XXVII, pp. 110–11.
44. Keynes, *CW* XXVII, p. 195.
45. J. R. Hicks, *Economic Perspectives: Further Essays in Money and Growth* (Oxford: Clarendon Press, 1977), p. 98.
46. Brandt Commission, *Common Crisis, North-South: Co-operation for World Recovery* (London: Pan Books, 1983).
47. N. Kaldor, 'The Role of Commodity Prices in Economic Recovery', *Lloyds Bank Review*, 149 (1983), pp. 21–34.
48. Kaldor, 'The Role of Commodity Prices in Economic Recovery', p. 34.
49. J. M. Keynes, *The Economic Consequences of the Peace* (London: Macmillan, 1919). Reprinted as *CW* II. The depiction of Germany as the rapidly growing industrial sector held back by the inadequate supply of food and other wage-goods is an early expression of the situation modelled by Kaldor.
50. Brandt Report: A Summary, at http://www.sharing.org/information-centre/reports/brandt-report-summary, final paragraph [accessed 17 June 2014].

5 Ghosh and Ruziev, 'Cost-Determined and Demand-Determined Prices: Lessons for the Globalized World from Development Economics'

1. Credit for the original contribution of this chapter should go to Dipak alone. When Kobil Ruziev first saw the draft of this chapter in 2008, Dipak had almost completed it; it had lacked only a concluding section. Dipak then invited him to become a co-author and help to complete it. As for more recent updates of references, data and also minor adjustments to other parts of the chapter to avoid overlap with Chapter 2, we hope that Dipak would have approved them.

2. The problem of persistent unemployment was thought to belong to the past during the golden era of Great Moderation. See B. Bernanke, '*Great Moderation*', Remarks at the Meeting of Eastern Economic Association, Washington DC, February 2004, at http://www.federalreserve.gov/boarddocs/speeches/2004/20040220/ [accessed 26 May 2013].

3. A. Bagchi, *The Political Economy of Development* (Cambridge: Cambridge University Press, 1982), p. 3.

4. See for example, among others, G. Ranis and J. C. H. Fei, 'A Theory of Economic Development', *American Economic Review*, 51:4 (1961), pp. 533–565; J. C. H. Fei and G. Ranis, *Development of the Labour Surplus Economy* (Illinois: Irwin, 1964); D. W. Jorgenson, 'Testing Alternative Theories of the Development of a Dual Economy', in I. Adelman and E. Thorbeck (eds), *Theory and Design of Economic Development* (Baltimore, MD: Johns Hopkins University Press, 1966), pp. 45–60; and D. W. Jorgenson, 'Surplus Agricultural Labour and the Development of a Dual Economy', *Oxford Economic Papers*, 19:3 (1967), pp. 288–312. A comprehensive list can be found in A. K. Dixit, 'Models of Dual Economies', in J. A. Mirrlees and N. H. Stern (eds), *Models of Economic Growth* (New York: John Wiley & Sons, 1973), pp. 325–7 and S. M. R. Kanbur and J. P. McIntosh, 'Dual Economy Models: Retrospect and Prospect', *Bulletin of Economic Research*, 40:2 (1988), pp. 83–113. For open and closed systems, see B. J. Loasby, 'Closed Models and Open Systems', *Journal of Economic Methodology*, 10:3 (2003), pp. 285–306 and V. Chick, 'On Open Systems', *Brazilian Journal of Political Economy*, 24:1 (2004), pp. 3–16.

5. A. O. Hirschman, *Essays in Trespassing: Economics to Politics and Beyond* (Cambridge: Cambridge University Press, 1981), p. 23.

6. A. Sen, 'Development: Which Way Now?', *Economic Journal*, 93 (1983), pp. 745–62, on p. 746.

7. For instance, see A. Gerschenkron, *Economic Backwardness in Historical Perspective: A Book of Essays* (Cambridge, MA: Harvard University Press, 1966); W. A. Lewis, 'Economic Development with Unlimited Supplies of Labour', *Manchester School*, 22:2 (1954), pp. 139–91; W. A. Lewis, 'Unlimited Labour: Further Notes', *Manchester School*, 26:1 (1958), pp. 1–32; and H. Myint, *The Economics of the Developing Countries* (London: Hutchinson, 1968).

8. See C. Kirkpatrick and A. Barrientos, 'The Lewis Model after 50 Years', *Manchester School*, 72:6 (2004), pp. 679–90, on p. 679 .

9. Though some neoclassical authors treat them as identical. See for example Jorgenson, 'Surplus Agricultural Labour and the Development of a Dual Economy'.

10. J. Robinson, 'Disguised Unemployment', *Economic Journal*, 46:184 (1936), pp. 225–37, on p. 226 (original emphasis).

11. Lewis, 'Economic Development with Unlimited Supplies of Labour', p. 140.

12. For the discussion of how Lewis's main contribution lost its central message in the hands of the neoclassical economists, see D. Ghosh, 'Metamorphosis of Lewis's Dual Economy Model', *Journal of Economic Methodology*, 14:1 (2007), pp. 5–25.

13. A. Sen, *Employment, Technology and Development* (Oxford: Clarendon Press, 1975), p. 85). They are called 'necessities' in M. Kalecki, '"Cost-determined" and "Demand Determined" Prices', *Selected Essays on the Dynamics of the Capitalist Economy, 1933–1970* (Cambridge: Cambridge University Press, 1971), pp. 43–61.

14. Lewis, 'Economic Development with Unlimited Supplies of Labour', p. 173.

15. M. Kalecki, 'Unemployment in Underdeveloped Countries', in *Collected Work of Michael Kalecki, Volume V, Developing Economies* (Oxford: Clarendon Press, 1993), pp. 3–5, on p. 3.

16. See for example V. K. R. V. Rao, 'Investment, Income and Multiplier in an Underdeveloped Economy', in A. N. Agarwala and S. P. Singh (eds), *The Economics of Underdevelopment* (New York: Oxford University Press, 1952), pp. 205–18, and A. K. Dasgupta, 'Keynesian Economics and Underdeveloped Countries', *Economic Weekly* (26 January 1954), pp. 29–37.

17. Rao, 'Investment, Income and Multiplier in an Underdeveloped Economy', pp. 206–7. See also P. N. Mathur and H. Ezekiel, 'Marketed Surplus for Food and Price Fluctuations in a Developing Economy', *Kyklos*, 14:3 (1961), pp. 396–408, and I. Ahluwalia, 'An Analysis of Price and Output Behavior in the Indian Economy: 1951–1973', *Journal of Development Economics*, 6:3 (1979), pp. 363–90.

18. Sen, *Employment, Technology and Development*, p. 85.

19. N. Kaldor, 'What is Wrong with Economic Theory', *Quarterly Journal of Economics*, 89:3 (1975), pp. 347–57.

20. See M. Dobb, *Soviet Economic Development Since 1917* (London: Routledge and Kegan Paul, 1966), chs 8, 9.

21. All quotes of Stalin are from M. Ellman, *Socialist Planning* (Cambridge: Cambridge University Press, 1989), p. 96.

22. Kaldor, 'What is Wrong with Economic Theory', p. 350.

23. Lewis, 'Economic Development with Unlimited Supplies of Labour', p. 173.

24. Kaldor, 'What is Wrong with Economic Theory', p. 354.

25. Brandt Commission, *Common Crisis, North-South: Co-operation for World Recovery* (London: Pan Books, 1983).

26. J. R. Hicks, *Economic Perspectives: Further Essays in Money and Growth* (Oxford: Clarendon Press, 1977).

27. Hicks, *Economic Perspectives: Further Essays in Money and* Growth, p. 98 (emphasis added).

28. J. M. Keynes, 'Economic Possibilities for Our Grandchildren', in *The Collected Writings of John Maynard Keynes*. Vol. IX: *Essays in Persuasion* (London: Macmillan, 1972), p. 325 (original emphasis).

29. Keynes, 'Economic Possibilities for Our Grandchildren', p. 326.

30. J. M. Keynes, 'The Policy of Government Storage of Food-Stuffs and Raw Materials', *Economic Journal*, 48:191 (1938), pp. 449–60. The quote is from p. 455. See also chapter 3 of J. M. Keynes, *The Collected Writings of John Maynard Keynes*. Vol. XXVII: *Activities 1940–1946, Shaping the Post-war World Employment and Commodities*, ed. D. E. Moggridge (London: Macmillan, 1980), which contains materials on Keynes's war-time plan for commodity price stabilization. These papers came to be known much later under the thirty-year rule as the war-time government papers could not be

published when these were written.

31. Keynes, *The Collected Writings of John Maynard Keynes*, p. 172.
32. N. Kaldor, 'The Role of Commodity Prices in Economic Recovery', *Lloyds Bank Review*, 149 (1983), pp. 21–34, on p. 34.
33. Keynes, 'The Policy of Government Storage of Food-Stuffs and Raw Materials'.
34. See H. Bloch and D. Sapsford, 'Whither the Terms of Trade?', *Cambridge Journal of Economics*, 24 (2000), pp. 461–81, and H. Bloch, A. M. Dockery and D. Sapsford, 'Commodity Prices, Wages and US Inflationin the 20th Century', *Journal of Post Keynesian Economics*, 26:3 (2004), pp. 523–45.
35. H. Bloch, A. M. Dockery, C. W. Morgan and D. Sapsford, 'Growth, Commodity Prices, Inflation and the Distribution of Income', *Metroeconomica*, 58:1 (2005), pp. 3–44.
36. See also the International Monetary Fund (IMF), *World Economic Outlook, April 2008: Housing and the Business Cycle* (Washington, DC: IMF, 2008), p. 197.
37. N. Krichene, '*Recent Inflationary Trends in World Commodities Markets*', IMF Working Paper WP/08/130 (Washington DC: IMF, 2008) and the IMF, *World Economic Outlook, April 2008: Housing and the Business Cycle*, p. 47.
38. Food and Agriculture Organization of the United Nations (FAOUN), *Recent Trends in World Food Commodity Prices: Costs and Benefits. The State of Food Insecurity in the World 2011* (Rome: FAOUN, 2011). Also see T. Helbling and V. M. Blackman, *Commodity Price Moves and The Global Economic Slowdown* (Washington DC: IMF Survey Magazine, 2008).
39. See M. De Ceco, 'Origins of the Post-War Payment System', *Cambridge Journal of Economics*, 3:1 (1979), pp. 49–61; Kaldor, 'The Role of Commodity Prices in Economic Recovery', in J. Williamson, *The Failure of World Monetary Reform, 1971–74* (Middlesex: Nelson, 1977); and R. Skidelsky, 'Keynes, Globalisation and the Bretton Woods Institutions in the Light of Changing Ideas about Markets', *World Economics*, 6 (2005), pp. 15–30.
40. J. Cotis, 'Recent Development in Macroeconomic Analysis: Reviving the Case for Stabilisation Policies', *Économie Internationale*, 100:4Q (2004), pp. 85–98.
41. Brandt Commission, *Common Crisis, North-South: Co-operation for World Recovery*, p. 263.

6 Toporowski, 'Kalecki and the Savings Constraint on Economic Development'

1. See for example D. Ghosh, 'Fixprice-Flexprice in Development Economics', *Australian Economic Papers*, 25:46 (1986), pp. 122–7.
2. See M. Kula, 'Between Memory and Historical Inquiry: Kaleckiand the Warsaw Centre of Research on Underdeveloped Economies: 1962–1968', in R. Bellofiore, E. Karwowski and J. Toporowski (eds), *The Legacy of Rosa Luxemburg, Oskar Langeand Michał Kalecki, Volume 1 of Essays in Honour of Tadeusz Kowalik* (Basingstoke: Palgrave, 2013), pp. 165–79.
3. M. Manoilescu, *The Theory of Protection and International Trade* (London: P.S. King and Son, 1931).
4. M. Kalecki, 'Foreign Trade and the National Forces of Production', *Economic Journal*, 48:192 (1938), pp. 708–11 (orginal emphasis), on p. 711.
5. M. Kalecki, 'Report on the Main Current Economic Problems of Israel', In J. Osiatyński (ed.), *Collected Works of Michał Kalecki Volume V: Developing Economies* (Oxford:

Clarendon Press, 1993).

6. M. Kalecki, 'The Problem of Financing Economic Development', in J. Osiatyński (ed.), *Collected Works of Michał Kalecki Volume V: Developing Economies* (Oxford: Clarendon Press, 1993).

7. M. Kalecki, 'Observations on Social and Economic Aspects of "Intermediate Regimes"', in J. Osiatyński (ed.), *Collected Works of Michał Kalecki Volume V: Developing Economies* (Oxford: Clarendon Press, 1993).

8. See T. Skouras, 'The "Intermediate Regime" and Industrialization Prospects', *Development and Change*, 9 (1978), pp. 631–48, and J. Toye, *Dilemmas of Development* (Oxford: Blackwell, 1987).

9. M. Kalecki 'Problems of Financing Economic Development in a Mixed Economy', in J. Osiatyński (ed.), *Collected Works of Michał Kalecki Volume V: Developing Economies* (Oxford: Clarendon Press, 1993).

10. M. Kalecki, and I. Sachs 'Forms of Foreign Aid: An Economic Analysis', in J. Osiatyński (ed.), *Collected Works of Michał Kalecki Volume V: Developing Economies* (Oxford: Clarendon Press, 1993).

11. M. Kalecki, 'The Problem of Financing Economic Development', in J. Osiatyński (ed.), *Collected Works of Michał Kalecki Volume V: Developing Economies* (Oxford: Clarendon Press, 1993b), p. 25.

12. M. Kalecki, 'The Problem of Financing Economic Development', p. 26.

13. J. M. Keynes, *The General Theory of Employment Interest and Money* (London: Macmillan 1936), chs 6 and 7.

14. V. Chick, 'The Evolution of The Banking System and the Theory of Saving, Investment and Interest', *Economies et Sociétés*, 3 (1986), pp. 111–26.

15. M. Kalecki, 'The Problem of Financing Economic Development', pp. 24–5.

16. J. M. Keynes, *A Treatise on Money Volume I The Pure Theory of Money* (London: Macmillan, 1930), p. 125.

17. M. Kalecki, *Selected Essays on the Economic Growth of the Socialist and the Mixed Economy* (Cambridge: Cambridge University Press 1972), ch. 10.

18. M. Kalecki, 'Problems of Financing Economic Development in a Mixed Economy', in W. A. Eltis, M. F. G. Scott and J. N. Wolfe (eds), *Induction, Growth and Trade Essays in Honour of Sir Roy Harrod* (Oxford: Clarendon Press, 1970), pp. 96–104.

19. H. B. Chenery and A. M. Strout, 'Foreign Assistance and Economic Development', *American Economic Review*, 56:1 (1966), pp. 679–733. A. P. Thirlwall, *Growth and Development with Special Reference to Developing Economies* (Basingstoke: Palgrave Macmillan, 2005).

7 Ruziev and Dow, 'A Re-Evaluation of Banking Sector Reforms in Transition Economics: Intentions and Unintended Consequences'

1. S. Fries and A. Taci, 'Banking Transition: A Comparative Analysis', in L. Bokros, A. Fleming and C. Votava (eds), *Financial Transition in Europe and Central Asia: Challenges of the New Decade* (Washington, DC: World Bank, 2001), pp. 173–87, on p.173.

2. A. Zwass, *Money, Banking, and Credit in the Soviet Union and Eastern Europe* (London: Macmillan, 1979).

3. G. Garvy, *Money, Financial Flows, and Credit in the Soviet Union* (Cambridge: Ballinger, 1977), p. 42.

4. J. Kornai, *Growth, Shortage and Efficiency* (Oxford: Basil Blackwell, 1982).

5. S. Peachey and A. Roe, 'Financial Deepening and the Role of Financial Crises', in L. Bokros, A. Fleming and C. Votava (eds), *Financial Transition in Europe and Central Asia: Challenges of the New Decade* (Washington DC: World Bank, 2001), pp. 189–207.

6. S. Fischer and A. Gelb, 'The Process of Socialist Economic Transformation', *Journal of Economic Perspectives*, 5:4 (1991), pp. 91–104, on p. 95.

7. M. Ellman, 'Transition: Intended and Unintended Processes', *Comparative Economic Studies*, 47:4 (2005), pp. 595–614, on p. 595.

8. See, among others, G. Calvo and J. Frenkel, 'From Centrally Planned to Market Economy', *IMF Staff Papers*, 38:2 (1991), pp. 268–99; G. Calvo and J. Frenkel, 'Credit Markets, Credibility, and Economic Transformation', *Journal of Economic Perspectives*, 5:4 (1991), pp. 139–48; and Fischer and Gelb, 'The Process of Socialist Economic Transformation'.

9. EBRD, *Transition Report: Finance in Transition* (London: European Bank for Reconstruction and Development, 2006).

10. See B. Fischer and H. Reisen, 'Towards Capital Account Convertibility', *OECD Development Centre, Policy Brief No. 4* (Paris: OECD, 1992), EBRD, *Transition Report*, and K. Ruziev, 'Emerging Markets', in J. Toporowski and J. Michell (eds), *Handbook of Critical Issues in Finance* (Cheltenham: Edward Elgar, 2012), pp. 77–85.

11. See V. Chick, 'The Evolution of The Banking System and the Theory of Saving, Investment and Interest', *Economies et Sociétés*, 3 (1986), pp. 111–26, and V. Chick 'The Evolution of the Banking System and the Theory of Monetary Policy', in S. F. Frowen (ed.), *Monetary Theory and Monetary Policy: New Tracks in the 1990s* (Basingstoke: St Martin's Press, 1993), pp. 79–92. An application of Chick's analysis to transition economiesis developed in S. C. Dow, D. Ghosh and K. Ruziev, 'A Stages Approach to Banking Development in Transition Economies', *Journal of Post Keynesian Economics*, 31:1 (2008), pp. 3–34.

12. D. Yergin and J. Stanislaw, *The Commanding Heights: The Battle for the World Economy* (New York: Touchstone, 2002).

13. L. Abalkin, 'Economic Realities and Abstract Schemes. On Conceptual Principles of the Monetarist Financial Program', *Problems of Economic Transition*, 39:10 (1997), pp. 5–23, on p.6

14. See a study by B. Kim, 'The Income, Savings, and Monetary Overhang of Soviet Households', *Journal of Comparative Economics*, 27:4 (1999), pp. 644–68. Kim estimated the size of the monetary overhang in the FSU in 1991 to be around 40 per cent of the household sector's monetary balances. Since the monetary overhang was seen as financial assets not backed by goods and services, it was thought to represent suppressed inflation, which was seen as a source of imbalance, and needed to be unleashed sooner or later. He argued that more than 60 per cent adjustment in the price level would be necessary to remove it. However, the monetary overhangdid not need to cause any inflationary pressure if it was perceived as title also to private property, which was banned in almost all forms under central planning, not simply to goods and services alone. In other words, by allowing private proprietorship and the gradual sale of public assets to the private sector through step-by-step privatization, any possible inflationary consequences of the monetary overhang could have been prevented. Furthermore, the existence of the grey economy in general, also referred to as 'the second economy', and the kolkhoz market in particular in the Soviet Union casts shadow on the accuracy of the estimated size of monetary overhang. Since prices in these markets were determined freely by market forces of supply and demand, one would expect them to have played an equilibrating role. For more on the 'second economy' see G. Grossman, 'The "Second

Economy" of the USSR', *Problems of Communism*, 26:5 (1977), pp. 25–40.

15. For instance, Russia and Poland chose a shock therapy approach to transition and removed almost all price controls overnight.

16. See W. Carlin, M. Schaffer and P. Seabright, 'Barter and Non-monetary Transactions in Transition Countries: Evidence from a Cross-country Survey', in P. Wachtel (ed.), *The Vanishing Rouble: Barter Networks and Non-Monetary Transactions in Post-Soviet Societies* (Cambridge: Cambridge University Press, 2000), pp. 236–56.

17. See S. Aukutsionek, 'Industrial Barter in Russia', *Communist Economies and Economic Transformation*, 10:2 (1998), pp. 179–188, on p. 181.

18. See V. Ivanenko and D. Mikheyev, 'The Role of Non-Monetary Trade in Russian Transition', *Post-Communist Economies*, 14:4 (2002), pp. 405–19, on p. 409.

19. For detailed discussion, see Dow, Ghosh and Ruziev, 'A Stages Approach to Banking Development in Transition Economies'.

20. The distinction between outside and inside money, originally made by J. Gurley and E. S. Shaw, *Money in a Theory of Finance* (Washington, DC: Brookings Institution, 1970), pp. 72–3. Inside money is both an asset and liability of the private sector, whereas outside money is its asset only. Outside money may be a pure asset (such as gold) or an asset that is the liability of the central bank. For instance, while the fiat money of the central bank and gold can be classified as outside money, bank deposits can be classified as inside money.

21. The first of these shocks came before the political meltdown of the FSU in early 1991 and therefore was common to all other members of the FSU. During perestroika (and glasnost – freedom of information) it became public knowledge that corruption and bribery were deeply rooted in society. Since owning private property was banned in the FSU and keeping substantial amounts in bank accounts was not desirable, again for political reasons, it was believed that the bulk of wealth generated by individuals through various 'dubious' activities was hoarded in high-denomination banknotes. Therefore, in early 1991 the decision was taken to confiscate part of cash hoards of 'unjustifiably' wealthy individuals by withdrawing the high-denomination banknotes from circulation. As a result, individuals, who either did not bother about financial return offered on bank deposits or did not trust the political system and thus kept their wealth in cash hoards, suffered heavily.

22. S. Glaz`ev, 'The Central Bank versus Russian Industry', *Problems of Economic Transition*, 41:1 (1998), pp. 72–92, on p. 75.

23. See C. Rock and V. Solodkov, 'Monetary Policies, Banking, and Trust in Changing Institutions: Russia's Transition in the 1990s', *Journal of Economic Issues*, 35:2 (2001), pp. 451–8.

24. By 1997 total short-term and long-term debt issue had reached 296 trillion roubles ($51.3 billion), of which 25 per cent was held by foreign investors. The growing fiscal deficit financed in this way meant that the resulting obligations were financed in Ponzi fashion by sales of new GKOs. The only way out of this situation was to either return to printing huge amounts of money or to cut government spending and improve tax collection. As the consequence of the former option was clear from the hyperinflation of the early 1990s, successive governments decided to choose the latter option. For more please see C. S. Poirot, 'Financial Integration under Conditions of Chaotic Hysteresis: The Russian Financial Crisis of 1998', *Journal of Post Keynesian Economics*, 23:3 (2001), pp. 485–507, and D. Gros and A. Steinherr, *Economic Transition in Central and Eastern Europe: Planting the Seeds* (Cambridge: Cambridge University Press, 2004), pp. 252–3.

25. Except for Estonia, Latvia, Lithuania and Moldova which joined the Soviet Union in 1940 but effectively started central planning experience after World War II.

26. J. Marangos, 'Price Liberalization, Monetary and Fiscal Policies for Transition Econo-
    mies: A Post Keynesian Perspective', *Journal of Post Keynesian Economics*, 25:3 (2003),
    pp. 449–70, on p. 453.
27. Fischer and Gelb, 'The Process of Socialist Economic Transformation', pp. 92–3.
28. R. W. Anderson, and C. Kegels, *Transition Banking: Financial Development of Central
    and Eastern Europe* (Oxford: Clarendon, 1998), on p. 75.
29. See J. Bonin, I. Hasan and P. Wachtel, 'Banking in Transition Countries', in A. N.
    Berger, P. Molyneux and J. O. S. Wilson (eds), *The Oxford Handbook of Banking*
    (Oxford: Oxford University Press, 2010).
30. Bonin, Hasan and Wachtel, 'Banking in Transition Countries'.
31. See EBRD, *Transition Report: Transition in Crisis?* (London: European Bank for
    Reconstruction and Development, 2009), p. 43 and EBRD, *Transition Report:
    Integration Across Boarders* (London: European Bank for Reconstruction and
    Development, 2012), p. 45.
32. IMF, 'Russian Federation: Financial System Stability Assessment', IMF Country Report
    No 11/291 (Washington, DC: IMF, 2011), p. 12.
33. See J. Peek and E. S. Rosengren, 'The International Transmission of Financial Shocks:
    The Case of Japan', *American Economic Review*, 87:4 (1997), pp. 495–505, and EBRD,
    Transition Report: Finance in Transition.
34. EBRD, *Transition Report: Finance in Transition*, p. 43.
35. EBRD, *Transition Report: Transition in Crisis?*, p. 42.
36. See EBRD, *Transition Report: Finance in Transition*, p. 48, and Bonin, Hasan and
    Wachtel, 'Banking in Transition Countries', p. 18.
37. EBRD, *Transition Report: Transition in Crisis?*, p. 46.
38. For the experiences of Hungary and Kazakhstan, see, respectively, EBRD, *Transition
    Report: Integration Across Boarders* (London: European Bank for Reconstruction and
    Development, 2012), and K. Ruziev and T. Majidov, 'Differing Effects of the Global
    Financial Crisison the Central Asian Countries: Kazakhstan, the Kyrgyz Republic, and
    Uzbekistan', *Europe-Asia Studies*, 65:4 (2013), pp. 682–716.
39. EBRD, *Transition Report: Recovery and Reform* (London: European Bank for
    Reconstruction and Development, 2010), p. 49.
40. D. Gabor, 'Managing Capital Accounts in Emerging Markets: Lessons from the Global
    Financial Crisis', *Journal of Development Studies*, 48:6 (2012), pp. 714–31.
41. In comparison, foreign currency loans and deposits are only of marginal importance in
    advanced economies where the general public's trustin outside moneyas well as inside
    moneyis strong. See also EBRD, *Transition Report: Recovery and Reform*, p. 48.
42. Dow, Ghosh and Ruziev, 'A Stages Approach to Banking Development in Transition
    Economies'.
43. See S. Claessens and N. Van Horen, 'Foreign Banks: Trends, Impact and Financial
    Stability', IMF Working Paper No. 12/10 (Washington, DC: IMF, 2012), and R.
    De Haas and I. Van Lelyveld, 'Multinational Banks and the Global Financial Crisis:
    Weathering the Perfect Storm', EBRD Working Paper No. 135 (London: EBRD, 2011).
44. See H. Kamil and K. Rai, 'The Global Credit Crunch and Foreign Banks' Lending to
    Emerging Markets: Why Did Latin America Fare Better?', IMF Working Paper No.
    10/102 (Washington, DC: IMF, 2010), and S. Ongena, J. Peydró and N. Van Horen,
    'Shocks Abroad, Pain at Home? Bank-firm Level Evidence on Financial Contagion
    during the 2007–2009 Crisis', 2012, at https://www.ecb.int/events/pdf/conferences/
    mar_net/Ongena_Peydro_vanHoren_2012–03.pdf?3815db28ec6e314d333d288d70
    8ec2b7 [accessed 27 May 2013].

8 Djalilov and Hölscher, 'Dynamics of Risk, Concentration and Efficiency in Banking Sectors of Transition Economies'

1. K. Djalilov and J. Piesse, 'Financial Development and Growth in Central Asia', *Emerging Market Trade and Finance*, 47:6 (2011), pp. 4–23.
2. E. Kraft and D. Tirtiroğlu, 'Bank Efficiency in Croatia: A Stochastic-Frontier Analysis', *Journal of Comparative Economics,* 26:2 (1998), pp. 282–300.
3. I. Jemric and B. Vujcic, 'Efficiency of Banks in Croatia: A DEA Approach', *Comparative Economic Studies*, 44:2–3 (2002), pp. 169–93.
4. Please see, among others, S. Fries and A. Taci, 'Cost Efficiency of Banks in Transition: Evidence from 289 Banks in 15 Post-Communist Countries', *Journal of Banking and Finance,* 29:1 (2005), pp. 55–81; K. Tochkov and N. Nenovsky, 'Institutional Reforms, EU Accession, and Bank Efficiency in Transition Economies. Evidence from Bulgaria', *Emerging Markets Finance and Trade*, 47:1 (2011), pp. 113–29; A. Karas, K. Schoors and L. Weill, 'Are Private Banks More Efficient than Public Banks?', *Economics of Transition*, 18:1 (2010), pp. 209–44; J. P. Bonin, I. Hasan and P. Wachtel, 'Bank Performance, Efficiency and Ownership in Transition Countries', *Journal of Banking and Finance*, 29:1 (2005), pp. 31–53; E. M. Nikiel and T. P. Opiela, 'Customer Type and Bank Efficiency in Poland: Implications for Emerging Market Banking', *Contemporary Economic Policy*, 20:3 (2002), pp. 255–71; and I. Hasan and K. Marton, 'Development and Efficiency of the Banking Sector in a Transitional Economy: Hungarian Experience', *Journal of Banking and Finance*, 27:12 (2003), pp. 2249–71.
5. Y. Fang, I. Hasan and K. Marton, 'Bank Efficiency in Transition Economies: Recent Evidence from South-Eastern Europe', *BOFIT Discussion Papers* 5/2011 (2011).
6. S. Brissimis, M. Delis and N. Papanikolaou, 'Exploring the Nexus between Banking Sector Reform and Performance: Evidence from Newly Acceded EU Countries', *Bank of Greece Working Paper*, 73 (2008).
7. M. Keeley, 'Deposit Insurance, Risk and Market Power in Banking', *American Economic Review*, 80:5 (1990), pp. 1183–200.
8. C. Matutes and X. Vives, 'Imperfect Competition, Risk Taking and Regulation in Banking', *European Economic Review*, 44:1 (2000), pp. 1–34.
9. J. Boyd and G. De Nicolo, 'The Theory of Bank Risk Taking and Competition Revisited', *Journal of Finance*, 60:3 (2005), pp. 1329–43.
10. D. Martinez-Miera and R. Rupello, 'Does Competition Reduce the Risk of Bank Failure?', *Review of Financial Studies,* 23:10 (2010), pp. 3638–64.
11. Martinez-Miera and Rupello, 'Does Competition Reduce the Risk of Bank Failure?'
12. Please see, among others, A. Kanas, 'Bank Dividends, Risk, and Regulatory Regimes', *Journal of Banking and Finance,* 37:1 (2013), pp. 1–10, and G. Jimenez, J. Lopez and J. Saurina, 'How Does Competition Affect Bank Risk-taking?', *Journal of Financial Stability,* 9:2 (2013), pp. 185–95.
13. Please see, among others, A. Berger, L. Klapper and G. Udell, 'The Ability of Banks to Lend to Informationally Opaque Small Businesses', *Journal of Banking and Finance,* 25:12 (2001), pp. 2127–67; A. Berger and G. Udell, 'Small Business Credit Availability and Relationship Lending: The Importance of Bank Organisational Structure', *Economic Journal*, 112:477 (2002), pp. F32–F53; and R. Haselmann and P. Wachtel, 'Risk Taking by Banks in the Transition Countries', *Comparative Economic Studies*, 49:3, (2007), pp. 411–29.
14. Please see, among others, D. A. Grigorian and V. Manole, 'Determinants of Commercial Bank Performance in Transition. An Application of Data Envelopment Analysis', *The*

World Bank. Working Paper 2850 (2002), pp. 1–36; A. Peresetskiy, 'Bank Cost Efficiency in Kazakhstan and Russia', *BOFIT Discussion Papers* 1/2010 (2010); A. Pruteanu-Podpiera, L.Weill and F. Schobert, 'Banking Competition and Efficiency: A Micro-Data Analysis on the Czech Banking Industry', *Comparative Economic Studies*, 50: 2 (2008), pp. 253–73; and L. Weill, 'Banking Efficiency in Transition Economies, The Role of Foreign Ownership', *Economics of Transition*, 11: 3 (2003), pp. 569–92.

15. Haselmann and Wachtel, 'Risk Taking by Banks in the Transition Countries'.
16. M. K. Agoraki, M. D. Delis and P. Fotios, 'Regulations, Competition and Bank Risk-taking in Transition Countries', *Journal of Financial Stability*, 7:1(2011), pp. 38–48.
17. Fries and Taci, 'Cost Efficiency of Banks in Transition: Evidence from 289 Banks in 15 Post-Communist Countries'.
18. A. Berger, L. Klapper and R. Turk-Ariss, 'Bank Competition and Financial Stability', *Journal of Financial Services Research*, 35:2 (2009), pp. 99–118.
19. G. Battese and T. Coelli, 'A Model for Technical Inefficiency Effects in a Stochastic Frontier Production Function for Panel Data', *Empirical Economics,* 20:2 (1995), pp. 325–32.
20. Please see, among others, J. Boyd, G. De Nicolo and A. M. Jalal, 'Bank Risk-Taking and Competition Revisited: New Theory and New Evidence, *IMF Working Paper*, WP/06/297 (2006), and L. B. Marquez, R. Correa, and H. Sapriza, 'International Evidence on Government Support and Risk Taking in the Banking Sector', *IMF Working Paper* WP/13/94 (2013), p. 46.
21. Please see, among others, Boyd, De Nicolo and Jalal, 'Bank Risk-Taking and Competition Revisited: New Theory and New Evidence', and Marquez, Correa and Sapriza, 'International Evidence on Government Support and Risk Taking in the Banking Sector', p. 46.
22. Marquez, Correa and Sapriza, 'International Evidence on Government Support and Risk Taking in the Banking Sector', p. 46.
23. Marquez, Correa and Sapriza, 'International Evidence on Government Support and Risk Taking in the Banking Sector', p. 46.
24. B. Bai, and J. Hölscher, 'Banking Reform in China', in R. W. McGee (ed.), *Accounting Reform in Transition and Developing Economies* (New York: Springer, 2009), pp. 45–65.
25. In particular, the EU membership required the reduction of state aid (see J. Hölscher, N. Nulsch and J. Stephan, 'Ten Years after Accession: State Aid in Eastern Europe', *European State Aid Law Quarterly*, EStAL:2, (2014), pp. 305–9).

9 Gabor, 'Fictions of Transition: On the Role of Central Banks in Post-Socialist Transformations'

1. S. Fischer and A. Gelb, 'The Process of Socialist Economic Transformation', *Journal of Economic Perspectives*, 5:4 (1991), pp. 91–105, and R. Ericson, 'The Classical Soviet-Type Economy: Nature of the System and Implications for Reform', *Journal of Economic Perspectives*, 5:4 (1991), pp. 11–27.
2. C. Ban, 'Neoliberalism in Translation: Economic Ideas and Reforms in Spain and Romania' (PhD dissertation, University of Maryland, 2011).
3. A. Ben-Ner and J. M. Montias, 'The Introduction of Markets in a Hypercentralized Economy: The Case of Romania', *Journal of Economic Perspectives*, 5:4 (1991), pp. 163–70.
4. L. Cernat, *Europeanization, Varieties of Capitalism and Economic Performance in Central and Eastern Europe* (Basingstoke: Palgrave Macmillan, 2006). See also A. Nolke

and A. Vliegenhart, 'Enlarging Varieties of Capitalism: the Emergence of Dependent Market Economies in East and Central Europe', *World Politics*, 61:4 (2009), pp. 670–702.

5. D. Gabor, *Central Banking and Financialization. A Romanian Account of How Eastern Europe became Subprime* (Basingstoke: Palgrave Macmillan 2010).

6. A. Boot, 'Relationship Banking: What Do We Know?', *Journal of Financial Intermediation*, 9:1 (2000), pp. 7–25.

7. P. Hall and D. Soskice, *Varieties of Capitalism: The Institutional Foundations of Comparative Advantage* (London: Oxford University Press, 2001). See also C. Ban, 'Brazil's Liberal Neo-developmentalism: New Paradigm or Edited Orthodoxy?', *Review of International Political Economy*, 20:2 (2013), pp. 298–331.

8. D. Demekas and M. S. Khan, 'The Romanian Economic Reform Program', IMF Working Paper No 91/80 (Washington, DC: IMF, 1991). See also International Monetary Fund, *A Study of the Soviet Economy* (Washington, DC: IMF, 1991).

9. A. Amsden, *The Market Meets Its Match: Restructuring the Economies of Eastern Europe* (Cambridge, MA: Harvard University Press, 1994).

10. M. Blyth, *Great Transformations: Economic Ideas and Institutional Change in the Twentieth Century* (Cambridge: Cambridge University Press, 2002).

11. J. Kornai, E. Maskin and G. Roland, 'Understanding the Soft Budget Constraint', *Journal of Economic Literature* (2003), pp. 1095–136.

12. J. Pickles, 'Restructuring State Enterprises', in J. Pickles and A. Smith (eds), *Theorising Transition: The Political Economy of Post-Communist Transformations* (London: Routledge, 1998).

13. Pickles, 'Restructuring State Enterprises'.

14. M. Burawoy and J. Lukács, *The Radiant Past: Ideology and Reality in Hungary's Road to Capitalism* (Chicago, IL: University of Chicago Press, 1992).

15. J. Persky, 'Retrospectives: Langeand von Mises, Large-Scale Enterprises, and the Economic Case for Socialism', *Journal of Economic Perspectives* (1991), pp. 229–36.

16. O. Lange, *On the Economic Theory of Socialism* (Minneapolis, MN: University of Minnesota, 1968), p. 121. Lange argued that 'the most important part of economic life is just as far removed from free competition as it is from socialism; it is chocked up with restrictions of all sorts ... when it will be recognized that it is impossible to return to free competition, or to have successful public control of enterprise and of investment without taking them out of private hands, then socialism will remain as the only solution available'.

17. L. von Mises, 'Economic Calculation in the Socialist Commonwealth', in F. A. Hayek (ed.), *Collectivist Economic Planning* (London: Routledge, 1937), pp. 87–130.

18. See R. Portes, *Macroeconomic Equilibrium and Disequilibrium in Centrally Planned Economies* (London: Centre for Economic Policy Research, 1987).

19. J. Kornai, 'The Soft Budget Constraint', *Kyklos*, 39:1 (1986), pp. 3–30.

20. See Ericson, 'The Classical Soviet-Type Economy: Nature of the System and Implications for Reform'.

21. J. K. Galbraith, *The New Industrial State* (Princeton, NJ: Princeton University Press, 1967).

22. G. Gereffi, J. Humphrey and T. Sturgeon, 'The Governance of Global Value Chains', *Review of International Political Economy*, 12:1 (2005), pp. 78–104.

23. M. Mazzucato, 'The Entrepreneurial State', *Soundings*, 49:49 (2011), pp. 131–42.

24. J. Kornai, *The Road To a Free Economy: Shifting From a Socialist System: The Example of Hungary* (New York: Norton, 1990).

25. Ericson, 'The Classical Soviet-type Economy: Nature of the System and Implications

for Reform', p. 17.

26. Ericson, 'The Classical Soviet-Type Economy: Nature of The System and Implications for Reform'.

27. Burawoy and Lukács, *The Radiant Past: Ideology and Reality in Hungary's Road To Capitalism*.

28. K. Ruziev and S. Dow, 'A Re-Evaluation of Banking Sector Reforms in Transition Economies: Intentions and Unintended Consequences', in K. Ruziev and N. Perdikis (eds), *Development and Financial Reform in Emerging Economies* (London: Pickering & Chatto Publishers), forthcoming. See also M. Ellman, 'Transition: Intended and Unintended Processes', *Comparative Economic Studies*, 47:4 (2005), pp. 595–614.

29. R. McKinnon, 'Financial Control in the Transition from Classical Socialism to a Market Economy', *Journal of Economic Perspectives*, 5:4 (1991), pp. 107–22.

30. T. A. Wolf, 'The Lessons of Limited Market-Oriented Reform', *Journal of Economic Perspectives*, 5:4 (1991), pp. 45–58.

31. J. Marangos, 'A Political Economy Approach to the Neoclassical Model of Transition', *American Journal of Economics and Sociology*, 61:1 (2002), pp. 259–76.

32. McKinnon, 'Financial Control in the Transition from Classical Socialism to a Market Economy', argued that low productivity of physical capital in socialist economies could worsen during liberalization.

33. Fischer and Gelb, 'The Process of Socialist Economic Transformation'. See also Kornai, Maskin and Roland, 'Understanding the Soft Budget Constraint'.

34. Ericson, 'The Classical Soviet-Type Economy: Nature of the System and Implications for Reform', p. 21.

35. See M. Long and I. Rutkovska, *The Role of Commercial Banks in Enterprise Restructuring in Eastern Europe* (London: Centre for Economic Policy Research, 1995).

36. Boot, 'Relationship Banking: What Do We Know?'

37. McKinnon, 'Financial Control in the Transition from Classical Socialism to a Market Economy'.

38. See Long and Rutkovska, 'The Role of Commercial Banks in Enterprise Restructuring in Eastern Europe'.

39. See Nolke and Vliegenhart, 'Enlarging Varieties of Capitalism: The Emergence of Dependent Market Economies in East and Central Europe'.

40. C. Ban, *Ruling Ideas. How Global Economic Paradigms Go Local and Survive Adversity* (Mimeo, MA: Boston University, 2014).

41. Gabor, *Central Banking and Financialization. A Romanian Account of How Eastern Europe Became Subprime*.

42. F. Stilwell, 'Four Reasons for Pluralism in the Teaching of Economics', *Australasian Journal of Economics Education*, 3:1 (2006), pp. 42–55.

43. Gabor, *Central Banking and Financialization. A Romanian Account of How Eastern Europe Became Subprime*.

44. D. Gabor, 'The Road to Financialization in Central and Eastern Europe: The Early Policies and Politics of Stabilizing Transition', *Review of Political Economy*, 24:2 (2012), pp. 227–49.

45. R. Anderson, E. Berglof and K. Mizsei, *Banking Sector Development in Central and Eastern Europe* (London: Centre for Economic Policy Research, 1996).

46. G. W. Kolodko 'Economic Liberalism Became Almost Irrelevant', *Transition*, 9:3 (1998), pp. 1–6.

47. J. Winiecki, *The Distorted World of Soviet-Type Economies* (London: Routledge, 1998).

48. J. Sachs, 'Economic Transition and the Exchange-rate Regime', *American Economic*

Review, 86:2 (1996), pp.147–52.

49. According to Sachs, 'Economic Transition and the Exchange-rate Regime', p.150, 'Economic transition and the exchange-rate regime': 'the reluctance of the IMF to advise in favor of pegged rates at the outset of stabilization from high inflation seems to be the result of the institution's reluctance to support the international provision of stabilization funds to countries that lack adequate foreign reserves to defend a pegged rate'.

50. Allen and de Haas, 2001, quoted in Gabor, *Central Banking and Financialization. A Romanian Account of How Eastern Europe Became Subprime.*

51. Gabor, 'The Road to Financialization in Central and Eastern Europe: The Early Policies and Politics of Stabilizing Transition'.

52. International Monetary Fund, *A Study of the Soviet Economy*. See also Gabor, *Central Banking and Financialization. A Romanian Account of How Eastern Europe Became Subprime*; Gabor, 'The Road to Financialization in Central and Eastern Europe: The Early Policies and Politics of Stabilizing Transition'.

53. Fischer and Gelb, 'The Process of Socialist Economic Transformation'.

54. International Monetary Fund, *A Study of the Soviet Economy.*

55. D. Gabor, 'Learning from Japan: The European Central Bank and the European Sovereign Debt Crisis', *Review of Political Economy*, 26:2 (2014), pp. 190–209.

56. Sachs, 'Economic Transition and the Exchange-Rate Regime'. See also S. Schadler, 'IMF Conditionality: Experience under Stand by and Extended Arrangements, Part I: Key Issues and Findings', IMF Occasional Paper No. 128 (Washington, DC: IMF, 1995).

57. G. A. Calvo and F. Coricelli, 'Output Collapse in Eastern Europe: The Role of Credit', *IMF Staff Papers*, 40:1 (1993), pp. 32–52.

58. S. Dow, D. Ghosh and K. Ruziev, 'A Stages Approach to Banking Development in Transition Economies', *Journal of Post Keynesian Economics*, 31:1 (2008), pp 3–33.

59. G. A. Calvo and F. Coricelli, 'Stagflationary Effects of Stabilization Programs in Reforming Socialist Countries: Enterprise-Side and Household-Side Factors', *World Bank Economic Review*, 6:1 (1992), pp. 71–90.

60. For instance throughout 1993, during the second IMF programme, see Gabor, *Central Banking and Financialization: A Romanian Account of How Eastern Europe Became Subprime.*

61. G. Ibrahim and V. Galt, 'Bye-bye Central Planning, Hello Market Hiccups: Institutional Transition in Romania', *Cambridge Journal of Economics*, 26:1 (2002), pp. 105–18.

62. E. Berglof and P. Bolton, 'The Great Divide and Beyond: Financial Architecture in Transition', *Journal of Economic Perspectives*, 16:1 (2002), pp. 77–100.

63. Gabor, 'The Road to Financialization in Central and Eastern Europe: The Early Policies and Politics of Stabilizing Transition'.

10 Akimov, 'The Political Economy of Financial Reforms in Authoritarian Transition Economies: A Comparative Study of Kazakhstan and Uzbekistan'

1. G. Roland, *Transition and Economics: Politics, Firms, Markets* (Cambridge: MIT Press, 2000) and G. Roland, 'The Political Economy of Transition', *Journal of Economic Perspectives*, 16:1 (2002), pp. 29–50.

2. A. Akimov and B. Dollery, 'Financial Policy in Transition Economies. Architecture, Pace and Sequencing', *Problems of Economic Transition*, 50:9 (2008), pp. 6–26.

3. P. J. Luong, *Institutional Change and Political Continuity in Post Soviet Central Asia:*

Power, Perceptions and Pacts (Cambridge: Cambridge University Press, 2002).

4.   B. Islamov, *The Central Asian States Ten Years After: How to Overcome Traps of Development, Transformation and Globalisation?* (Tokyo: Maruzen Co, 2001).

5.   I. Karimov, *Uzbekistan – an Own Model of Transition to Market Relations* (Tashkent: Sharq, 1993) and I. Karimov, *Uzbekistan on the Way of Deepening of Economic Reforms* (Tashkent: Sharq, 1995).

6.   R. Pomfret, *The Central Asian Economies Since Independence* (Princeton, NJ: Princeton University Press, 2006).

7.   A. Akimov, and B. Dollery, *Financial Sector Reform in Uzbekistan: Theoretical Foundations and Policy Analysis* (Cologne: Lambert Academic Publishing, 2009).

8.   N. Sirajiddinov, 'Main Stages of Economic Reforms in Uzbekistan', *Proceedings of the International Policy Conference on Transition Economies* (Hanoi: United Nations Development Programme, 2004).

9.   V. Chjen, *Fundamentals of Privatisation (in Russian)* (Tashkent: State Property Committee of the Republic of Uzbekistan, 1996).

10. A. Akimov and B. Dollery, 'Uzbekistan's Financial System: Evaluation of Twelve Years of Transition', *Problems of Economic Transition*, 48:12 (2006), pp. 6–31.

11. Sirajiddinov, 'Main Stages of Economic Reforms in Uzbekistan'.

12. R. Pomfret, *The Economies of Central Asia* (Princeton, NJ: Princeton University Press, 1995).

13. EBRD, *Transition Report: Ten Years of Transition?* (London: European Bank for Reconstruction and Development, 1999).

14. Economist Intelligence Unit, *Country Profile: Uzbekistan* (London: Economist Intelligence Unit, 2005).

15. Karimov left the PDPU in 1996. Akimov and Dollery, *Financial Sector Reform in Uzbekistan: Theoretical Foundations and Policy Analysis*.

16. A. Akimov and B. Dollery, 'Financial Development Policies in Uzbekistan: An Analysis of Achievements and Failures', *Economic Change and Restructuring*, 42:4 (2009), pp. 293–318.

17. K. Ruziev, Ghosh, D. and S. Dow, 'The Uzbek Puzzle Revisited: An Analysis of Economic Performance in Uzbekistan Since 1991', *Central Asian Survey*, 26:1 (2007), pp. 7–30.

18. Akimov and Dollery, 'Financial Development Policies in Uzbekistan: An Analysis of Achievements and Failures'.

19. Akimov and Dollery, 'Uzbekistan's Financial System: Evaluation of Twelve Years of Transition'.

20. Pomfret, *The Central Asian Economies Since Independence*.

21. See, for example, Asian Development Bank, *Asian Development Outlook 2006* (Hong Kong: Asian Development Bank, 2006).

22. K. Ruziev, and D. Ghosh, 'Banking Sector Development in Uzbekistan: A Case of Mixed Blessings?', *Problems of Economic Transition*, 52:2 (2009), pp. 3–41.

23. J. Kakhkharov and A. Akimov, 'Estimating Remittances in the Former Soviet Union: Methodological Complexities and Potential Solutions', Discussion Paper 2014–03 (Brisbane: Griffith University, 2014).

24. Central Election Committee of Uzbekistan, 'In Central Election Committee (in Russian)', 2007, at http://elections.uz/rus/news/v_entralnoy_izbiratelnoy_komissii_respubliki_uzbekistan_11.mgr [accessed 20 March 2014].

25. K. Ruziev and T. Majidov, 'Differing Effects of the Global Financial Crisison the Central Asian Countries: Kazakhstan, the Kyrgyz Republic and Uzbekistan', *Europe-Asia Studies*, 65:4 (2013), pp. 682–716.

26. Kakhkharov and Akimov, 'Estimating Remittances in the Former Soviet Union: Meth-

odological Complexities and Potential Solutions'.

27. M. lcott, 'Kazakhstan: Pushing for Eurasia', in I. Bremmer and R. Taras (eds), *New States, New Politics: Building the Post-Soviet Nations* (Cambridge: Cambridge University Press, 1997), pp. 547–50.

28. Pomfret, *The Economies of Central Asia.*

29. G. Gleason, *Markets and Politics in Central Asia: Structural Reform and Political Change* (London: Routledge, 2003).

30. D. Furman, 'The Regime in Kazakhstan', in B. Rumer (ed.), *Central Asia: At the End of the Transition* (New York: M. E. Sharpe, 2005), pp. 195–266.

31. EBRD, *Transition Report: Investment and Enterprise Development* (London: European Bank for Reconstruction and Development, 1995).

32. IMF, 'Republic of Kazakhstan: Selected Issues and Statistical Appendix', IMF Country Staff Report 00/29 (Washington, DC: International Monetary Fund, 2000).

33. EBRD, *Transition Report: Investment and Enterprise Development.*

34. Cummings, *Kazakhstan: Power and the Elite.*

35. Gleason, *Markets and Politics in Central Asia: Structural Reform and Political Change.*

36. Furman, 'The Regime in Kazakhstan'.

37. D. Furman, 'The Regime in Kazakhstan' and Gleason, *Markets and Politics in Central Asia: Structural Reform and Political Change.*

38. A. Akimov and B. Dollery, 'Financial System Reform in Kazakhstan from 1993 to 2006 and its Socioeconomic Effects', *Emerging Market Finance and Trade,* 44:3 (2008), pp. 81–97.

39. D. Hoelscher, 'Banking System Restructuring in Kazakhstan', Working Paper WP/98/96 (Washington, DC: International Monetary Fund, 1998).

40. Such as Gleason, *Markets and Politics in Central Asia: Structural Reform and Political Change.*

41. M. Olcott, *Kazakhstan: Unfulfilled Promise?* (Washington, DC: Carnegie Endowment for International Peace, 2010).

42. S. Barisitz and M. Lahnsteiner, From Stromy Expansion to Riding out the Storm: Banking Development in Kazakhstan, Financial Stability Report No 19 (Vienna: Austrian National Bank, 2010).

43. A. Bissenova, 'Construction Boom and Banking Crisis in Kazakhstan', *Central Asia and Caucasus Analyst,* 2009, at http://old.cacianalyst.org/?q=node/5117 [accessed 1 March 2014].

44. EBRD, *Transition Report: Integration Across Borders* (London: European Bank for Reconstruction and Development, 2012) and IMF, 'Republic of Kazakhstan: Staff Report for the 2013 Article IV Consultation', IMF Country Staff Report 13/290 (Washington, DC: International Monetary Fund, 2013).

45. Luong, *Institutional Change and Political Continuity in Post Soviet Central Asia: Power, Perceptions and Pacts.*

46. Political rights include assessment of electoral process, political pluralism and participation and functioning of the government. Civil liberties include freedom of expression and belief, association and organization rights, rule of law, personal autonomy and individual rights. More details are available at http://www.freedomhouse.org/report/methodology-fact-sheet#.U2ZQe_mSyta.

47. N. Lubin and A. Joldaosn, 'Central Asians Take Stock. Part II. Comparison o the Results from Public Opinion Survey, Uzbekistan and Kazakhstan, 1993 & 2007' (Seattle, WA: National Council for Eurasian and East European Research).

48. Heritage Foundation, Index of Economic Freedom, 2014, at http://www.heritage.org/

index/country/kazakhstan [accessed 1 March 2014].

49. Heritage Foundation, Index of Economic Freedom, 2014, at http://www.heritage.org/
     index/country/uzbekistan [accessed 1 March 2014].

50. B. Rumer, 'Central Asia: At the End of Transition', in B. Rumer (ed.), *Central Asia: At
     the End of the Transition* (New York: M. E. Sharpe, 2005), pp. 3–70.

51. Transition indicator methodologydescription is avialble at http://www.ebrd.com/
     pages/research/economics/data/macro/ti_methodology.shtml.

52. R. Wintrobe, *The Political Economy of Dictatorship* (Cambridge: Cambirdge University
     Press, 1998).

53. See, for example, Karimov, *Uzbekistan – an Own Model of Transition to Market Relations*
     and Karimov, *Uzbekistan on the Way of Deepening of Economic Reforms*.

54. Wintrobe, *The Political Economy of Dictatorship*.

55. For example, R. Pomfret, 'The Uzbek Model of Economic Development 1991–9', 2000,
     at http://www.economics.adelaide.edu.au/staff/pomfret/eotzub.pdf [accessed 2 Sep-
     tember 2006] and M. Spechler, K. Bektemirov, S. Chepel and F. Suvankulov, 'The Uzbek
     Paradox: Progress without Neo-Liberal Reform', in G. Ofer and R. Pomfret (eds),*The
     Economic Prospects of the CIS* (Cheltenham: Edward Elgar, 2004), pp. 177–97.

56. E. Abdullaev, 'Uzbekistan: Between Traditionalism and Westernisation', in B. Rumer
     (ed.), *Central Asia: At the End of the Transition* (New York: M. E. Sharpe, 2005),
     pp. 267–96.

57. A. Matveea, 'Legitimasing Central Asian Authoritarianism: Political Manipulation and
     Symbolic Power', *Europe-Asia Studies*, 61:7 (2009), pp. 1095–121.

58. L. Adams and A. Rustemova, 'Mass Spectacle and Styles of Governmentality in
     Kazakhstan and Uzbekistan', *Europe-Asia Studies*, 61:7 (2009), pp. 1249–76.

59. R. Gilson and C. Milhaupt, 'Economically Benevolent Dictators: Lessons for Developing
     Democracies', *American Journal of Comparative Law*, 59:1 (2011), pp. 227–88.

60. Radio Freedom, 'Gulnara Karimova's assets are nationalized (in Uzbek)', 2014, at
     www.ozodlik.org/content/article/25329725.html [accessed 14 April 2014].

11 Dey and Wang, 'An Overview of the Securities Market Reform in Post-Liberalization China and India'

1. For a definition of and comprehensive discussion on financial liberalization, refer to
    United Nations, *Rethinking Poverty, Report on World Social Situation 2010*, ch. 6, pp.
    97–111, at http://www.un.org/esa/socdev/rwss/docs/2010/fullreport.pdf [accessed
    30 June 2014].

2. To trace the literature on finance and growth from the beginning, please refer to: R. I.
    McKinnon, *Money and Capitalin Economic Development* (Washington, DC: Brookings
    Institution, 1973); E. Shaw, *Financial Deepening in Economic Development* (New York:
    Oxford University Press, 1973); J. Stiglitz, 'Capital Market Liberalization, Economic
    Growth, and Instability', *World Development*, 78:6 (2000), pp. 1075–86; R. Levine,
    'More on Finance and Growth: More Finance, More Growth?', *St. Louis Federal Reserve
    Review*, 85:4 (2003), pp. 31–46; and I. Hasan, P. Wachtel and M. Zhou, 'Institutional
    Development, Financial Deepening, and Economic Growth: Evidence from China',
    Journal of Banking and Finance, 33:1 (2009), pp. 157–70.

3. For empirical evidence on the asymmetric effect of financial market development on
    economic growth, please refer to: C. Calderon and L. Liu, 'The Direction of Causality

Between Financial Development and Economic Growth', *Journal of Development Economics*, 72:1 (2003), pp. 321–34; M. K. Hassan, B., Sanchez and J. Yu, 'Financial Development and Economic Growth: New Evidence from Panel Data', *Quarterly Review of Economics and Finance*, 51:1 (2011), pp. 88–104; Q. Liang and J. Teng, 'Financial Development and Economic Growth: Evidence from China', *China Economic Review*, 17:4 (2006), pp. 395–411.

4. Arguably, this 'one size fits all' Western style approach to market reforms fails to recognize the myriad of subtle differences across countries and is one of the reasons for the inconsistent and unconvincing empirical evidence on the relation between economic growth and financial development. For example, market liquidity requires wide participation by opportunistic investors, who need to be sufficiently informed, interested in, and have sufficient funds available for investment. Both information and interest are functions of many social parameters like education, access to and familiarity with technology, entrepreneurship etc.; while fund availability is constrained by disposable income. All of these parameters vary widely among countries, even after controlling for factors like income level, growth, and legal system.

5. The International Monetary Fund (IMF) proclaims that securities market regulation targets private and public issue of securities, secondary markets, asset management products, and market intermediaries (brokers, dealers, and advisors). In terms of regulatory model, there are two basic forms: i) a government regulatory body that prescribes and mandates socially desirable behavior for securities market participants; and ii) self-regulation, social regulation, co-regulation, third-party regulation, certification, and accreditation by industry and trade associations. Most countries choose one of the two, while some choose their combination. For instance, both the UK and the USA have self-regulated financial markets like the London Stock Exchange and the New York Stock Exchange along network of government agencies such as Securities and Exchange Commission and Commodity Futures Trading Commission in the USA and Financial Conduct Authority in the UK, which exercise control and supervision over a variety of securities market activities.

6. Please refer to: A. Shleifer and R. W. Vishny, 'Large Shareholders and Corporate Control', *Journal of Political Economy*, 94:3 (1986), pp. 461–88, and R. La Porta, F. Lopez-de-Silanes, A. Shleifer and R. W. Vishny, 'Investor Protection and Corporate Governance', *Journal of Financial Economics,* 58:1–2 (2000), pp. 3–28. For recent comprehensive surveys of corporate governance practices and issues around the world, please refer to R. V. Aguilera and G. Jackson, 'Comparative and International Corporate Governance', *Academy of Management Annals*, 4:1 (2010), pp. 485–556; and S. Claessens and B. Yurtuglu, 'Corporate Governance in Emerging Markets: A Survey', *Emerging Markets Review*, 15:C (2013), pp. 1–33.

7. The constant and widespread allegations of corruption and violations among all levels of elected officials, bureaucrats, civil servants, and business leaders down to the cab driver, the street vendor, and the pedestrian (understandably, not every violation has the same effect on others) point to the pervasiveness of the problem of law and order enforcement in India.

8. K. D. Lal, 'India and China: Contrasts in Economic Liberalization?', *World Development*, 23:9 (1995), pp. 1475–94; N. Rajagopalan and Y. Zhang, 'Corporate Governance Reforms in China and India: Challenges and Opportunities', *Business Horizons*, 51:1 (2008), pp. 55–64.

9. The concept of "property rights" was re-introduced in Constitution of The People's Repub-

lic of China in 1982, see Article 13 'The state protects the right of citizens to own lawfully earned income, savings, houses and other lawful property'. And it was in the Fourteenth National Congress of the Communist Party of China in 1992 that 'declared that our socialist economy was a planned commodity economy based on public ownership'. (See http://www.bjreview.com.cn/document/txt/2011–03/29/content_363504.htm).

10. The World Justice Project Annual Rule of Law Report 2014, at http://www.worldjustice-project.org/publication/rule-law-index-reports/rule-law-index-2014-report [accessed 30 June 2014].

11. P. Bardhan, *Awakening Giants, Feet of Clay: A Comparative Assessment of the rise of China and India* (Princeton, NJ: Princeton University Press, 2010); J. Felipe, E. Lavina and E. X. Fan, 'The Diverging Patterns of Profitability, Investment and Growth of China and India during 1980–2003', *World Development*, 36:5 (2008), pp. 741–74; Y. Huang and T. Khanna, 'Can India Overtake China?', *Foreign Policy* (July–August 2003), pp. 74–81.

12. G. J. Fernald and J. H. Rogers, 'Puzzles in the Chinese Stock Market', *Review of Economics and Statistics*, 84:3 (2002), pp. 416–32; F. Allen, J. Qian and M. Qian, 'Law, Finance, and Economic Growth in China', *Journal of Financial Economics*, 77:1 (2005), pp. 57–116.

13. The history of China's stock markets is one of 'wading across the stream by feeling the way' – as enunciated by the Chinese leader Deng Xiaopingand has been the guiding principle for economic liberalization in post-Mao era. In China, stocks were introduced in the late 1970s during the time the farmers built the earliest joint-work township enterprises.

14. The concept of stocks and markets, virtually non-existent for decades in China, were reintroduced after 1990. During this time, China had just begun her open-up policy aimed at transition from a planned economy to a market economy. Property rights were reintroduced in the public arena for the first time since its abolition in 1949, when the Chinese Communist Party took power. Nevertheless, the spirit of socialist ideology and centrally planned economy was still high in the minds of the government officials, who were more interested in improving the performance of the state owned enterprises rather than outright transfer of their ownership to the private sector. The initial mission of the stock exchanges was to broaden external financing opportunities for State-Owned-Enterprises (SOEs).

15. See the World Federation of Exchange, at http://www.world-exchanges.org/statistics/monthly-reports for more [accessed 30 June 2014].

16. A listed firm can issue A, B and H-shares; A-shares are exclusively for domestic investors, while B and H-shares are for foreign investors only. Note that H-shares belong to firms with primary listing in the Hong Kong Stock Exchange (SEHK) that is considered as a 'foreign' stock exchange for listing purpose.

17. The SSE index is comprised of all the A shares and B shares listed on the SSE.

18. The international community used the WTO membership as a lever to force China's government to take concrete and tangible steps towards economic reform. This exposed the true extent of non-performing loansin the banking sector, which originated primarily from loans extended to SOEs. As a result, reforms envisaged to impose harder budget constraints on SOEs.

19. In the words of Zhou Zhengqing, former China's chief securities regulator from 1995 to 1999, the CSRC must ensure that securities markets serve the state-owned enterprises but not the shareholders. see Zhou Zhengqing, *Actively and Prudently Develop Securities Market*. An article published on the People's Bank of China website in Chinese language on 16 October 1997, at http://www.pbc.gov.cn/ [accessed 9 July 2014].

20. See Fernald and Rogers, 'Puzzles in the Chinese Stock Market'.

21. See *China Securities and Futures Statistical Yearbook 2006* (Beijing: Securities Regulatory Commission of China, 2006).

22. See *China Securities and Futures Statistical Yearbook 2006*.

23. For evidence on expropriation of minority by majority shareholders in China, please see G. Tong and C. J. Green, 'Pecking Order or Trade-off Hypothesis? Evidence on the CapitalStructure of Chinese Companies', *Applied Economics,* 37:19 (2005), pp. 2179–89; L. Gao and G. Kling, 'Corporate Governance and Tunneling: Empirical Evidence from China', *Pacific-Basin Finance Journal,* 16:5 (2008), pp. 591–605.

24. The World Justice Project Annual Rule of Law Report 2014.

25. For detailed definition and use of RFs and BRs, please refer to S. Barua and J. Varma, 'Securities Scam: Genesis, Mechanics, and Impact', *Vikalpa,* 18:1 (1993), pp. 3–12.

26. For a complete analysis of how the scam happened, please refer to Barua and Varma, 'Securities Scam: Genesis, Mechanics, and Impact', pp. 3–12. For a broad comprehensive description with a few disconcerting details about the Indian securities market, please refer to A. Shah and S. Thomas, 'Policy Issues in Indian Securities Markets', in A. Krueger and S. Z. Chinoy (eds), *Reforming India's External, Financial and Fiscal Policies, Stanford Studies in International Economics and Development* (Stanford, CA: Stanford University Press, 2003), pp. 129–47.

27. See the article *Transformation of the Indian CapitalMarkets by Dr. R. H. Patil,* at http://suchetadalal.com/?id=ada00779–864d-0ae4-492e8bb2019c&base=sections&f &t=TRANSFORMATION+OF+THE+INDIAN+CAPITAL+MARKET [accessed 30 June 2014].

28. See the speech made by SEBI chairman U.K. Sinha in 2013, at http://www.powerpolitics .in/Issues/January2014/page48.php [accessed 30 June 2014].

29. See the speech made by SEBI chairman U. K. Sinha in 2013, at http://www.powerpolitics .in/Issues/January2014/page48.php [accessed 30 June 2014].

30. R. Chakravarti, W. Megginson and P. Yadav, 'Corporate Governance in India', *Journal of Applied Corporate Finance,* 20:1 (2008), pp. 59–72.

31. The 1956 Companies Act replaced all prior companies acts and amendments thereof related to corporations.

32. Rajagopalan and Zhang, 'Corporate Governance Reforms in China and India: Challenges and Opportunities'.

33. Chakravarti, Megginson and Yadav, 'Corporate Governance in India'.

34. L. A. Bebchuk and J. M. Fried, 'Executive Compensation as an Agency Problem', *Journal of Economic Perspectives,* 17:3 (2003), pp. 71–92.

35. The World Justice Project Annual Rule of Law Report 2014.

36. The World Justice Project Annual Rule of Law Report 2014.

37. S. Bose, 'Securities Regulations: Lessons from US and Indian Experience', *Money and Finance,* 2:20–1 (January–June 2005), pp. 1–42.

12 Upadhyaya, 'Financial Sector Development in Sub-Saharan Africa: A Survey of Empirical Literature'

1. T. Mkandawire and C. Soludo, *Our Continent, Our Future: African Perspectives on Structural Adjustment* (Dakar: CODESRIA, 1999), p. vii.

2. T. Mkandawire, 'The Political Economy of Financial Reform in Africa', *Journal of*

International Development, 11:3 (1999), pp. 321–42; M. Nissanke and E. Aryeetey, *Financial Integration and Development: Liberalisation and Reform in Sub-Saharan Africa* (London: Routledge, 1998); and J. Serieux, 'Financial Liberalisation and Domestic Resource Mobilization in Africa: An Assessment', *International Poverty Centre Working Paper No. 45* (Brasilia: International Poverty Centre, 2008).

3.   M. Brownbridge and C. Harvey, *Banking in Africa* (Trenton, NJ: World Press, Inc., 1998), and P. Honohan and T. Beck, *Making Finance Work for Africa*. (Washington, DC: World Bank, 2007).

4.   R. Upadhyaya, 'Analysing the Sources and Impact of Segmentation in the Banking Sector: A Case Study of Kenya' (PhD dissertation, School of Oriental and African Studies, University of London, 2011).

5.   T. Beck, S. Maimbo, I. Faye and T. Triki, *Financing Africa: Through the Crisis and Beyond* (Washington, DC: World Bank, 2011), and Serieux, 'Financial Liberalisation and Domestic Resource Mobilization in Africa: An Assessment'.

6.   This paper focuses on formal financial sector, more specifically banking, developments in the SSA region.

7.   There are two main measures of financial system size and depth: the ratio of liquid liabilities to GDP and the ratio of private credit to GDP respectively. The former is a measure of monetary resources mobilized by banks. The latter is a measure of banks' ability to channel resources to productive uses. Interest rate spread, which is measured as the difference between the average lending rate and the average deposit rate, is the most common measure of bank (in)efficiency. The spread is often thought of as the cost of external funds introduced due to informational and enforcement frictions. A more commonly used measure of inefficiency is the interest rate margin measured as net interest income as a percentage of total earning assets.

8.   The classifications are based on the World Bank database, at http://data.worldbank.org/about/country-and-lending-groups [accessed 1 July 2014]. Low-income economies are defined as those with a GNI per capita, of $1,035 or less in 2012; middle-income economies are those with a GNI per capita of more than $1,035 but less than $12,616; high-income economies are those with a GNI per capita of $12,616 or more. Lower-middle-income and upper-middle-income economies are separated at a GNI per capita of $4,085.

9.   L. Harris, 'From Financial Development to Economic Growth and Vice Versa: A Review of International Experience and Policy Lessons for Africa', *Journal of African Economics*, 21:1 (2012), pp. i89–i106.

10. T. Beck and R. Levine, 'Stock markets, Banks, and Growth: Panel Evidence', *Journal of Banking and Finance*, 28:3 (2004), pp. 423–42.

11. J. Ndebbio, 'Financial Deepening, Economic Growth and Development: Evidence from Selected Sub-Saharan African Countries', *AERC Research Paper No. 142* (Nairobi: AERC, 2004).

12. T. Ghirmay, 'Financial Development and Economic Growth in Sub-Saharan African Countries: Evidence from Time Series Analysis', *African Development Review*, 16:3 (2004), pp. 415–32.

13. O. Akinboade, 'The Relationship between Financial Deepening and Economic Growth in Tanzania', *Journal of International Development*, 12:7 (2000), pp. 939–50.

14. It is not clear, however, why Akinboade places the commencement of financial liberalization in 1982, nearly a decade earlier than most authors.

15. N. Odhiambo, 'Financial Depth, Savings and Economic Growth in Kenya: A Dynamic Causal Linkage', *Economic Modelling*, 25:4 (2008), pp. 704–13.

16. N. Odhiambo, 'Interest Rate Reforms, Financial Deepening and Economic Growth in Kenya: An Empirical Investigation', *Journal of Developing Areas*, 43:1 (2009), pp. 295–313.

17. N. Odhiambo, 'Interest Rate Reforms, Financial Deepening and Economic Growth in Kenya: An Empirical Investigation', p. 311. Despite the contrasting conclusions of the papers, the author makes no attempt to reconcile them.

18. C. Kenny and D. Williams, 'What Do We Know About Economic Growth? Or, Why Don't We Know Very Much?' *World Development*, 29:1 (2001), pp. 1–22.

19. V. Murinde, 'Financial Development and Economic Growth: Global and African Evidence', *Journal of African Economics*, 21:1 (2012), pp. i10–i56.

20. Harris, 'From Financial Development to Economic Growth and Vice Versa: A Review of International Experience and Policy Lessons for Africa'.

21. R. McKinnon, *Money and Capital in Economic Development* (Washington DC: Brookings Institute, 1973), and E. Shaw, *Financial Deepening in Economic Development* (New York: Oxford University Press, 1973).

22. F. Mwega, 'An Econometric Study of Selected Monetary Policy Issues in Kenya', *ODI Working Paper 42* (London: ODI, 1990).

23. See for example M. Brownbridge, 'Financial Distress in Local Banks in Kenya, Nigeria, Uganda and Zambia: Causes and Implications for Regulatory Policy', *Development Policy Review*, 16 (1998), pp. 173–88; Mkandawire, 'The Political Economy of Financial Reform in Africa'; N. Ndung'u and R. Ngugi, 'Adjustment and Liberalisation in Kenya: The Financial and Foreign Exchange Markets', *Journal of International Development*, 11:3 (1999), pp. 465–91; R. Ngugi and J. Kabubo, 'Financial Sector Reforms and Interest Rate Liberalisation: The Kenya Experience', *AERC Research Paper No. 72* (Nairobi: AERC, 1998); Nissanke and Aryeetey, *Financial Integration and Development: Liberalisation and Reform in Sub-Saharan Africa*; A. Soyibo, 'Financial Liberalisation and Bank Restructuring in Sub-Saharan Africa: Some Lessons for Sequencing and Policy Design', *Journal of African Economies*, 6:1 (1997), pp. 100–150; and World Bank, *Adjustment in Africa: Reforms, Results and the Road Ahead* (Washington, DC: World Bank, 1994).

24. Brownbridge, 'Financial Distress in Local Banks in Kenya, Nigeria, Uganda and Zambia: Causes and Implications for Regulatory Policy'; Brownbridge and Harvey, *Banking in Africa*; and A. Soyibo and F. Adekanye, 'The Nigerian Banking System in the Context of Policies of Financial Regulation and Deregulation', *AERC Research Paper No. 17* (Nairobi: AERC, 1992).

25. Nissanke and Aryeetey, *Financial Integration and Development: Liberalisation and Reform in Sub-Saharan Africa* and Serieux, 'Financial Liberalisation and Domestic Resource Mobilization in Africa: An Assessment'.

26. G. Caprio, I. Atiyas, and J. Hanson (eds), *Financial Reform* (Cambridge: Cambridge University Press, 1994).

27. E. Aryeetey, H. Hettice, M. Nissanke and W. Steel, 'Informal Financial Markets under Liberalization in four African Countries', *World Development*, 25:5 (1997), pp. 817–30; E. Chirwa, 'Market Structure, Liberalisation and Performance of the Malawian Banking Industry', *AERC Research Paper No. 108* (Nairobi: AERC, 2001); and Nissanke and Aryeetey, *Financial Integration and Development: Liberalisation and Reform in Sub-Saharan Africa*.

28. J. Stiglitz, 'The Role of the State in Financial Markets', in M. Bruno and B. Pleskovic (ed.), *Proceeding of the World Bank Conference on Development Economics* (Washington, DC: World Bank 1993), pp. 41–6, and J. Stiglitz and A. Weiss, 'Credit Rationing

in Markets with Imperfect Information', *American Economic Review*, 71:3 (1981), pp. 393–410.

29. J. Stiglitz, T. Helmann, and K. Murdoch, 'Liberalization, Moral Hazard in Banking and Prudential Regulation: Are Capital Requirements Enough?', *American Economic Review*, 90:1 (2000), pp. 147–65.

30. C. Reinhart and I. Tokatlidis, 'Financial Liberalisation: The African Experience', *Journal of African Economies*, 12:2 (2003), pp. 53–88, and World Bank, *Adjustment in Africa: Reforms, Results and the Road Ahead*.

31. G. Caprio, I. Atiyas, and J. Hanson, *Financial Reform*.

32. G. Caprio, 'Banking on Financial Reform? A Case of Sensitive Dependence on Initial Conditions', in G. Caprio, I. Atiyas and P. Honohan (ed), *Financial Reform*, pp. 1–9, and World Bank, *Adjustment in Africa: Reforms, Results and the Road Ahead*.

33. World Bank *Adjustment in Africa: Reforms, Results and the Road Ahead*, p. 204.

34. A. Fosu, M. Kimenyi and N. Ndung'u, 'Economic Reforms and Restructuring in Sub-Saharan Africa: An Overview', *Journal of African Economies*, 12:2 (2003), pp. ii1–ii11.

35. M. Nissanke, 'Financing Enterprise Development in sub-Saharan Africa', *Cambridge Journal of Economics*, 25:3 (2001), pp. 343–67.

36. Brownbridge and Harvey, *Banking in Africa*, Nissanke and Aryeetey, *Financial Integration and Development: Liberalization and Reform in sub-Saharan Africa* and A. Soyibo, 'Financial Liberalization and Bank Restructuring in Sub-Saharan Africa: Some Lessons for Sequencing and Policy Design'.

37. S. Claessens and L. Laeven, 'What Drives Bank Competition? Some International Evidence', *Journal of Money, Credit and Banking*, 36:3 (2004), pp. 563–583 and X. Vives, 'Competition in the Changing World of Banking', *Oxford Review of Economic Policy*, 17:4 (2001), pp. 535–47.

38. T. Buchs and J. Mathisen, 'Competition and Efficiency in Banking: Behavioural Evidence from Ghana', *IMF Working Paper 05:17* (Washington, DC: IMF, 2005).

39. Vives, 'Competition in the Changing World of Banking'.

40. M. Ncube, 'Financial Services and Economic Development in Africa', *Journal of African Economies*, 16:1 (2007), pp. 13–57.

41. Chirwa, 'Market Structure, Liberalisation and Performance of the Malawian Banking Industry'.

42. Ngugi and Kabubo, 'Financial Sector Reforms and Interest Rate Liberalisation: The Kenya Experience'.

43. Competitive outcomes are possible in concentrated systems and collusive actions can be sustained when numerous firms are present. Therefore, it is the threat of entry, i.e. contestability that is more important. See W. Baumol, J. Panzar and R. Willig, *Contestable Markets and the Theory of Industrial Structure* (San Diego, CA: Harcourt Brace Jovanovich, 1982) and D. Besanko and A. Thakor, 'Banking Deregulation: Allocational Consequences of Relaxing Entry Barriers', *Journal of Banking and Finance*, 16:5 (1992), pp. 909–32.

44. J. Panzar and J. Rosse, 'Testing For 'Monopoly' Equilibrium', *Journal of Industrial Economics*, 35:4 (1987), pp. 443.

45. Claessens and Laeven, 'What Drives Bank Competition? Some International Evidence'.

46. Buchs and Mathisen, 'Competition and Efficiency in Banking: Behavioural Evidence from Ghana'.

47. See for example Buchs and Mathisen, 'Competition and Efficiency in Banking: Behavioural Evidence from Ghana', on p. 20. They find that bank profits are highly correlated to

the treasury bill rate and banks and governments are trapped in a co-dependency scheme.

48. A. Mugume, 'Market Structure and Performance in Uganda's Banking Industry', *AERC Biannual Workshop* (Nairobi: AERC, 2006).

49. A. Musonda, 'Deregulation, Market Power and Competition: An Empirical Investigation of the Zambian Banking Industry', *CSAE Conference 2008 – Economic Development in Africa* (Oxford: CSAE, 2008).

50. S. Maimbo, 'The Diagnosis and Prediction of Bank Failures in Zambia 1990–98', *Development Policy Review*, 20:3 (2002), pp. 261–78.

51. CAMELs is an acronym that stands for Capital, Assets, Management, Earnings and Liquidity.

52. Z. Hasan, 'Evaluation of Islamic Banking Performance: On the Current Use of Econometric Models', *Munich Personal RePEc Archive 7272* (Malaysia: International Islamic University, 2005)

53. R. Fare, S. Grosskopf, B. Lindgren and P. Roos, 'Productivity Developments in Swedish Hospitals: A Malmquist Output Index Approach', in A. Charnes, W. Cooper, W. Lewin and L. Seifor (eds), *Data Envelopment Analysis: Theory, Methodology, and Application* (Boston, MA: Kluwer Academic Publishers, 1994), pp. 253–74.

54. A. Berger and D. Humphrey, 'Efficiency of Financial Institutions: International Survey and Directions for Future Research', *European Journal of Operational Research*, 98:2 (1997), pp. 175–212.

55. K. Egesa, 'Financial Sector Liberalisation and Productivity Change in Uganda's Commercial Banking Sector', *AERC Biannual Research Workshop* (Nairobi: AERC, 2006), and J. Aikaeli, 'Commercial Banks Efficiency in Tanzania', CSAE *Conference – Economic Development in Africa* (Oxford: CSAE, 2008).

56. The author gives results for three different estimates, a random period effects model, a fixed cross section and random period effects model and a fixed cross section and period effects. The results quoted here are for the third – fixed cross section and period effects model which has the highest goodness of fit measure.

57. With a t value of 4.09, it is significant even at the 0.1 per cent level.

58. But, it is not clear why under the non-parametric approach banks are divided into three groups – large banks, international banks and small banks; and, for the parametric approach they are divided only into two groups – large banks and small banks.

59. Therefore core capital divided by total risk weighted assets is a key variable that bank regulators monitor closely.

60. The accounting identity that is at the basis of all double entry bookkeeping is Assets = Equity + Liability.

61. A. Berger, W. Hunter and S. Timme, 'The Efficiency of Financial Institutions: A Review and Preview of Research Past, Present, and Future', *Journal of Banking and Finance*, 17:2–3 (1993), pp. 221–49.

62. K. Egesa, 'Financial Sector Liberalisation and Productivity Change in Uganda's Commercial Banking Sector'.

63. D. Vittas, 'Measuring Commercial Bank Efficiency', *World Bank Policy Research Working Paper No. 806* (Washington, DC: World Bank, 1991).

64. J. Aikaeli, 'Efficiency and the Problem of Excess Liquidity in Commercial Banks in Tanzania' (PhD dissertation, University of Dar es Salaam, 2006).

65. Berger, Hunter and Timme, 'The Efficiency of Financial Institutions: A Review and Preview of Research Past, Present, and Future'.

66. P. dos Santos, 'Foreign Capital and Familial Control in Philippine Banking' (PhD dis-

sertation, University of London, 2007).

67. G. Hodgson, *How Economics Forgot History: The Problem of Historical Specificity in Social Science* (London and New York: Routledge, 2001), T. Lawson, *Economics and Reality* (London: Routledge, 1997) and D. Milonakis and B. Fine, *From Political Economy to Economics: Method, the Social and the Historical in the Evolution of Economic Theory* (New York: Routledge, 2008).

68. P. Arestis and J. Eatwell (eds), *Issues in Finance and Industry: Essays in Honour of Ajit Singh* (New York: Palgrave Macmillan, 2008). Ajit Singh also emphasizes that it is possible to carry out high quality research without using mathematical equations or formalistic modelling methods. See A. Singh, 'Better to be Rough and Relevant than to be Precise and Irrelevant: Reddaway's Legacy to Economics', *Cambridge Journal of Economics*, 33:3 (2009), pp. 363–79.

69. M. Mamdani, 'There Can be no African Renaissance without and African-focused Intelligentsia', in M. Makgoba (ed), *African Renaissance: The New Struggle* (Cape Town: Mafube Publishing, 1999), pp. 125–42.

70. Studies in microfinance have shown the importance of social factors and trust in increasing outreach of microfinance institutions. See S. Johnson, 'Understanding Kenya's Financial Landscape: The Missing Social Dimension' (Nairobi: FSD Kenya, 2011).

13 Chowdhury, 'Microcredit, Micro-Enterprises, and Self-Employment of Women: Experience from the Grameen Bank in Bangladesh'

1. F. M. Ssewamala, M. Lombe and J. C. Curley, *Using Individual Development Accounts for Microenterprise Development*, CSD Working Paper 06-05, Center for Social Development, George Warren Brown School of Social Work (USA: Washington University at St Louis, St Louis, 2006).

2. In Bangladesh those enterprises are regarded as micro-enterprises which have total number of employees less than 10.

3. A. K. M. H. Zaman and M. J. Islam, 'Small and Medium Enterprises Development in Bangladesh: Problems and Prospects', *ASA University Review*, 5:1 (2011), pp. 145–60.

4. Bangladesh Bureau of Statistics, *Cottage Industry Survey* (Dhaka: Bangladesh Bureau of Statistics, 2011).

5. D. B. Audretsch and M. Keilbach, 'Entrepreneurship Capital and Regional Growth', *Annals of Regional Science*, 39:3 (2005), pp. 457–69.

6. P. Mueller, 'Exploiting Entrepreneurial Opportunities: The Impact of Entrepreneurship on Growth', *Small Business Economics*, 28:4 (2007), pp. 355–62.

7. P. K. Wong, Y. P. Ho and E. Autio, 'Entrepreneurship, Innovation and Economic Growth: Evidence from GEM Data', *Small Business Economics*, 24:3 (2005), pp. 335–50.

8. G. Yamada, 'Urban Informal Employment and Self-Employment in Developing Countries: Theory and Evidence', *Economic Development and Cultural Change*, 44:2 (1996), pp. 289–314. M. F. Iyigun and A. L. Owen, 'Risk, Entrepreneurship and Human Capital Accumulation', *American Economic Review*, 88:2 (1998), pp. 454–7.

9. Z. J. Acs, D. B. Audretsch and D. S. Evans, '*Why Does the Self-Employment Rate Vary Across Countries and Over Time?*', Discussion Paper No. 871 (London: CEPR, 1994); M. A. Carree, A. J. van Stel, A. R. Thurik and A. R. M. Wennekers, 'Economic Development and Business Ownership: An Analysis Using Data of 23 OECD Countries in

the Period 1976–1996', *Small Business Economics*, 19:3 (2002), pp. 271–90.

10. The larger enterprises become cost efficient as these firms achieve the economies of scale as per unit fixed costs reduces with the increase in the size of the production. On the other hand, small enterprises fail to achieve the economies of scale and due to this reason, these enterprises become less cost efficient.

11. R. E. Lucas, 'On the Size Distribution of Firms', *BELL Journal of Economics*, 9:2 (1978), pp. 508–23.

12. Z. J. Acs, L. Szerb and E. Autio (2011), *Global Entrepreneurship and Development Index 2013* (Cheltenham: E, Edward Elgar, 2013).

13. D. Evans and B. Jovanovic, 'An Estimated Model of Entrepreneurial Choice under Liquidity Constraints', *Journal of Political Economy*, 97:4 (1989), pp. 808–27; D. Holtz-Eakin, D. Joulfian and H. S. Rosen, 'Sticking it Out: Entrepreneurial Survival and Liquidity Constraints', *Journal of Political Economy*, 102:1 (1994), pp. 53– 75; S. Carter and P. Rosa, 'The Financing of Male- and Female-owned Businesses', *Entrepreneurship and Regional Development*, 10:3 (1998), pp. 225–41; and I. Verheul and R. Thurik, 'Start-Up Capital: Does Gender Matter?', *Small Business Economics*, 16:4 (2001), pp. 329–45.

14. A. Bhaduri, *The Economic Structure of Backward Agriculture* (India: Macmillan India Limited, 1983); J. M. Rao, 'Interest Rates in Backward Agriculture', *Cambridge Journal of Economics*, 1:4 (1980), pp. 159–67; P. K. Bardhan, 'Interlocking Factor Markets and Agrarian Development: A Review of Issues', *Oxford Economic Papers*, 23:1 (1980), pp. 82–98; D. Ghosh, 'Monetary Dualism in Developing Countries', *Economies ET. Societes* (1986), pp. 19–30; P. Ghate, *Informal Finance: Some Findings from Asia* (Manila: Oxford University Press for the Asian Development Bank, 1992); J. Flotz, 'Credit Market Access and Profitability in Tunisia Agriculture', *Agricultural Economics*, 30 (2004), pp. 229–40; and M. Petrick, 'Empirical Measurement of Credit Rationing in Agriculture: A Methodological Survey', *Agricultural Economics*, 33:2 (2005), pp. 191–203.

15. L. Mayoux, 'Questioning Virtuous Spirals: Microfinance and Women's Empowerment in Africa', *Journal of International Development*, 11:7 (1999), pp. 957–84, and S. M. Hashemi, S. R. Schuler and A. P. Riley, 'Rural Credit Programmes and Women's Empowerment in Bangladesh', *World Development*, 24 (1996), pp. 635–53.

16. M. Pitt and S. R. Khandker, *Household and Intra Household Impacts of the Grameen Bank and Similar Targeted Credit Programmes in Bangladesh*, World Bank Discussion Paper No. 320 (USA: World Bank, Washington, DC, 1996).

17. R. D. M. Panjaitan-Drioadisuryo and K. Cloud, 'Gender, Self-Employment, and Microcredit Programs: An Indonesian Case Study', *Quarterly Review of Economics and Finance*, 39:5 (1999), 769–79.

18. M. J. A. Chowdhury, D. Ghosh and R. E. Wright, 'The Impact of Micro-credit on Poverty: Evidence from Bangladesh', *Progress in Development Studies*, 5:4 (2005), pp. 1–12.

19. A. Counts, *Give Us Credit: How Small Loans Today can Shape Our Tomorrow* (New Delhi: Research Press, 1996), and M. Yunus with A. Jolis, '*Banker to the Poor: The Autobiography of Muhammad Yunus*' (UK: Founder of the Grameen Bank, London: Aurum Press, 1998).

20. Grameen Bank, *Annual Report of Grameen Bank* (Dhaka: Grameen Bank, 2013).

21. A. L. Paulson and R. Townsend, 'Entrepreneurship and Financial Constraints in Thailand', *Journal of Corporate Finance*, 10:2 (2004), pp. 229–62.

22. D. Evans and B. Jovanovic, 'An Estimated Model of Entrepreneurial Choice under Liquidity Constraints'. T. Bates, 'Entrepreneur Human Capital Inputs and Small Business Longevity', *Review of Economics and Statistics*, 72:4 (1990), pp. 551–9.

23. D. Holtz-Eakin, D. Joulfian and H. S. Rosen., 'Sticking it Out: Entrepreneurial Survival and Liquidity Constraints', and Paulson and Townsend, 'Entrepreneurship and Financial Constraints in Thailand', pp. 229–62.

24. R. C. Cressy, 'Are Business Startups Debt-Rationed?', *Economic Journal*, 106:438 (1996), pp. 1253–70.

25. Verheul and Thurik, 'Start-up Capital: Does Gender Matter?', N. M. Carter, M. Williams and P. D. Reynolds, 'Discontinuing among New Firms in Retail: The Influence of Initial Resources, Strategy, and Gender', *Journal of Business Venturing*, 12:2 (1997), pp. 125–45.

26. L. M. Tiggers, and G. P. Green, 'Small Business Among Men- and Women-Owned Firms in Rural Areas', *Rural Sociology*, 59:2 (1994), pp. 289–310.

27. Carter, Williams and Reynolds, 'Discontinuing among New Firms in Retail: The Influence of Initial Resources, Strategy, and Gender'.

28. D. Fletschner, 'Rural Women's Access to Credit: Market Imperfections and Intrahousehold Dynamics', *World Development*, 37:3 (2009), pp. 618–31.

29. Fletschner, 'Rural Women's Access to Credit: Market Imperfections and Intrahousehold Dynamics'.

30. M. J. A. Chowdhury, 'The Determinants of the Entrepreneurship in a Conflict Region: Evidence from the Chittagong Hill Tracts in Bangladesh', *Journal of Small Business and Entrepreneurship*, 24:2 (2011), pp. 265–81.

31. Z. Lin , G. Picot and J. Compton, 'The Entry and Exit Dynamics of Self-Employment in Canada', *Small Business Economics*, 15:2 (2000), pp. 105–25; J. Block and P. Sandner, 'Necessity and Opportunity Entrepreneurs and their Duration in Self-Employment: Evidence from German Micro Data', *Journal of Industry, Competition and Trade*, 9:2 (2009), pp. 117–37; and M. Haapanen and H. Tervo, 'Self-Employment Duration in Urban and Rural Locations', *Applied Economics*, 41 (2009), pp. 2449–61.

32. M. P. Taylor, 'Self-Employment in Britain: When, Who and Why?', *Swedish Economic Policy Review*, 11:2 (2004), pp. 139–73; Block and Sandner, 'Necessity and Opportunity Entrepreneurs and their Duration in Self-Employment: Evidence from German Micro Data'; and Haapanen and Tervo, 'Self-Employment Duration in Urban and Rural Locations'.

33. X. Yang, Y. Cheng and J. Gao, 'The Changing Motives for Nascent Entrepreneurship in China: Using Global Entrepreneurship Monitor Data', Institute of Electrical and Electronics Engineers ICC 2008 Proceedings, 2008, pp. 5474–8.

34. G. Calvo and S. Wellisz, 'Technology, Entrepreneurship and Firm Size', *Quarterly Journal of Economics*, 95:4 (1980), pp. 663–78; D. Carr, 'Two Paths to Self Employment? Women's and Men's Self –Employment in the United States, 1980', *Work and Occupations*, 23:1 (1996), pp. 26–53; and A. L. Dolinsky, R. K. Captuto, K. Pasumarty and H. Quazi, 'The Effects of Education on Business Ownership: A Longitudinal Study of Women', *Entrepreneurship Theory and Practice*, 18:2 (1993), pp. 43–53.

35. J. van der Sluis, M. van Praag and W. Vijverberg, 'Entrepreneurship Selection and Performance: A Meta-Analysis of the Impact of Education in Less Developed Countries', *World Bank Economic Review*, 19:2 (2005), pp. 225–61; T. Dunn and D. Holz-Eakin, *Capital Market Constraints, Parental Wealth and the Transition to Self-Employment among Men and Women*, Discussion Paper (Washington, DC: Bureau of Labor Statistics, 1995); and L. Renzulli, H. Aldrich and J. Moody, 'Family Matters: Gender, Networks, and Entrepreneurial Outcomes', *Social Forces*, 79:2 (2000), pp. 523–46.

36. Lin, Picot and Compton, 'The Entry and Exit Dynamics of Self-Employment in

Canada'; and A. Demirguc-Kunt, L. F. Klapper and G. A. Panos, 'Entrepreneurship in Post-Conflict Transition: The Role of Informality and Access to Finance', *Policy Research Working Paper 4935* (USA: World Bank, 2009).

37. Yang, Cheng and Gao, 'The Changing Motives for Nascent Entrepreneurship in China: Using Global Entrepreneurship Monitor Data'.

38. D. B. Audretsch, W. Bönte, and J. P. Tamvada, '*Religion and Entrepreneurship*', CEPR Discussion Papers, 6378 (London: CEPR, 2007).

39. H. Taniguchi, 'Determinants of Women's Entry into Self-Employment', *Social Science Quarterly*, 83:3 (2002), pp. 875–93.

40. G. J. Borjas, 'The Self-Employment Experience of Immigrants', *Journal of Human Resources*, 21:4 (1986), pp. 485–506; Lin, Picot and Compton, 'The Entry and Exit Dynamics of Self-Employment in Canada'; R. W. Fairlie, 'The Absence of the African-American Owned Business: An Analysis of the Dynamics of Self-Employment', *Journal of Labor Economics*, 17:1 (1999), pp. 80–108; Demirguc-Kunt, Klapper and Panos, 'Entrepreneurship in Post-Conflict Transition: The Role of Informality and Access to Finance'; Block and Sandner, 'Necessity and Opportunity Entrepreneurs and their Duration in Self-Employment: Evidence from German Micro Data'; and Haapanen and Tervo, 'Self-Employment Duration in Urban and Rural Locations'.

41. T. J. Devine, 'Characteristics of Self-Employed Women in the United States', *Monthly Labor Review* (March 1994), pp. 20–34, and Carr, 'Two Paths to Self Employment? Women's and Men's Self – Employment in the United States, 1980'.

42. D. Bruce, 'Do Husbands Matter? Married Women Entering Self-Employment', *Small Business Economics*, 13:4 (1999), pp. 317–29.

43. Paulson and Townsend, 'Entrepreneurship and Financial Constraints in Thailand'.

44. J. Bruderl and P. Preisendorfer, 'Network Support and the Success of Newly Founded Businesses', *Small Business Economics*, 10:3 (1998), pp. 213–25.

45. Chowdhury, 'The Determinants of the Entrepreneurship in a Conflict Region: Evidence from the Chittagong Hill Tracts in Bangladesh'.

46. Evans and Jovanovic, 'An Estimated Model of Entrepreneurial Choice under Liquidity Constraints'.

47. Chowdhury, 'The Determinants of the Entrepreneurship in a Conflict Region: Evidence from the Chittagong Hill Tracts in Bangladesh'.

48. J. Yu and R. R. Stough, 'The Determinants of Entrepreneurship Development in China', *International Journal of Management and Enterprise Development*, 3:1–2 (2006), pp. 30–52.

49. 50 decimals are equal to approximately 0.20 Acre.

50. B. E. Coleman, 'The Impact of Group Lending in Northeast Thailand', *Journal of Development Economics*, 60:1 (1999), pp. 105–41, and Chowdhury, Ghosh and Wright, 'The Impact of Micro-Credit on Poverty: Evidence from Bangladesh'.

51. A. M. Goetz and R. S. Gupta, 'Who Takes Credit? Gender, Power, and Control Over Loan Use in Rural Credit Programs in Bangladesh', *World Development*, 24:1 (1996), pp. 45–63.

INDEX

For Product Safety Concerns and Information please contact our EU
representative GPSR@taylorandfrancis.com Taylor & Francis Verlag GmbH,
Kaufingerstraße 24, 80331 München, Germany

Printed and bound by CPI Group (UK) Ltd, Croydon, CR0 4YY
03/05/2025
01860118-0001